Catalogue of the extraordinary library, unique of its kind, formed by the late Rev. F.J. Stainforth : consisting entirely of works of British and American poetesses, and female dramatic writers, together with some interesting unpublished manuscripts...

Francis John Stainforth

CATALOGUE

OF THE

EXTRAORDINARY LIBRARY,

UNIQUE OF ITS KIND,

FORMED BY THE LATE

REV. F. J. STAINFORTH,

CONSISTING ENTIRELY OF

𝔚orks of 𝔅ritish & 𝔄merican 𝔓oetesses,

AND

FEMALE DRAMATIC WRITERS,

TOGETHER WITH

SOME INTERESTING UNPUBLISHED MANUSCRIPTS
AND AUTOGRAPH LETTERS,

ALSO

𝔄 few 𝔈ngravings, 𝔉ramed and 𝔊lazed

WHICH WILL BE SOLD BY AUCTION
BY MESSRS

SOTHEBY, WILKINSON & HODGE,

Auctioneers of 𝔏iterary 𝔓roperty and 𝔚orks illustrative of the 𝔉ine 𝔄rts

AT THEIR HOUSE, No. 13, WELLINGTON STREET, STRAND, W.C.

On MONDAY, the 1st of JULY, 1867, and five following Days

AT ONE O'CLOCK PRECISELY.

May be Viewed Two Days prior, and Catalogues had

Printed by J. Davy & Sons, 137, Long Acre.

CONDITIONS OF SALE

I. The highest bidder to be the buyer; and if any dispute arise between bidders, the lot so disputed shall be immediately put up again, provided the seller cannot decide the said dispute.

II. No person to advance less than 6d.; above ten shillings, 1s.; above five pounds, 2s. 6d., and so on.

III. The purchasers to give in their names and places of abode, and to pay down 10s. in the pound, if required, in part payment of the purchase-money; in default of which the lot or lots purchased to be immediately put up again and re-sold.

V. The lots to be taken away at the buyer's expense, immediately after the conclusion of the sale, in default of which Messrs SOTHEBY, WILKINSON & HODGE will not hold themselves responsible if lost, stolen, damaged or otherwise destroyed, but they will be left at the sole risk of the purchaser. If, at the expiration of ONE WEEK after the conclusion of the sale, the books or other property are not cleared or paid for, they will then be catalogued for immediate sale, and the expense, the same as if re-sold, will be added to the amount at which the books were bought. Messrs SOTHEBY, WILKINSON and HODGE will have the option of re-selling the Lots uncleared, either by public or private sale, without any notice being given to the defaulter.

V. The books are presumed to be perfect, unless otherwise expressed; but if, upon collating, any should prove defective, the purchaser will be at liberty to take or reject them, provided they are returned within ONE WEEK after the conclusion of the sale, when the purchase-money will be *returned*.

VI. The sale of any book or books is not to be set aside on account of any stained or short leaves of text or plates, want of list of plates, or on account of the publication of any subsequent volume, supplement, appendix, or plates. All the manuscripts, autographs, all magazines, and reviews, all books in lots, and all tracts in lots or volumes, will be sold with all faults, imperfections and errors of description. The sale of any lot of prints or drawings is not to be set aside on account of any error in the enumeration of the numbers stated, or errors of description.

VII. No IMPERFECT BOOKS will be taken back, unless a note accompanies each book, stating its imperfections, with the number of lot and date of the sale at which the same was purchased.

VIII. To prevent inaccuracy in the delivery, and inconvenience in the settlement of the purchases, no lot can on any account be removed during the time of sale.

IX. Upon failure of complying with the above Conditions, the money required and deposited in part of payment shall be forfeited, and *if any loss is sustained in the re-selling of such lots as are not cleared or paid for, all charges on such re-sale shall be made good by the defaulters at this Sale*.

- - -

Gentlemen who cannot attend the Sale may have their Commissions faithfully executed by their humble Servants,

SOTHEBY, WILKINSON & HODGE,
Wellington Street, Strand.

PREFACE.

This celebrated and unrivalled series of the Poetical Compositions of British and American Female Writers, exhibiting in a complete form the growth and progress of the genius of Woman in the department of Poetry, has been selected, with great zeal, industry, and toil, with a view to rescue our fair Poetesses from oblivion.

The Collection in its range extends over three hundred years, and contains many productions of remarkable interest and bibliographical rarity, from which the following may be selected among the numerous examples worthy of especial note:—Book of Hawking, Hunting, and Fishing, by Lady Juliana Berners, printed by Copland; Queen Katherine's Prayers and Lamentation of a Sinner 1563; Tragedie of Antonie translated by the Countess of Pembroke 1595; Lady Diana Primrose's Chaine of Pearle, 1630, Triumphs of Petrarch, by Anna Hume 1644, Tenth Muse of America, by Anne Bradstreet, 1650; Bentley's Monument of Matrons, 1582, Original Edition of Bale's Examinacyon of Anne Askewe 1546-7. There will also be found an extraordinary collection of Local and Privately Printed Effusions rarely to be met with, a vast assemblage of the Works of American Poetesses, the completest collection that could possibly be formed of the Works of Female Dramatic Writers, and of the Single Plays, and many other Compositions of writers in a superior grade of life, the whole forming AN ASSEMBLAGE WITHOUT PRECEDENT.

The Collection may, therefore, be justly designated unique, as no other of similar pretensions is known, nor would it be possible to get together another assemblage of works of a kindred nature, even with the most anxious and laborious research. Many of the volumes are enriched and their value greatly enhanced by the Biographical and Bibliographical remarks of the late possessor, whose successful exertions we trust will be duly appreciated by the curious Collector and Amateur.

It may be added, that the books are all in neat Bindings, and in the best condition.

Wellington Street, Strand,
1867

CATALOGUE

OF

THE UNIQUE LIBRARY

OF THE LATE

REV. F. J. STAINFORTH,

CONSISTING ENTIRELY OF WORKS OF

BRITISH AND AMERICAN POETESSES.

※※ As a mark of distinction the name of the Authoress is printed in Small Capitals

FIRST DAY'S SALE.

OCTAVO ET INFRA,

UNLESS OTHERWISE EXPRESSED

LOT
1 A (C E) Grace and Glory delineated 1855—A (C L) Widow's Tale, n d —A (M N) Leisure Moments, 1813   3 vol
2 ABDY (Mrs) Poetry, seven series, printed for private circulation 7 vol with autograph letter of the poetess inserted, 1834-55—Arthur's Ninth Birthday, and other Stories, n d   8 vol.
3 Abelard and Eloisa, Letters, with Poems by Pope and Mrs Madan, plates, 1776—Another Edition, 1783—Another Edition, plates, 1788—Another Edition, 1805   4 vol.
4 Achilles to Chiron By the Lady ****   folio 1738
5 Acrostics, Enigmas, and Charades
    privately printed   Kensington, 1849

B

6 Acting Drama. a Selection of Standard Plays by popular Authors (including Mrs Inchbald, Mrs Centlivre, and Mrs. Brooks), *plates*   *G. Virtue, n d*

7 ACTON (ELIZA) Poems   *Ipswich,* 1826

8 —— *second edition presentation copy, with autograph of the poetess*   *ib.* 1827

9 —— Voice of the North, *privately printed*   royal 8vo 1842

10 ACTON (HARRIET and ROSE) Poems *red morocco*   *printed for the author,* 1846

11 —— Poems, *second edition*   *ib* 1847

12 ADAMS (JANE) Miscellany Poems by Mrs Jane Adams in Crawfords-dyke
VERY RARE, *unfortunately wanting a corner off pages* 59-60   *Glasgow, by J Duncan,* 1734

13 ADAMS (MARY) Warning to the Inhabitants of England and London in particular By M A.   4to. *Printed in the year* 1676
*** At the end is a page in verse, commencing "Oh London I once more to thee do speak"

14 ADAMS (SARAH FLOWER) Vivia Perpetua A Dramatic Poem in five Acts   1841

15 Adversity; or, The Tears of Britannia, a Poem, by a Lady, *curious satirical etching of a celebrated Poet on horseback*   4to 1789

16 AGNEW (E C) Saint Mary and Her Times; a Poem in fourteen Cantos, *plate*   1851

17 Agreeable Variety, containing Discourses, Characters and Poems (by Mrs Behn, Lady Chudleigh, &c)   1717

18 —— The same, *second edition*   1724

19 —— The same, *third edition*   1742

20 AIKIN (LUCY) Epistles on Women, exemplifying their Character and Condition in various Ages and Nations With miscellaneous Poems, *with an autograph letter of the poetess inserted,* 4to 1810—Poetry for Children, *two editions,* 1808-25   3 vol

21 AINSLIE (ANN MARIA) Letters from the Dead to the Living, and Moral Letters, *second edition*   *Edinb* 1812

22 AIRD (MARION PAUL) Home of the Heart, and other Poems, Moral and Religious   *Kilmarnock,* 1846

23 —— Home of the Heart, &c.   *ib.* 1863

24 —— Heart Histories, Violets from the Greenwood, &c &c. in prose and verse, *with portrait (a carte de visite) inserted*   *ib* 1853

25 —— Sun and Shade, *with an autograph letter of the poetess inserted*   *ib.* 1860

26 Albert the Good a Nation's Tribute of Affection to the Memory of a truly Virtuous Prince, *portraits*   4to. 1862

27 ALCOCK (MARY) Poems, &c. edited by Joanna Hughes 1799
28 ALDERSON (R.) Lines, written and printed at the request of a Friend, by whom the Melancholy Story is related *Newcastle-upon-Tyne*, 1825
29 ALEXANDER (A.) Selection of Hymns for the use of Prisoners *York*, 1819
30 ALEXANDER (CECIL FRANCES) Baron's Little Daughter, and other Tales, in prose and verse, edited by W. Gresley, *printed within borders* 1848
31 —— Baron's Little Daughter, &c. *second edition, plates morocco, g. e* n. d.
32 —— Verses for Holy Seasons, 1846—Third Edition, 1849—Fourth Edition, *morocco, g. e.* 1858—Hymns, Descriptive and Devotional, 1858   1 vol
33 —— Hymns for Little Children, 1st, 2nd, 5th, 6th, 10th and 14th Editions, 1848-57—Moral Songs, 1st, 2nd, 3rd, 4th and 5th Editions, *woodcuts, n. d.*—Narrative Hymns, 3rd and 8th Editions, 1857-64—Verses in the Jubilee Year for 1851, 1852—Poems on Subjects in the Old Testament, two parts, 1854-7   12 vol
34 —— Hymns for Little Children, 25th Edition, *with illustrations by W. Chappell, engraved by Messrs. Dalziel* 4to n. d.
35 —— Legend of the Golden Prayers, and other Poems 1859
36 ALLEN (CHARLOTTE) Poems *Boston (in America)*, 1841
37 ALLEN (E.) *Loutherton*, Beauties of the Border, being a Description of the principal Gentlemen's Seats in Cumberland, Annandale, Nithsdale, Galloway, and Ayrshire *Annan: printed for the author*, 1846
38 ALLEN (ELEANOR) Siege of Agrigentum, a Poem *a present from the author* *Boston (in America)*, 1841
39 ALLEN (ELIZABETH) Silent Harp; or Fugitive Poems *Burlington (in America)*, 1832
40 Allibone (S. A.) Critical Dictionary of English Literature, and British and American Authors, vol. I *imp. 8vo* *Philadelphia*, 1859
41 ALLIN (ABBY) Home Ballads a Book for New Englanders, in 3 parts *Boston and Cambridge (in America)*, 1851
42 ALLINGHAM (HELEN MARIA) Closet Companion for the Daughters of Zion, 2 parts, 1850-1—Poem for the Times, n. d.   2 vol
43 ALLNUTT (Mrs. ALFRED) Day-Star Prophet 1865
44 ALLOM (ELIZABETH ANNE) Death Scenes, and other Poems *Hackney*, 1844
45 Almeda, or, The Neapolitan Revenge, a Tragic Drama, by a Lady 1801

46 Amaranth (The), a Miscellany of Original Prose and Verse, contributed by distinguished writers, and edited by T. K. Hervey, *plates* *folio.* 1839
47 Amethyst (The), or Christian's Annual for 1832 and 1833, (containing Poems by Mrs Opie, Mrs Mackay, and Mary Susanna Haynes), 2 vol *Edinb* 1832-3
48 Amulet (The); or Christian and Literary Remembrancer for the years 1826 to 1836 inclusive, 11 vol *plates,* 1826-36
49 Amusing Moralist, a Collection of Fables from Æsop, by a Lady *Doncaster,* 1806
50 Amusing Moralist, *woodcuts* *ib* 1816
51 Ancient Ballads, selected from Percy's Collection, with explanatory notes, by a Lady, *plates* 1807
52 ANDREW (Mrs) Original Poems on various and interesting Subjects, *not printed for publication* *Paisley,* 1852
53 ANDREWS (HANNAH) Miscellaneous Pieces, in verse *printed by T. Jones,* 1805
54 ANDREWS (MARY J.) Quiet Hour *Brighton,* 1850
55 Angel Visits, and other Poems *Edinb* 1865
56 Anglo-Indian Family, or Aunt Lucy's Journal, *plate and cuts* *Croydon,* 1853
57 ANNE BOLEYN (QUEEN) Memoirs of her Life, by Miss Benger, *portrait* 1827
58 —— The Star of the Court, by Miss S Bunbury, *port* 1844
59 Anniversary (The), or, Poetry and Prose for 1829, edited by Allan Cunningham, *plates, large paper* *royal 8vo* 1829
60 Annual Monitor for 1813, 1814, 1815, 1829, 1850, 1860 and 1866, and Obituary of the Society of Friends, 4 vol *York and Bradford,* 1850-66
61 Annual Souvenir for 1834, *plates,* 1834—Atlantic Souvenir, *plates, Philadelphia,* 1830—Aurora Borealis, a Literary Annual, *plates, Newcastle,* 1833 3 *vol*
62 ANSPACH (ELIZABETH LADY CRAVEN, MARGRAVINE OF,) Sleep-Walker, a Comedy, in two Acts
VERY RARE, ONLY A VERY SMALL NUMBER PRINTED FOR PRESENTS *Strawberry Hill, by T. Kirgate,* 1778
63 —— Fashionable Day, dedicated to Lord Berkeley, her brother, *privately printed,* VERY RARE 1780
64 —— Journey through the Crimea to Constantinople, *map and plates, with autograph letter of the Margravine inserted* 4to 1789
65 —— Songs, Duets, Trios, &c. in the Silver Tankard, or, the Point at Portsmouth, 1781—Sketch of the Pantomime, n d —The Robbers, with a Prologue and Epilogue by the Margravine of Anspach, 1799—Airs and Choruses in the Princess of Georgia, *privately printed,* 1798— The Miniature Picture, a Comedy, 1781 *in one vol*

66 ANSPACH (ELIZABETH LADY CRAVEN, MARGRAVINE OF,) Nourjad, a Comedy, with Bill of the Performers, *Hammersmith*, 1803—Release of Eblis, a Pantomime, *ib.* 1803—Bill of Performance at Brandenburgh House Theatre, *ib* 1804, *privately printed* — *in one vol.*
67 —— Memoirs, written by herself, 2 vol *portraits* 1826
68 —— Memoirs, 2 vol *portraits* *Paris,* 1826
69 APPLETON (ELIZABETH) Spring Bud, or Rural Scenery, in verse, *frontispiece by Scott* 1818
70 ARLY (H E G) Household Songs, and other Poems *New York,* 1855
71 Aristodemus, a Tragedy *Edinb* 1838
72 ARKWRIGHT (MRS ROBERT) Set of Six Songs, the words selected from the Poems of Byron, Campbell and Wordsworth, Mrs Arkwright and Miss Twiss *folio n d*
73 ARMSTRONG (ELIZA) Affection's Token, *plate* (*Otley*) *n d*
74 ARNOLD (JANE E) Lyra Evangelica Hymns from the French of Dr Malan 1866
75 ARNOLD (M E) Painted Window, a Poem, *first and second editions,* 2 vol. 1856
76 Arraignment of lewde, idle, froward and unconstant Women, 1615, *repr* 1807—Ester hath hang'd Haman, by Ester Sowernam (with a Defence of Women, in verse, by JOANE SHARP), 1617, *repr* 1807 *4to in one vol*
77 ARTHINGTON (MARIA) Remarks on Christian Faith, *Leeds,* 1836—Queries for Women Friends, 1847—To Mary Wright on completing her 100th year, *Leeds,* 1855—Rhymes for Harry and his Nursemaid, *coloured plates,* 1851—Poetry of Bye-gone Days, and other Selected Pieces, *not published,* 1861 *4 vol.*
78 ASHBY (ELIZABETH C) Scripture Teachings for Young Children 1857
79 Ask Mamma, 1813—Affectionate Mother, 1803—Adonia, 4 vol in 2, 1801—Aphorisms for Youth, 1801 *5 vol*
80 ASKEWE (ANNE) Bale (J.) First examinacyon of Anne Askewe, lately martyred in Smythfelde, by the Romysh Popes upholders, *with the voyce of Anne Askewe out of the 54 Psalme, in verse, Marpurg in the lande of Hessen, Nov* 1546. The lattre examinacyon by the wycked Synagoge of Antichrist, *with her songe in Newgate, ib Jan* 1547 black letter, ORIGINAL EDITION OF BOTH PARTS, OF EXTREME RARITY, *folio 19 in the first part supplied in facsimile* *in one vol.*
81 —— Bale, Examinations, and other Select Pieces, *reprinted for the Parker Society* *Camb* 1849
82 ASTELL (MARY) Serious Proposal to the Ladies, by a Lover of her Sex, *with a Poem on Pleasure, 3 pages in MS* 1694

83 Asylum for Fugitive Pieces, in prose and verse, 4 vol 1785-98
84 ATTERSOLL (MRS) Peter the Cruel, King of Castile and Leon, an Historical Play *Angers*, 1818
85 AUBER (MISS) Spirit of the Psalms 1829
86 ALBERT (MRS) Harlequin-Hydaspes or the Greshamite, a Mock-Opera 1719
87 Aunt Carrie's Rhymes for Children, *plates* *New York*, 1854
88 Aunt Mary's Poetry, *Reading*, 1840—The same, *second edition, plate, ib n d*—Aunt Mary's Verses, *woodcuts, New York*, 1855—Aunt Ann's Gift, *woodcuts, n d*—Aunt Rosamond's Enigmas, 1850 5 vol
89 AUSTIN (SARAH) Characteristics of Goethe, from the German of Falk, Von Muller, &c. 3 vol *portrait and plates*, 1833—AUSTIN (ELLEN) Stirring Hymns for Stirring Times, n d 4 vol
90 AVELINE (E. L) Mother's Fables, in verse, and Tales and Fables, *illustrations by W. Harvey* 1861
91 AVELINE (M G) Fairy Tale Charades for Acting, *two copies* 1858
92 AVERY (SARAH) *of Lyme Regis, Dorset*, Divine Hymns *Bridport*, 1795
93 AYRE (ELIZABETH GEORGIANA) Wild Flowers, *Stokesley*, 1842—Memoir of Mary Ayres, by David Ives, *Chalfont St. Peter, n d.* 2 vol
94 Ayrshire Wreath, for 1843, 4 and 5, and a collection of pieces, in prose and verse, by Native Authors, on subjects relating to Ayrshire, 3 vol. *plates* *Kilmarnock*, 1843-5
95 B (A L) Ôeone, or, Before the Dawn *privately printed* n d.
96 B. (E L) Original Sketches in Poetry *Thames Ditton*, 1845
97 B (F.) Miscellaneous Verses, adapted to Youth and Childhood, *privately printed* *Florence*, 1863
98 B (F. M.) Mildred, or, The Wandering Spirit *illustrations in outline by C B. B* 4to 1852
99 ——— Lady's Bay, and other Poems 1853
100 B. (L. M) Poems, *privately printed* 1830
101 B (M E) Poems and Tales, under the noms de Plume of Mary Campbell, Mary Mel, &c. *New York*, 1851
102 B. (M H) *of Kelso*, Rokesburghe Castle· a Metrical Romance of the Twelfth Century, in Six Cantos *privately printed* 1851
103 B. (M P) Legend of the Rhone· a Poem in Five Cantos, *two copies* 1858
104 B. (MRS) Poems, appropriate for a sick or a melancholy Hour, *frontispiece, Wellington, Salop*, 1824—Tribute of Affection to the Memory of a Beloved Sister, *ib* 1836 2 vol

105 B (S. A.) Love's Chosen Few, a Tale in verse, *privately printed, Birmingham, n d*—Emma, by M A B, *Sheffield*, 1850—Poems on various Subjects, by Mrs. B, 1826   3 *vol*
106 B—N (Mrs.) *of Carnock, near Dunfermline,* Collection of Miscellaneous Poems   *Edinb.* 1819
107 B—N (S) Serious Reflections, with the addition of a few Poems on several occasions   1801
108 Baby Ballads, by a Lady, 1839 — Babe and Princess, 1864 — BACHE (ANNA) Clara Howell, *Edinb.* 1857   3 vol
109 BACON (M A) Poetry in Winged Thoughts, Flowers and their kindred Thoughts, Fruits from the Garden and Field, 3 vol. *beautifully printed in colours, and illuminated by Owen Jones, fancy embossed calf, g e.*   1848-51
110 BAGEHOT (EDITH) Echo for the commencement of a subscription to build a New Church
privately printed   *Langport* (1841)
111 BAILEY (ELIZABETH RAINIER) Lady Jane Grey, and other Poems, 2 vol *portrait and plate*   1854
112 BAILEY (Mrs) Months, and other Poems, *second edition,* 1833 —Musæ Sacræ Hymns and Sacred Poetry, *Ballingdon, n. d*   2 *vol*
113 BAILLIE (E C C) Way of the Wilderness   (1862)
114 BAILLIE (JOANNA) Plays on the Passions of the Mind   1798
115 —— The same, *second edition*   1799
116 —— The same, *third edition*   1800
117 —— The same, *fourth edition,* 1802, Vol II, *second edition,* 1802, Vol III, 1812—Family Legend, a Tragedy, *Edinb.* 1810—Miscellaneous Plays, 1804, *calf*   4 *vol*
118 —— The same, *fifth edition,* 1806, Vol II, *third edition,* 1806, Vol III, 1812—Miscellaneous Plays, *second edition,* 1805, *calf gilt*   4 *vol*
119 —— The same, *new edition,* 3 vol.   1821
120 —— Miscellaneous Plays, 1804—De Monfort, with remarks by Mrs Inchbald, *Edinb n d.*   2 *vol*
121 —— Family Legend, *Edinb* 1810—Metrical Legends, 1821   2 *vol*
122 —— Family Legend, *second edition, Edinb* 1810—Metrical Legends, *second edition,* 1821   2 *vol*
123 —— Collection of Poems from Living Authors   1823
124 —— Dramas, 3 vol *calf*   1836
125 —— The Martyr, 1826—The Bride, 1828—Fugitive Verses, 1842   3 *vol*
126 —— Fugitive Verses, 1840—The Bride, *second edition,* 1828   2 *vol*
127 —— Ahalya Baee, *privately printed*   1849

128 BAILLIE (JOANNA) Dramatic and Poetical Works, complete in 1 vol *portrait and view of Bothwell Manse, with signature of the Poetess pasted on the title-page, calf gilt* 1851
129 —— The same, *second edition, portrait and plate* 1853
130 BAILLIE (MARIANNE) Guy of Warwick a Legende, and other Poems, *privately printed*   *Kingsbury*, 1817
131 —— Trifles in Verse, *vignette on title-page privately printed* 1825
132 Baker (D E) Biographia Dramatica, continued by Reed and Jones, 4 vol 1812
133 BAKER (MRS E A) Fruits of the Spirit, & other Poems 1847
134 BALDWIN (ELIZABETH) *of Wolverton, Bucks,* Selection from several Books of Poetry   *Stony Stratford*, 1823
135 —— Selection, *second edition*   *ib* 1824
136 BALFOUR (CLARA LUCAS) Garland of Water Flowers, 1844—Sketches of English Literature, 1852—Working Women of the last Half Century, 1856   3 *vol.*
137 BALFOUR (Miss) Hope, with other Poems   *Belfast*, 1810
138 BALL (ELIZA CRAUFURD) Christian Armour, *embellished and illuminated with beautiful borders, &c*   4to   *New York*, 1866
139 Ballads and Songs of Yorkshire, with Notes and Glossary by C J Davison Ingledew 1860
140 BALLANTYNE (MRS) Kelso Souvenir, or Selections from her Scrap Book   *Kelso*, 1832
141 Ballard (G) Memoirs of British Ladies 1775
142 BALMANNO (MARY) Pen and Pencil, *beautifully illustrated*   4to   *New York*, 1858
143 Balmford (William) Seaman's Spiritual Companion, in verse, *with a metrical Epistle to the Reader, by a Gentlewoman* VERY SCARCE 1678
144 BANKS (MRS G L) *formerly Isabella Varley,* Ivy Leaves a Collection of Poems, *Manchester*, 1844—Daisies in the Grass a Collection of Songs and Poems, 1865   2 vol
145 BANNERMAN (ANNE) Poems   *Edinb* 1800
146 —— Poems Another Edition   4to   *ib* 1807
147 —— Tales of Superstition and Chivalry, *plates* 1802
148 BARBAULD (ANNA LETITIA) Poems, *port inserted* 4to 1773
149 —— Poems, *third edition, old calf gilt* 1773
150 —— Poems, *fourth edition* 1774
151 —— Poems, *fourth edition*, 1774—Miscellaneous Pieces, in prose, by J & A L Aikin, *second edition*, 1777 *in 1 vol*
152 —— Poems, *fifth edition*, 1777—Miscellaneous Pieces, 1775, *with autograph of Sylvester Douglas*   *in one vol*
153 —— Poems, to which is added an Epistle to W Wilberforce *calf gilt by Kalthoeber* 1792
154 —— Poems   *Boston (in America)* 1820

155 BARBAULD (ANNA LAETITIA) Devotional Pieces, compiled from the Psalms and Book of Job, &c. 1775
156 ———— Epistle to W. Wilberforce on the rejection of the Bill, for abolishing the Slave Trade, *second edition, portrait inserted* 4to. 1791
157 ———— Dr Watts's Hymns and Moral Songs, revised and altered 1791
158 ———— Hymns, in prose, for Children 1799
159 ———— Eighteen Hundred and Eleven, a Poem 4to 1812
160 ———— Works, with Memoir by Lucy Aikin, 2 vol *portraits, and an autograph note of Mrs. Barbauld inserted* calf 1825
161 ———— Legacy for Young Ladies, 1826—Hymns in Rhyme, 1838—Hymns in Prose, 1850 3 vol
162 BARBER (MARY) Poems on several occasions *old red morocco, g. e* 4to 1734
163 ———— Poems 1735
164 ———— Poems 1736
165 BARCLAY (RACHEL) Select Pieces of Poetry 1793
166 ———— Poems, *second edition* 1797
167 BARKER (H A.) Crown Jewels 1854
168 BARKER (JANE) Poetical Recreations 1688
169 ———— Exilius, or The Banish'd Roman, a Romance, 2 parts E Curll, 1715
170 ———— Christian Pilgrimage, from the French of Fenelon *ib* 1718
171 ———— Patch-Work Screen for the Ladies, a Collection of Novels, interspersed with Poems *ib* 1723
172 ———— Entertaining Novels, with the Amours of Bosvil and Galetia, *third edition* 1743
173 BARKER (JEMIMA) Poems 1822
174 BARKER (MISS) Lines to Lord Byron (His Lordship will know why), by one of the Small Fry of the Lakes, *presentation copy from the authoress to Hartley Coleridge* 1815
175 BALLAND (KATHARINE) Poems *Glasgow*, 1815
176 ———— Songs of Consolation *Edinb* 1851
177 BARNARD (ANNE) *born Lady Anne Lindsay of Balcarres*, Auld Robin Gray, a Ballad, *frontispiece designed by C. K Sharpe, Esq* *privately printed for the Bannatyne Club, with part of an autograph letter of Lady Ann Lindsay inserted* *ib.* 1825
178 BARNARD (FRANCES C [*Mrs Alfred*]) Embroidered Facts, *cuts* 1836
179 ———— Doleful Death and Flowery Funeral of Fancy *Yarmouth,* 1837
180 BARNES (CHARLOTTE M. S) The Night of the Coronation *New York,* 1838

181 BARNES (CHARLOTTE M. S) Plays, Prose, and Poetry
    Philadelphia, 1848
182 BARNES (ESTHER) *of Shepton Mallett, Somersetshire*, The
    Disengaged Fair   *Bristol*, 1796
183 BARNARD (ELIZABETH) The Willows of Amwell
    *privately printed, with autograph copy of the poetess's letter
    to Queen Victoria, &c inserted*   *Hertford*, 1853
184 BARRELL (MARIA) *formerly Weylar*. Reveries du Cœur; or
    Feelings of the Heart, attempted in Verse
    Printed for the author, 1770
185 ——— British Liberty Vindicated, or a Delineation of the
    King's Bench   4to. 1788
186 ——— The Captive (a Play), *privately printed*   1790
187 BARRELL (Miss P) Riches and Poverty, a Tale, *frontispiece*,
    1808—Test of Virtue and other Poems, *frontispiece*,
    1811   2 vol
189 BARRETT (ELIZABETH G. BARBER) Poems, *portrait*
    New York, 1866
190 BARTHOLOMEW (JULIA MERSILVIA) The Young Poet's Offering
    Winchester, n d
191 BARTITY (Mrs) *formerly Smith*, Lady of the Lake, a Drama,
    frontispiece, Dublin, n d—Border Feuds, or the Lady
    of Buccleuch, a Drama, *frontispiece, green morocco, g e
    with autograph of the Princess Elizabeth in both, ib n d*
    2 vol.
192 BARTON (LUCY) The Reliquary, 1836—The Oratory, 1841
    2 vol
193 BARWELL (Mrs) Childhood's Hours, *plates*   1851
194 BASSETT (MATILDA) Bible Gleanings, *Woolwich*, 1849—
    Another Edition, 1851   2 vol
195 BATCHELOR (HARRIET) Original Poetry, *printed and manu-
    script, unpublished*   (1862)
196 BATH (ELIZABETH) Poems   *Bristol*, 1806
197 BATTIER (HENRIETTA) Protected Fugitives, a Collection of
    Miscellaneous Poems   *Dub printed for the author*, 1791
198 BAYFIELD (E G) Fugitive Poems, 1805—Gleanings from
    Zimmerman's Solitude, &c 1806   2 vol.
199 BAYLEY (CATHARINE) Vacation Evenings, with the Addition
    of A Visitor from Eton, 3 vol   1809
200 BEACH (ELIZABETH T PORTER) Pelayo, an Epic of the Olden
    Moorish Time, *plates*   *New York*, 1864
201 BLAIR (ANN) Poems, 1842—The Rescued, and other Poems,
    1848   2 vol.
202 BLAIR (Mrs MARY) Four Psalms paraphrased, (in the Second
    Edition of Woodford), *frontispiece*   1678
203 BRANCROFT (SUSANNA) Eva of Chepstow, a New Year's Tale
    in Verse   *Richmond*, 1844
204 Beautiful Poetry, selected by the Editors of the Critic, 6 vol
    1853-9

205 BEATTIE (ANNE) Songs in the Desert   *Manchester*, 1815
206 BEHN (APHRA) Amorous Prince, or the Curious Husband, a Comedy   4to   1671
207 —— Forc'd Marriage, or Jealous Bridegroom, a Tragi-Comedy, *head line partly cut off*   4to   1671
208 —— Forc'd Marriage   4to   1688
209 —— Forc'd Marriage   4to   1690
210 —— Dutch Lover, a Comedy   4to   1673
211 —— Abdelazer, or The Moor's Revenge, a Tragedy   4to   1677
212 —— Abdelazer   4to   1693
213 —— Debauchee, or Credulous Cuckold, a Comedy   4to   1677
214 —— Rover, or Banish't Cavaliers, a Comedy   4to   1697
215 —— The same, 1677—The same, second edition, 1697—Second Part of the Rover 1681   4to   *in one vol*
216 —— The same, 1677—Second Part, *wants last leaf*, 1681   4to   *in one vol*
217 —— The same, another Edition, 1729—Another Edition, *frontispiece, two copies*, 1735—Another Edition, 1737—Another Edition, *Dublin*, 1741—Another Edition, 1757—Love in Many Masks, as altered from the Rover by J P Kemble (1790)   7 vol
218 —— Town Fopp, or Sir Timothy Tawdrey, a Comedy   4to   1677
219 —— Town Fopp   4to.   1699
220 —— Sir Patient Fancy, a Comedy, *head lines mended in manuscript*   4to   1678
221 —— Feign'd Curtizans, or A Nights Intrigue a Comedy   4to   1679
222 —— City-Heiress, or Sir Timothy Treat-all, a Comedy   4to   1682
223 —— False Count, or A New Way to play an Old Game   4to   1682
224 —— False Count   4to   1697
225 —— Roundheads; or The Good Old Cause, a Comedy   4to   1682
226 —— Roundheads   4to   1698
227 —— Young King, or The Mistake   4to.   1683
228 —— Poems upon several Occasions, with a Voyage to the Island of Love, *portrait inserted*   1684
229 —— Pindarick Poem on the Happy Coronation of James II and Queen Mary   folio   1685
230 —— Pindarick on the Death of our late Sovereign 1685—The same, *second edition*, 1685—Poem to Catherine, Queen Dowager, on the Death of King Charles II, 1685—Congratulatory Poem to Queen Mary upon her Arrival in England, 1689—Ode on the Death of Her Majesty, by a Young Lady, 1695   folio   *in one vol*

231 BEHN (APHRA) Miscellany, a Collection of Poems by several hands, *portrait inserted* 1685
232 ------ La Montre, or The Lover's Watch, *frontispiece* 1686
233 ------ To Christopher Duke of Albemarle, on his Voyage to his Government of Jamaica, a Pindarick 4to 1687
234 ------ Luckey Chance, or An Alderman's Bargain, a Comedy, *the Roxburghe copy* 4to 1687
235 ------ Emperor of the Moon, a Farce 4to 1687
236 ------ The same, *second edition, portrait inserted*, 4to. 1688— Another Edition, *Dublin*, 1757 2 vol
237 ------ Two Congratulatory Poems on the Hopes and Birth of the Prince of Wales, *second edition* 4to 1688
238 ------ Lycidus, or The Lover in Fashion, being an Account from Lycidus to Lysander of his Voyage from the Island of Love, with a Miscellany of Poems, *portrait inserted* 1688
239 ------ Widdow Ranter, or History of Bacon in Virginia, a Tragi-Comedy 4to. 1690
240 ------ Younger Brother, or Amorous Jilt, a Comedy 4to 1696
241 ------ The same. Another copy 4to 1696
242 ------ Histories and Novels, viz Oroonoko, Fair Jilt, Agnes de Castro, Lover's Watch, Ladies Looking Glass, Lucky Mistake, and Love Letters 1696
243 ------ Poems upon Several Occasions, with a Voyage to the Island of Love, also The Lover in Fashion, &c *second edition, portrait* 1697
244 ------ Lady's Looking-Glass to dress herself by, or the whole Art of Charming 1697
245 ------ Wandering Beauty, a Novel, 1698—Unfortunate Bride, a Novel, 1700—Unfortunate Happy Lady, a True History, 1700—Dumb Virgin, a Novel, 1700 *in one vol*
246 ------ Plays, entire, 2 vol *portrait inserted* 1702
247 ------ Plays, entire, *second edition*, 2 vol. *portrait*, 1716— Poems, with a Voyage to the Island of Love, *portrait inserted*, 1684—Lycidus, or Lover in Fashion, &c 1688 —Histories and Novels, *fifth edition*, 1705, *calf gilt* 4 vol
248 ------ Theory or System of several New Inhabited Worlds, in five Nights Conversation with the Marchioness of ***, from the French of Fontenelle, 1718—History of Oracles, and the Cheats of the Pagan Priests, 1718— Unfortunate Bride, 1718—Dumb Virgin, 1718—Unfortunate Happy Lady, 1718—Wandering Beauty, 1718—Unhappy Mistake, 1718 *in one vol.*
249 ------ Incouragement for Sinners, or Instructions for Saints 1719

250 BEHN (APHRA) Plays, *third edition*, 4 vol. *portrait, and an additional one inserted*, 1724—Histories and Novels, *eighth edition*, 2 vol. *portrait*, 1735; *calf gilt*   6 vol
251 ——. Romulus and Hersilia, or, The Sabine War, a Tragedy, *the Epilogue by Mrs. Behn*   4to   1683
252 —— Valentinian, a Tragedy, as alter'd by the late Earl of Rochester, *the Prologue by Mrs Behn*   4to   1685
253 —— Æsop's Fables, with his Life, in English, French, and Latin, by Francis Barlow, 112 *sculptures and* 31 *plates* (*No* 17 *wanting*) *representing his life, the verses under the engravings to the life written by Mrs Behn*
   russia extra, g e   folio   1687
254 —— Fane (Sir F.) Sacrifice, a Tragedy, with commendatory Poem by Mrs Behn   4to   1687
255 —— Poems to the Memory of Edmond Waller (including one by Mrs. Behn)   4to.   1688
256 —— Dunton (J) Athenian Mercury (No. 23, June 18, 1695, contains Poems by Mrs Behn), and other old Newspapers   *folio a thick vol*
257 —— Tryon (Tho) Way to Health, Long Life and Happiness, *with introductory Poem by Mrs Behn*   1697
258 —— Memoirs of the Life of Mr Tho Tryon, late of London, Merchant, *with Epitaph by Mrs Behn, portrait*   1705
259 —— Poems by George Duke of Buckingham (including Sappho addrest to the Duke in 1681, translated by Madam Behn, and a Poem to his Memory by Mrs Behn in 1687, *with her portrait*, 1711—Poem to Higden on his Translation of Juvenal, 4to   2 vol
260 BELL (A [Mrs Colonel]) Lays of a Lady or Poetical Tales and Poems   1840
261 BELL (A S) Fanny, or True Benevolence and Miscellaneous Poems, *frontispiece*   *Whitby*, 1821
262 BELL (FRANCES AUGUSTA) Memoir, with specimens of her compositions by Rev J Grant   1827
263 BELL (Miss) Edinburgh Literary Album   *Edinb* 1811
264 Bell's Classical Arrangement of Fugitive Poetry, 18 vol   1789-1800
265 BELLAMY (D) Love Triumphant or, The Rival Goddesses, a Pastoral Opera perform'd by the young Ladies of Mrs Bellamy's School, with some original Poems, &c
   Printed for and sold only by Mrs Bellamy at her School in Old Boswel Court, near Clement's Inn, 1722
266 Belle Assemblée (La), or Bell's Court and Fashionable Magazine, vol XXIII, *new series, plates, some coloured* 1821
267 BELT (Miss) Sons of the Martyrs, and other Poems
   Jewish Industrial Press, 1847

268 Bengal Annual, a Literary Keepsake for 1830, 1833, and 1834, edited by D. L. Richardson, 3 vol *plates*
Calcutta, 1830-4

269 BENGER (ELIZABETH OGILVY) Memoir, by Miss Aikin *privately printed, portrait and specimen of Miss Benger's autograph inserted* n. d

270 —— Poems on the Abolition of the Slave Trade, by Montgomery, Grahame, and Miss Benger, *portraits and plates after Smirke, russia, g. c.* 4to. 1809

271 BENN (MARY) The Solitary, or, a Lay from the West, 1853— Lays of the Hebrews, *Bath*, 1854 2 vol.

272 BENNET (GEORGIANA) Ianthe and other Poems, *Birmingham*, 1841—The same, *second edition*, ib 1841—A Lay and Songs of Home, ib 1843—The Poetess, ib. 1844—The Studio, ib. 1846 5 vol

273 BENNET (GRACE) Memoirs, &c by W. Bennet
Macclesfield, 1803

274 BENNETT (ELIZABETH) My Mothers' Meetings 1863

275 BENNETT (EMILY T B) Song of the Rivers *New York*, 1865

276 BENNISON (D M) Poems
Boston (in America), printed for the author, 1847

277 BENSON (MRS) Lays of Memory, Sacred and Social, by a Mother and Son 1856

278 BENTLEY (C. C) Cambria· a Poem, Raymond, a Metrical Romance, &c *Newark-upon-Trent*, 1830

279 BENTLEY (ELIZABETH) Genuine Poetical Compositions, *portrait* *Norwich*, 1791

280 —— Poems, *portrait, and an additional one inserted* ib 1821

281 —— Tales for Children, part II, *Norwich*, 1831—Miscellaneous Poems, third volume, ib 1835 2 vol.

282 Bentley (Thomas) Monument of Matrones. conteining seven severall Lamps of Virginitie, or distinct treatises, whereof the first five concerne praier and meditation· the other two last, precepts and examples, as the woorthie works parthe of men, parthe of women, 3 vol.
black letter, EXCESSIVELY RARE, QUITE COMPLETE, IN WHICH STATE ONLY TWO OTHER COPIES ARE KNOWN, *old russia, from the Libraries of Mr Herbert, Mr Woodhouse, Mr Heber, and Dr Bliss, with two autograph Letters of the Rt Hon. T Grenville inserted*
4to *H Denham*, 1582

⁎⁎ This book contains several valuable pieces or prayers, viz. of Queen Katharine Parr, Queen Elizabeth, Margaret Queen of Navarre, Lady Jane Dudley, Lady Abergavenny, Lady Tirwit, Ann Askew, Mrs Bradford, &c.

283 BERNERS (JULIANA) Booke of Haukyng, Huntyng, and Fysshyng, with all the properties and medecynes that are necessary to be kept
black letter, with woodcuts, the first title-page, A 4, and small corner of last leaf supplied in facsimile, morocco, g e. by Riviere 4to. *Wyllyam Copland, n. d.*

₊ OF EXCESSIVE RARITY, THE ONLY COPY NOTICED IN LOWNDES'S MANUAL *is that priced in the Bibliotheca Anglo-Poetica at £35*

284 —— Book of Hawking, Hunting, Coat Armour, Fishing, and Blasing of Arms, as printed by Wynkyn de Worde, 1496, with Biographical and Bibliographical Notices by Joseph Haslewood, *150 copies only printed russia, g. e very scarce* small folio. 1810

285 BERRY (SARAH) Thoughts, in prose and verse, on the Grace and Love of God *Ramsgate*, 1837

286 BETHAM (MATILDA) Elegies and other small Poems *Ipswich* (1797)

287 —— Biographical Dictionary of celebrated Women, *portraits* 1804

288 —— Poems 1808

289 —— Lay of Marie, *with two pages of Poetry in the autograph of the poetess inserted* 1816

290 —— Vignettes, in verse *Ipswich*, 1818

291 BEVAN (E F) Songs of Eternal Life, translated from the German, *plates in outline* 4to. 1858

292 —— Songs of Praise for Christian Pilgrims, &c *Chichester*, 1859

293 BEVERLEY (CHARLOTTE) Poems, *frontispiece and vignette* *Hull*, 1792

294 BEVERLEY (ELIZABETH, [*Mrs R*]) Poetical Olio, &c 1819— Modern Times, *sixth edition*, 1818 *in one vol*

295 —— The Actress's Ways and Means to industriously raise the Wind, *fourth edition* 1822

296 —— The same, *tenth edition* n. d

297 —— Book of Variety, laughable Anecdotes, &c. 1823

298 —— The same, *fifth edition* 1824

299 —— Odd Thoughts on a variety of Odd Subjects *fourth edition* 1826

300 —— Entertaining Moral Poems 1826

301 —— The same, *fifth edition* n. d.

302 —— The Indefatigable, bound on a Voyage to the Island of Liberality 1830

303 BEWSHER (AMELIA) Early Musings, a Collection of Sacred and other Poems 1854

304 BIDDLE (ESTHER) The Trumpet of the Lord sounded as a Warning from the Spirit of Truth to England and the great and famous City of London, &c. 4to 1662
305 BIGELOW (MARION ALBINA) Northern Harp, containing Songs from the St. Lawrence, and Forest Melodies
New York, 1853
306 Bijou (The) or Annual of Literature and the Arts for 1828, 1829, and 1830, 3 vol *plates* *Pickering*, 1828-30
307 BILLER (SARAH) Holkham, the Scenes of my Childhood, and other Poems 1839
308 —— The same, *second edition* 1839
309 BINGHAM (JANE) Amy of the Peak, *plate, Chesterfield*, (1847) —Joys and Sorrows, *plate, ib. n d* 2 vol.
310 BINGHAM (MARY HELEN) Memoir, by J. Bustard, *imperfect in preface, Sevenoaks*, 1827—The same, *second edition,* 1832—The same, *third edition*, 1834 2 vol.
311 Biographical Dictionary of the Living Authors of Great Britain and Ireland (by Upcott, &c) 1816
312 Biographium Fœmineum. The Female Worthies; or Memoirs of Illustrious Ladies, 2 vol 1766
313 BIRCH (ELIZA) Poems and a Selection of Hymns
Manchester, 1800
314 BIRCH (MRS WALTER) Job Paraphrased 1838
315 BIRKETT (MARY) Poem on the African Slave Trade, 2 parts
Dublin, 1792
316 —— The same, first part, *second edition, Dublin*, 1792— Lines to the Memory of Joseph Williams, *ib.* 1807
in one vol.
317 Birth-Day Reflections, written by a Young Lady, Nov. 25, 1767 *Bath*, 1801
318 BISHOP (MARY) Poetic Tales and Miscellanies *Liverpool*, 1812
319 BLACKALL (ELIZABETH) Psalms and Hymns *Dublin*, 1835
320 BLACKWELL (ANN) Poems 1853
321 BLAIR (FRANCES) Christian Bouquet *South Shields*, 1832
322 BLAIR (MRS.) Poemata Melica. Original Odes, by Kennett Lea *n d.*
323 BLAKE (MARTHA) Elegy upon the Death of Mrs. Mary Blake (at the end of a Sermon at her Funeral, by T. Brooks)
1657
324 BLAMIRE (SUSANNA) Poetical Works, *portrait* *Edinb* 1842
325 BLANCHARD (ANNE) Midnight Reflections, *morocco, g. e.* 1822
326 —— The same, *second edition* 1823
327 BLEASE (ELIZABETH BOWER) Poems, 1817 — Tribute to the Memory of the Duke of Kent, 1820 2 vol.
328 BLEECKER (ANN ELIZA) Posthumous Works, and Collection of Essays by Margaretta V. Faugeres, *portrait, New York*, 1793—Bleecker's Miscellaneous Works, *imperfect* 2 vol.

329 BLESSINGTON (COUNTESS OF) Works, 2 vol. *portrait*
    Philadelphia, 1838
330 —— Diary of an Ennuyée   1826
331 —— Rambles in Waltham Forest, *plates*   4*to*. 1827
332 —— Gems of Beauty, 4 vol. 48 *plates*   4*to* 1836-40
333 —— Desultory Thoughts and Reflections, 1839—The same, second edition, 1839   2 vol
334 —— The Belle of a Season, *illustrated by Chalon*   4*to*. 1840
335 —— Literary Life and Correspondence, by R. R. Madden, 3 vol. *portrait and plates*   1855
336 BLOODWORTH (EMMA) Thoughts, and other Poems
    Sudbury, n d
337 Blossoms of Fancy, *printed for the author*, 1811—Bible Sketches, by a Lady, 1831—Thoughts in Verse (by J. BESSEMERES), 1859—The same 1860—BENNETT (MARY) Poems, 1853—BECKENCROFT (MRS) Conversations, n d —Baths of Bagnole, *plates*, 1826   7 vol.
338 BLOTT (JULIA S) May Garland, or, Wayside Flowers 1860
339 BLUNT (ELLEN KEY) Bread to my Children
    Philadelphia, 1856
340 BLYTH (CHARLOTTE ISABELLA) Tour in Scotland in 1859 *privately printed*   1860
341 BLYTON (EMMA) Poetical Tributes to the Memories of British Bards, 1858—Pleasures of Freedom, 1860   2 vol
342 BOATE (MRS WELLINGTON) Carlo Marillo, and other Poems, including Recollections of Ireland   1857
343 BODDINGTON (MRS) Poems, *vignettes*
    red morocco, tooled on the sides, g e   1839
344 BODKIN (S. S) Scenes from Life   1860
345 BOLAINE (ELIZABETH) Life and History of Betty Bolaine, late of Canterbury, interspersed with Poetry, *portrait, last leaf slightly defective,* Canterbury, 1805—History of Betty Bolaine, *plate*, Rochester, n d   *in one vol*
346 —— Life, second edition
    green morocco, tooled on the sides   *Canterbury*, 1832
347 BOLDERO (CHRIST) Sacred Dramas
    Holt printed for the author, 1823
348 BOND (MRS HENRY) Sacred and Miscellaneous Poems, 2 vol
    Guernsey, n d
349 BONHOTE (ELIZABETH) Parental Monitor, 1 vol. in 2, *frontispieces*   1796
350 Book of Common Praise, being Select Hymns for Parochial Use, 1863—Book of Hymns for public and private devotion, *Boston*, 1853—Book of Praise, arranged by Roundell Palmer, 1866   3 vol
351 BOOKER (ELLEN) Meditations in Poetry and Prose, 1861— Selections from the Papers of Martha Boone, 1817 2 vol

352 Boot (Charlotte) The Pirate, and other Poems, 1859—
    Borron (Mrs.) Reminiscences, 1839   2 vol.
353 Booth (Mrs.) The Little French Lawyer, a Farce, *plate inserted*   1778
354 Boothby (Mrs F) Marcella: or, the Treacherous Friend, a Tragi-Comedy   4to   1670
355 Border Feuds. or the Lady of Buccleuch, a Musical Drama   *Dublin*, 1811
356 Borthwick (Jane) Hymns from the Land of Luther, *four series, Edinb* 1855-62—Thoughts for Thoughtful Hours, 1859—Thoughtful Hours, 1863   4 vol
357 —— Hymns, complete in one vol   *Edinb* 1862
358 Botsford (Margaret) Viola, Heiress of St. Valverde, an Original Romance   *Philadelphia*, 1823
359 Bouquet (The) or Flowers of Poetry, *plate Yarmouth*, 1837
360 Bourke (Hannah Maria) O'Donoghue, Prince of Killarney   *Dublin*, 1830
361 Bourne (Isabella) Lays of Labour's Leisure Hours   1858
362 Bourne (Mary Anne) Evergreen a Collection of Original Poetry, *two copies, Warminster*, 1839—Guide to Tenby, *Carmarthen*, 1843   3 vol
363 Bourne (Mrs) Northern Reminiscences, *Whitehaven*, 1832 —Noah's Ark, 1841   2 vol
364 Bousfield (F B) Admonitory Rhymes   1829
365 Bousfield (W C.) Elijah, a Poem, 1818—Poems on Scriptural Subjects, 1823   2 vol.
366 Bowden (Hannah) Poetical Remains, edited by her Sister (Priscilla Marsh), 1860—The same, *another edition*, 1861   2 vol.
367 Bowden (Samuel) Poems (with a Farewell to the Country, by a Lady)   *Bath*, 1754
368 Bowdler (H. M) Pen Tamar, or, History of an Old Maid, *plates*   1830
369 Bowdler (Jane) Poems and Essays, 2 vol   *Bath*, 1786
370 —— The same, *second edition*, 2 vol   *ib* 1786
371 —— The same, *third edition*, 2 vol *port inserted*   *ib.* 1787
372 —— The same, *fourth edition*, 2 vol   *ib* 1787
373 —— The same, *a surreptitious edition*   *Dublin*, 1787
374 —— The same, *fifth edition*, 2 vol   *Bath*, 1788
375 —— The same, *sixth edition*, 2 vol   *ib* 1788
376 —— The same, *seventh edition*   *ib* 1793
377 —— The same, *eighth edition, vignettes, &c painted calf, Etruscan pattern*   *ib.* 1793
378 —— The same, *ninth edition, large paper*   *ib* 1797
379 —— The same, *tenth edition, port inserted*   4to *ib* 1798
380 —— The same, *eleventh edition*   *ib* 1807
381 —— The same, *twelfth edition*   *ib.* 1809

382 BOWDLER (JANE) The same, *thirteenth edition*   *Bath*, 1811
383 —— The same, *first American edition*   *New York*, 1811
384 —— The same, *fourteenth edition*   *Bath*, 1815
385 —— The same, *fifteenth edition*   *ib* 1815
386 —— The same, *called the eleventh edition*   *Dublin*, 1815
387 —— The same, *sixteenth edition*   *Bath*, 1819
388 —— The same, *portrait and plate*   *Lond* 1824
389 —— The same, *seventeenth edition*   *Bath*, 1830
390 BOWEN (Miss M.) Original Poems, *plate of St Vincent's Rock, and woodcut vignettes*   *Chepstow*, 1808
391 BOWEN (Mrs.) Ystradffin, a Descriptive Poem *morocco extra, g e by Hayday*   *Llandovery*, 1839
392 BOWEN (Mrs LEWIS) Kenilworth Castle, and other Poems, *plate*   *Wellington, Salop*, 1818
393 BOWLES (MRS GEORGE CRANLEY) Life's Dissolving Views, *Hertford*, 1865—BOWLEY (MARY) Hymns, 1847—BOWMAN (ANNE) Charade Dramas, *plates*, 1857   3 vol
394 BOWMAN (ANNE) Charade Dramas, *plates*, 1856—Norman Invasion and Day of Rivalry, 1857—Poetry, 1857   3 vol
395 BOYD (ELIZABETH) Humorous Miscellany, or, Riddles for the Beaux, inscribed to the Earl of Cardigan
     4to   *printed for S Slow*, 1733
396 —— Don Sancho or, The Student's Whim, a Ballad Opera, with Minerva's Triumph, a Masque   1739
397 —— The Beau's Miscellany or, the Agreeable Variety (containing Zara and Churchill, William and Catherine, and Admiral Anson, three Poems, by E Boyd) 1743
   ⁎⁎⁎ The title-pages to the other pieces in this collection are cancelled
398 BOYLE (MARY LOUISA) Bridal of Melcha, a Dramatic Sketch
     1844
399 —— My Portrait Gallery, and other Poems
   privately printed   1849
400 BRADBURN (ELIZA WEAVER) Our Centenary, 1839—Stories in Rhyme, 1842   2 vol
401 BRADDON (M E) Garibaldi, and other Poems, *portrait inserted*   1861
402 BRADNACK (I R and M A) Lays of the Valley, *plate*
     Yarmouth, 1843
403 BRADSHAW (ANNA) Six Legends of King Goldenstar 1858
404 BRADSTREET (ANNE) Tenth Muse lately sprung up in America. Or severall Poems, compiled with great variety of Wit and Learning, full of delight. Also a Dialogue between Old England and New, concerning the late troubles. With divers other pleasant and serious Poems
   EXCESSIVELY RARE, *good copy, calf, panelled sides, by Hering*   1650

405 BRADSTREET (ANNE) Several Poems, &c. Third Edition, corrected by the author, and enlarged by an Addition of several other Poems found amongst her Papers after her Death

 EXCESSIVELY RARE, UNKNOWN TO LOWNDES
 (Boston in America) reprinted from the second edition, 1758
406 BRAGG (JANE) Lays of Early Years, &c., 1839 — Birds and Insects, 30 *engravings from designs by the authoress*, 1841 — Extracts, Religious and Secular, 1862 — Verses for Children, *Carlisle*, 1862   4 vol
407 BRAITHWAITE (MARTHA) Fireside Hymn-Book   1865
408 BRAND (HANNAH) Plays and Poems   *Norwich,* 1798
409 BRAWN (MARY ANN) *of Loughton, Essex,* Poems on various Subjects, in Manuscript, *and three privately printed single pieces*   1847-62
410 BRERETON (JANE) Poems and Letters, with Life   4to   1744
411 BRETTELL (MRS) *of Burslem, Staffordshire,* Susan Ashfield, &c   1820
412 BRETTINGHAM (CLARA M.) Devotions for the Hours from the Psalms   1852
413 Bridal Gift. Poems by British and American Poets, *Halifax,* 1859 — Bridal Gift, *Liverpool,* 1831 — Breathings of Consolation, *ib* 1854   3 vol.
414 BRISTOW (A) Maniac, a Tale, 1810 — Emma de Lissau, 2 vol 1829   3 vol
415 Britannia's Royal Chieftain   4to   *Leeds,* 1837
416 British Drama, a Collection of Tragedies, Comedies, Operas and Farces, 2 vol *portraits and plates*   1824-6
417 British Female Poets with Biographical and Critical Notes by G W Bethune, *port and plates Philadelphia,* 1851
418 British Poetical Miscellany, 30 Nos *published weekly, with a title and contents*
 very scarce   *Huddersfield, S Sikes and Co , n d*
419 British Theatre (New): a selection of Original Dramas, not yet acted, 4 vol   1814-15
420 BRITTLE (EMILY) India Guide or Journal of a Voyage to the East Indies in 1780, a Poetical Epistle to her Mother
 very scarce   *Calcutta, printed by George Gordon,* 1785
421 BLITTON (FRANCES) Short and True Sketches on the Conflicts of Life, &c   *printed for the author,* 1828
422 BROCK (MRS HENRY F) Christmas Eve, 1859 — Daily Readings for Passion-Tide, *Cambridge,* 1861   2 vol
423 BRODERIP (FRANCES FREELING) Way-Side Fancies
    Moxon, 1857
424 —— My Grandmother's Budget of Stories and Songs, *coloured illustrations by her brother, Thos Hood* 1863

425 BRODERIP (FRANCES FREELING) Crosspatch, the Cricket and the Counterpane, a Patchwork of Story and Song, *illustrations by T. Hood* 1865

426 —— Merry Songs for Little Voices, set to Music by T Murby, *illustrations by T Hood* 4to 1865

427 BROMFIELD (ELIZABETH) Recollections of Brittany, n d — The Gathered Flower, a Memoir of Miss SUSANNA BROMFIELD, with Poems, &c 1857   2 vol.

428 BROMLEY (M I) Poems, *only a very small number privately printed* Worcester, 1861

429 BRONTE (CHARLOTTE) Poems by Currer, Ellis and Acton Bell 1846

430 —— The same *Philadelphia*, 1848

431 —— The Professor, and Poems 1860

432 —— Life, by E C Gaskell, 2 vol *portrait and plate* 1857

433 BROOKE (CHARLOTTE) Reliques of Irish Poetry, translated into English verse 4to *Dublin*, 1789

434 —— The same, with Life by A C Seymour *ib* 1816

435 BROOKE (FRANCES) Virginia, a Tragedy, 1756—Siege of Sinope, 1781—Rosina, *two editions*, 1783 and 1790—Marian, 1800—Songs, &c in Marian, 1788   5 vol

436 —— Old Maid, by Mary Singleton, Spinster, *a new edition, revised by the Editor* 1764

437 —— Rosina, *sixteen different editions*, 1783-1815—Siege of Sinope, 1781—Songs, &c in Marian, 1789   (18)

438 BROOKS (MARIA) Judith, Esther, and other Poems, *Boston (in America)*, 1820—Zophiel, or, the Bride of Seven 1833—Verses on Schools, by SOPHIA BROOKS, 1854 — Dove on the Cross, by J E B, 1853   4 vol

439 BROOKS (MARY ELIZABETH) Rivals of Este, and other Poems, by James G and Mary E Brooks *New York*, 1829

440 Broomholme Priory, or, the Loves of Albert and Agnes, a Poem, *frontispiece* 4to *Holt*, 1801

441 BROTHERTON (MARY) Poems, *second edition, Brussels*, 1855 — The Brother and Sisters, by the Author of the Lily, 1858   2 vol

442 BROWN (D) Poetical Recreations   *Edinb printed for the authoress* 1851

443 BROWN (ELIZABETH) *of Woodend, Northamptonshire* Original Poems *Northampton*, 1811

444 —— The same *Banbury*, 1813

445 BROWN (FRANCES) Star of Attéghéi, Vision of Schwartz, and other Poems, 1844 — Lyrics and Miscellaneous Poems, *Edinb* 1848 — Pictures and Songs of Home (1865) — The same, *cuts coloured and illuminated, n d*   4 vol

446 Brown (Louisa) Heathen Mythology, in easy and pleasing verse, *woodcuts* *printed for the author, n d*
447 Brown (Margaret) Lays of Affection, *presentation copy, with autograph inscription by the Poetess* Edinb 1819
448 Browne (Rev A. W) Home Lyrics (the greater portion by Females of the Family)
printed for private circulation 1859
449 Browne (Frances Elizabeth) Poems
Cambridge (in America), 1846
450 —— The same, *frontispiece* Boston (in America), 1848
451 Browne (J E) Dove on the Cross, *six editions*, 1819-63—Aunt Effie's Gift, *with illustrations*, 1854 7 vol
452 —— Aunt Effie's Rhymes for Little Children, *24 illustrations by H K Browne* n. d.
453 —— The Child, *beautifully illustrated in chromo-lithography* 4to Day and Son, n d
454 Browning (Elizabeth Barrett) Essay on Mind, with other Poems 1826
455 —— The same, 1826—Prometheus Bound and Miscellaneous Poems, 1833, *green morocco extra, g e in one vol*
456 —— The Seraphim, and other Poems, *portrait* 1838
457 —— Poems, 2 vol Moxon, 1844
458 —— Poems, *new edition*, 2 vol 1850
459 —— Poems, *third edition*, 2 vol 1853
460 —— Poems, *fourth edition*, 3 vol *portrait* 1856
461 —— Poems, *fifth edition*, 3 vol 1862
462 —— Poems, *sixth edition*, 4 vol *portrait* 1864
463 —— Casa Guidi Windows, a Poem, 1851—Aurora Leigh, 1857—Poems before Congress, 1860—Last Poems 1862—Greek Christian Poets and English Poets, 1863 5 vol
464 —— Aurora Leigh, *second edition, port* 1857—The same, *third edition,* 1857—The same, *fourth edition,* 1859—The same, *fifth edition,* 1860 4 vol
465 —— Napoleon III in Italy, and other Poems, New York, 1860—Last Poems, *second edition,* 1862 2 vol
466 Bruce (Charlotte Ann Brownsword) Poems
privately printed Calcutta, 1846
467 Bruce (Mrs Henry) Scripture Sonnets 1863
468 Bruce (Jane) Sacred Poems, edited by her Son, W D Bruce 1846
469 —— Poems, *privately printed* 1851
470 —— Poems, *privately printed* Edinb 1857
471 Bruce (M) In Memoriam Annæ Mariæ Bruce, obiit Feb 18th, 1855 (a Volume of Poems) 1856
472 Brunton (Mary) Emmeline, with other pieces, *portrait* Edinb 1819
473 Brunton (Mrs) *formerly Anna Ross*, The Cottagers, a Comic Opera, 1st, 2nd, and 3rd editions, 1788 3 vol.

474 BRYAN (MARY) Sonnets and Metrical Tales *Bristol*, 1815
475 Bryant (William Cullen) Selections from the American Poets
   New York, 1840
476 Brydges (Sir Egerton) Restituta, or Titles, Extracts, and Characters of Old Books in English Literature revived, 4 vol *very scarce, calf gilt* 1814
477 —— Censura Literaria, containing Titles, Abstracts, and Opinions of Old English Books, &c SECOND EDITION, 10 vol
   very scarce, only 250 copies printed, fine copy, calf gilt, yellow edges, by F Bedford 1815
478 BUDGEN (LOUISA H) Grasshopper's Call, *illustrations n d* — Buds of Thought, a Century of Enigmas, Charades, &c by a Lady, 1844 *2 vol*
479 BUDGETT (MARY ELIZABETH) Lays and Legends of many Lands, 1848—The Priest, a Poem, *n d* *2 vol*
480 BULLOCK (CYNTHIA) Washington, and other Poems, *New York*, 1847—Bunch of Pansies, *ib* 1852 *2 vol*
481 BULMER (AGNES) Messiah's Kingdom, 1833 — The same, *New York*, 1833—Memoirs of Mrs Mortimer *portrait*, 1836—Memoir and Poem, Man the Offspring of Divine Providence, 1837—Select Letters, 1842 *5 vol*
482 BUNBURY (F T) Life and Times of Dante, translated from the Italian of Count Cesare Balbo, 2 vol 1852
483 Burder (Samuel) Memoirs of Eminently Pious Women, 3 vol *portraits* 1815
484 BURDER (SOPHIA MARIA) Poetical Efforts, *privately printed* 1826
485 BURDETT (SARAH) Poems, with Biographical Notes, *Camb* 1841—Pleasant Poems for the Young by Mrs BURDEN, *two editions, n d*—Language of Flowers, by Mrs BURKE, *plates*, 1838 *4 vol*
486 BURGESS (ELIZABETH) Life and History of Betty Bolaine, of Canterbury, interspersed with Poetry, *portrait*
   Canterbury, 1805
487 —— The same, Second Edition, *portrait* *ib* 1832
488 BURGESS (MRS) The Oaks, or the Beauties of Canterbury, a Comedy *ib* 1780
489 BURGH (MARIANNE DE, *formerly Tollemache*) Chimes *privately printed* 1858
490 BURNEY (FRANCES) Tragic Dramas, 1818—BURMAN (ELLEN ELIZABETH) Poetical Remains, *Bristol*, 1862—BURNSIDE (HELEN) Poems, 1864 *3 vol*
491 Burns Centenary Poems, a Collection of Fifty of the best, selected and edited by George Anderson and John Finlay, *portrait* 4to *Glasgow*, 1859
492 BURT (MARY ANN) Specimens of the German Poets, translated in English Verse, *second edition* *Zuric*, 1856

493 BURRELL (LADY SOPHIA) Comàla, a Dramatic Poem from Ossian, 1792—Poems, 2 vol 1793—Telemachus, 1794—The Thymbriad, 1794—Maximian, a Tragedy, from Corneille, 1800—Theodora, a Tragedy, 1800   5 vol

494 BURTON (HARRIET EMMA) White-Rose Wreath, with other Poems, 1833—Lindah, a Metrical Romance, and Minor Poems, *plates of Windsor, with autograph letter of the poetess inserted*, 1815   2 vol.

495 BURTON (MARGARET) of *Darlington*, Poetical Effusions, 1816—Life and Correspondence of Mrs Margaret Burton, by J Dungett, *Darlington* 1832   2 vol.

496 BURY (LADY CHARLOTTE) *formerly Campbell*, Poems on several Occasions, *privately printed*   *Edinb* 1797

497 —— Three Great Sanctuaries of Tuscany, a Poem, *portrait and plates from drawings by Rev E Bury*
   obl folio 1833

498 —— The Divorced, 1858—Racine and the French Drama by MADAME BLAIZE BURY, 1845—BURROWS (MARY) Sketches of Our Village, *two copies, Ipswich*, 1852—The same, Second Edition, 1856   5 vol

499 BUSH (BELLE) Voices of the Morning   *Philadelphia*, 1865

500 BUSK (Mrs. WILLIAM) Plays and Poems, 2 vol *with autograph letter of the poetess inserted*   1837

501 BUTLER (ANN) Fragments in Verse, *two copies*   *Oxf* 1826

502 BUTLER (CAROLINE H) Ice King and Sweet South Wind, *plates*   1854

503 —— The same, New Edition, *plates*   1855

504 —— The same, *plates*   *Boston (in America)*, 1857

505 BUTLER (FRANCES ANNE, *late Fanny Kemble*) Francis the First, an Historical Drama, *ten editions*, 10 vol   1832-3

506 —— Star of Seville, a Drama, *three editions*, 1837—Journal of a Residence in America, *Brussels*, 1835—Francis the First, 1832   3 vol

507 —— Poems, *portrait*   *Philadelphia*, 1844

508 —— Poems, 1844—Select Poems, n d—Star of Seville, 1837   3 vol

509 —— Poems   *Boston (in America)*, 1859

510 —— Poems   *Moxon*, 1866

511 —— Year of Consolation, 2 vol   *ib* 1847

512 —— Plays (An English Tragedy, Mary Stuart, and Mademoiselle de Belle Isle)   1863

513 BUTLER (HARRIETTE) Lays of the Heart *privately printed*   *Manchester*, 1833

514 BYRON (LADY) Responsive "Fare thee well,' 1816—Lord Byron in the other World, &c *portrait inserted*, in one vol—Byron, Salathiel and other Poems, by ÆMILIA JULIA, *portrait*, 1855—Leon de Beaumonon, by ÆMILIA JULIA, 1865   3 vol

SECOND DAY'S SALE.

OCTAVO ET INFRA.

UNLESS OTHERWISE EXPRESSED

LOT
515 C (A.) Peppa; or, The Reward of Constant Love, a Novel, with several Songs set to Musick, for Two Voices *very scarce* 1689
516 C. (A.) Fugitive Pieces, *privately printed* 1819
517 C (E S) Home Reminiscences, *unpublished, the title-page, &v cancelled* 1861
518 CAIRD (MRS) Christian Songs and Elegies, edited by John Caird, *privately printed* *Perth* 1846
519 CAIRNS (CHRISTIANA VICTORIA) Fugitive Poems, 1860—Calaf, a Rejected Drama, 1826 *2 vol.*
520 CALCOTT (J. BERKLEY) *eleven years of age*, Stanzas, *two series privately printed* *Dublin*, 1834-5
521 Caledoniad (The) a Collection of Poems, written chiefly by Scottish Authors, 3 vol 1775
522 Calliope and Euterpe, a Poem, by a Young Lady, *Durham*, 1817—Carthusian Friar, a Tragedy, by a Female Refugee, 1793 *2 vol.*
523 CAMBRIDGE (ADA) Hymns on the Litany, *Oxford*, 1865—Hymns on the Holy Communion, 1866 *2 vol*
524 CAMERON (JULIA M.) Leonora, translated from Burger, *with illustrations by Maclise* *4to* 1847
525 Camoens (Luis de) Memoirs of his Life and Writings, by J Adamson, with Translations and account of the Editions, 2 vol *plates* *Newcastle*, 1820
526 CAMPBELL (ANN) Wreath of Poesy *printed for the author*, 1828
527 CAMPBELL (ARABELLA GEORGINA) Cranmer, a Poem *Reading*, (1855)
528 CAMPBELL (DOROTHEA PRIMROSE) Poems *Inverness, printed for the authoress*, 1811
529 —— Poems *printed for the authoress*, 1816
530 CAMPBELL (ELIZABETH) Poems *privately printed* *Arbroath*, 1862
531 CAMPBELL (ELIZABETH ANNE) Life Unfolding, a Poem (1863) Life Triumphant, a Poem (1863) *2 vol.*

E

532 CAMHILL (Mrs Graham) One Hundred Voices from Nature, 1861—Louisa's Metrical English Grammar, 1861—Christabelle and Our Little White Rose, n d 2 vol.
533 Campbell (Isabella) of Fernicarry, Rosneath, Memoir
  Greenock, 1829
534 Candler (Ann) a Suffolk cottager, Poetical Attempts, with Life Ipswich, 1803
535 Canning (Mrs Charlotte) of Eastcourt, Wilts, Wood-Notes, together with the Siege of Cirta, an Opera, frontispiece 1850
536 Cannon (M Maria) Maria and St Flos, a Poem
  Newbury, 1825
537 Cantrell (Mrs. John Blackwall) Melodies from the Mountains 1861
538 Capp (Mary Elizabeth) African Princess, and other Poems
  Yarmouth, 1813
539 Capper (Miss) Poetical History of England 1810
540 Carey (Elizabeth Shlridan) Ivy Leaves
  privately printed 1837
541 Capey (H M) Echoes from the Harp of France, Caen, 1858—The same, ib 1860—Merry Evenings for Merry People, 1859—Matilda of Normandy, 1859 4 vol.
542 Capen (Phœbe) Poems and Parodies Boston (in America), 1854
543 Carmichall (Mary D. J) New Dress for an Old Friend, being a Fable of Æsop, in Rhyme, with illustrations by the Authoress 4to. 1857
544 Carmichael (Miss R.) Poems
  Edinburgh, printed for the Author, 1790
545 Carnes (Hannah) Widow's Cottage and other Poems, Glocester, 1829—Widow's Cottage, Camb 1810—The same, ib. 1814—Beauties of Walden, Saffron Walden, 1842—The same, Camb 1847—Juvenile Poems, Saffron Walden, 1846—Mysterious Travellers, Chelmsford, 1861—Beauties of Halstead, &c ib 1861—Truthful Pathetic Poetry, ib n. d—Life of Hannah Carnes, Weymouth, n d—Autograph Letter of the Poetess when Mrs Garwood, dated 1862 8 vol
546 Carpenter (Sarah Osmond) Poems, Canterbury, 1857—Carpenter (S S) Winter Flowers, privately printed, Exeter, 1860 2 vol.
547 Capr (Helen and Gabrielle) Ephemera, with illustrations, 2 copies Moxon, 1865
548 Carrington (E) Metrical Outline of Historical Events, Yarmouth, 1836—The same, 2nd edition, ib 1838—Thoughts of Many Minds, ib 1843 3 vol.
549 Carshore (Mrs. W S) Songs of the East Calcutta, 1855

550 CARSTAIRS (MISS) Original Poems, dedicated to Miss Ann Henderson, VERY RARE, *having been printed in detached portions at different times* 4to Edinb 1786

551 —— The Hubble-Shue, (with introductory notice by Mr. Maidment) *30 copies only printed* Edinb 1833

552 CARTER (A P) Songs in the Wilderness, *Kingsbridge,* (1816) —Sunshine and Shadow, 1861—Hymns for Children, *two editions,* and Catechism in Rhyme, n. d—CARTER (AUGUSTA MARIA) Poetic Reveries, *Winchester,* 1819 —CARTER (MARY ANN) Deluge, &c *Nottingham,* 1838
7 vol

553 CARTER (ELIZABETH) Works of Epictetus, translated from the Greek, *old russia gilt, Dr Heath's copy* 4to 1758

554 —— Poems, *first edition, portrait inserted* 1762

555 —— Poems, *second edition, portrait inserted old red morocco, g e* 1766

556 —— Poems, *third edition,* 1776, *fourth edition, Dublin,* 1777 —Another, *also called the fourth,* 1789 3 vol

557 —— Memoirs of her Life, with Poems, &c by Rev M Pennington, *portrait* 4to 1807

558 —— The same, *second edition,* 2 vol. *portrait* 1808

559 —— The same, *third edition,* 2 vol *portrait* 1816

560 —— The same, *fourth edition,* 2 vol *portrait* 1825

561 —— Letters between her and Miss Catherine Talbot, from 1741 to 1770, edited by Rev M Pennington, 4 vol *portrait* 1809

562 —— Letters to Mrs Montagu between 1755 and 1800, 3 vol *portrait* 1817

563 CARTWRIGHT (F D) Poems, chiefly Devotional, 1835— CARTWRIGHT (MRS ROBERT) Royal Sisters, 2 vol 1857 —Pilgrim Walks, a Chaplet of Memories, 1859 4 vol.

564 CARY (ALICE) Poems *Boston, (in America)* 1855

565 CARY (LADY E) Tragedie of Mariam, the Faire Queene of Jewry, *very scarce* 4to *by Thomas Creede,* 1613

566 CARY (MARY) *afterwards* Rande, Little Horns Doom and Downfall. or a Scripture Prophesie of King James, and King Charles, and of this present Parliament, unfolded —also, a new and more exact mappe or description of New Jerusalems Glory when Jesus Christ and his Saints with him shall reign on earth a Thousand years, and possess all Kingdoms &c *with 14 pages of Poems to the Court of Parliament, who are supreme, in England, Ireland, and elsewhere*
VERY RARE, *sold in Dr Bandinel's sale in 1861 for £8* 1651

567 CASELLI (ELIZABETH) Poems *Falmouth,* 1818

568 Casket (The) a Miscellany of Unpublished Poems 1829

569 CASSAN (MRS) Poems *privately printed* 4to. 1866

570 Catalogue of Living Authors and their publications 1788

571 CAULFEILD (MRS. EDWIN T.) Innocents, Ocean, and Earthquake at Aleppo, *Bath*, 1824—The Deluge, a Poem, 1837   2 vol.
572 CAULTON (ISABELLA) Domestic Hearth and other Poems, *Manchester*, 1843—The same, *second edition*, *ib.* 1844—Poems for Home, *Leamington Spa*, 1851   3 vol.
573 CAVE (JANE) *afterwards Mrs Winscomb*, Poems, *first edition, portrait*   *Winchester*, 1783
574 ——— The same, *portrait*   *Bristol*, 1786
575 ——— The same, *portrait*   *Shrewsbury*, 1789
576 ——— The same, *portrait*   *Bristol*, 1794
577 ——— The same, *portrait*   *ib* 1795
578 CECIL (MRS CHARLES) Juvenile Scrap Book, *plates*, 4to. n. d.—The Seraph, *n d.*—Sacred Melodies, *plate, n.d.* 3 vol
579 Celestial Harmony, or Songs of Grateful Praise to the ever blessed glorious King of Saints, &c. (*Muggletonian*) *scarce*   1794
580 CELISIA (MRS.) Almida, a Tragedy, *three editions*, 3 vol.   Lond. and Dub. 1771
581 CENTLIVRE (SUSANNAH) Dramatic Works, 3 vol *two portraits* VERY SCARCE   1761
582 ——— Perjur'd Husband, a Tragedy   4to. 1700
583 ——— The same, *front-spiece*   1737
584 ——— Beau's Duel, or a Soldier for the Ladies, a Comedy   4to 1702
585 ——— The same, *second edition, frontispiece*   1715
586 ——— The same, *third edition, frontispiece*   1735
587 ——— Love's Contrivance, a Comedy   4to. 1703
588 ——— Stolen Heiress, or the Salamanca Doctor Outplotted, a Comedy   4to n d.
589 ——— Gamester, a Comedy   4to. 1705
590 ——— The same, *second edition*   4to. 1708
591 ——— The same, *third edition, frontispiece*   1711
592 ——— The same, *other editions*, 7 vol.   1736-67
593 ——— Basset-Table, a Comedy, 1706, and 12 Plays by other Authors   4to. *in one vol.*
594 ——— The same, *third edition, frontispiece*   1735
595 ——— The same, *fourth edition, frontispiece*   1736
596 ——— Love at a Venture, a Comedy   4to. 1706
597 ——— Platonick Lady, a Comedy   4to. 1707
598 ——— Busie Body, a Comedy   4to. (1709)
599 ——— The same, *second edition*   4to n. d.
600 ——— The same, *third edition, frontispiece*   1711
601 ——— The same, *other editions*, 30 vol.   1727-1815
602 ——— Man's Bewitch'd; or The Devil to do about Her, a Comedy   4to (1710)
603 ——— The same, *another edition, frontispiece*   1737

604 CENTLIVRE (SUSANNAH) The Ghost (from Mrs Centlivre's Man Bewitched) *Corke, n. d. Another edition, n. d.*
  2 vol.
605 —— Bickerstaff's Burying, or Work for the Upholders, a Farce   4to   *n. d.*
606 —— The same, *another edition*   *Dublin,* 1724
607 —— Mar Plot, or the second part of the Busie-Body, a Comedy   4to   1711
608 —— The same, *another edition*   1737
609 —— Perplex'd Lovers, a Comedy   4to   1712
610 —— Wonder. a Woman keeps a Secret, a Comedy *frontispiece*   1714
611 —— The same, *second edition, frontispiece*   1734
612 —— The same, *third edition, frontispiece*   1736
613 —— The same, *other editions,* 25 vol.   1740-1847
614 —— Humours of Elections, and a Cure for Cuckoldom: or the Wife well Manag'd, two Farces, *portrait*   1715
615 —— Gotham Election, a Farce   1715
616 —— Humours of Elections, *frontispiece,* 2 copies   1737
617 —— Wife well Manag'd, *portrait inserted*   1715
618 —— The same, *another edition, frontispiece*   1737
619 —— Cruel Gift, a Tragedy, *frontispiece*   1717
620 —— The same, *second edition, frontispiece*   1734
621 —— The same, *third edition, frontispiece,* 2 copies   1736
622 —— Pastoral to the Memory of Nicholas Rowe in Musarum Lachrymæ   *for E Curll,* 1719
623 —— Artifice, a Comedy   1723
624 —— The same, *another edition, frontispiece*   1735
625 —— The same, *another edition, frontispiece*   1736
626 —— Bold Stroke for a Wife, a Comedy, *second edition, frontispiece*   1724
627 —— The same, *also called the second edition, frontispiece* 1728
628 —— The same, *third edition, frontispiece*   1729
629 —— The same, *another edition, frontispiece*   1735
630 —— The same, *other editions,* 24 vol.   1736-1826
631 —— Poem to King George, upon his Accession to the Throne   *folio.* 1715
632 —— Verses in the "Plurality of Worlds," *frontispiece* 1737
633 —— Answer of Abelard to Heloise in "The Lovers Cabinet, a Collection of Poems," *scarce*   *Dublin,* 1755
634 Ceres and Agenorica, a Poem, by a Young Lady *Hull,* 1822
635 CHADWICK (MRS) Rural and other Poems   *Ludlow,* 1828
636 CHALENOR (MARY) Walter Gray, and other Poems, 1841— Poetical Remains, 1843
  2 vol.
637 —— The same, *second edition,* including the Poetical Remains   1843

638 CHALMERS (GRACE PRATT) Road and Resting Place, *Edinb.* 1864
639 CHALMERS (MARGARET) *of Lerwick, Zetland,* Poems
Newcastle, 1813
640 CHAMBERS (MARIANNE) He deceives himself, a Domestic Tale, 3 vol. 1799
641 —— School for Friends, a Comedy, 1805—The same, *third edition,* 1806—The same, *fourth edition,* 1806—The same, *sixth edition, n. d.*—Ourselves, a Comedy, 1811
4 vol.
642 CHANDLER (ELIZABETH MARGARET) Poetical Works, with Life by B Lundy, *portrait, Philadelphia,* 1836—Essays on the Abolition of Slavery in America, *ib* 1836
in one vol.
643 CHANDLER (MARY) Description of Bath, and other Poems, *editions* 3, 4, 5, 6, 7 and 8, 6 vol. *Bath,* 1736-67
644 CHANTRELL (MARY ANN) Poems *printed for the Author,* 1798
645 CHAPMAN (JANE FRANCES) King René's Daughter, from the Danish of Hertz, 1845—CHANDLER (LOUISA) Poems, 1861 *2 vol.*
646 CHAPONE (HESTER) *formerly Mulso,* Miscellanies in Prose and Verse 1775
647 —— The same, *other editions,* 4 vol 1775-89
648 —— Letters on the Improvement of the Mind and Miscellanies, *third edition,* 2 vol. in 1 *Dublin,* 1777
649 —— Works, with Life, 4 vol. *portrait,* 1807—Posthumous Works, 2 vol. 1807 *6 vol.*
650 —— Works, *portrait, Edinb* 1807—Posthumous Works, 2 vol 1807—Letters, 1815 *4 vol.*
651 —— Memoirs, with Anecdotes of her Contemporaries by J. Cole, *Wellingborough,* 1839—Posthumous Works, 2 vol. *portrait,* 1808 *3 vol.*
652 CHAPPEL (SARAH) *of the Tabernacle,* Divine Poems, *two leaves* *n. d*
653 CHARKE (MRS. CHARLOTTE) *formerly Cibber,* Art of Management, or Tragedy expell'd, *portrait inserted* 1735

*** A Satire upon Mr Fleetwood, the Manager of Drury Lane Theatre, who bought up and destroyed nearly the whole impression.

654 —— Narrative of her Life, *first edition, portrait* 1755
655 —— The same, *second edition, inlaid in 4to and illustrated with scarce Portraits of Actors and Actresses of the Period in which she lived, Early Play Bills and Cuttings from Newspapers, curious engraving of Mrs Midnight's Animal Comedians, copies of the view of May Fair, 1712, and of Mr Maddox's performances at Sadler's Wells, and other engravings,*
half russia, g e *large 4to.* 1755

656 CHARLES (MRS. ELIZ.) Voice of Christian Life in Song, 1858
—Three Wakings, 1859   2 vol.
657 —— Three Wakings, with Hymns and Songs, *New York*, 1860
658 —— Voice of Christian Life in Song, *second edition* 1865
660 CHARLOTTE (PRINCESS) Memoirs, with specimens of her Poetry, Music, &c. by R Huish, *portraits and plates* 1818
661 CHATTERTON (GEORGIANA LADY) Leonore, a Tale, and other Poems, 1864
662 —— Leonore, *illustrated edition* 1865
663 Chaucer (Geoffrey) Poems modernized, 1811 — CHARLTON (Mrs) Pathetic Poetry, n d —CHARNOCK (MARY ANNA E) Legendary Rhymes, and other Poems, *Wakefield*, 1843   3 vol.
664 Cheap Repository Tracts, a volume containing 37, *mostly with a wood-cut on the title-page*, (written by HANNAH MORE, &c.) in 1 vol. *dark calf, from the Daniel Library* 1795-6
665 Cheap Repository Tracts Another volume containing 47, *mostly with a wood-cut on the title-page, similar to the preceding*
666 Cheap Repository Tracts Another lot unbound, and a volume entitled Cheap Repository Shorter Tracts, *woodcuts* 1817
667 CHETWYND (MRS. HENRY) Poetical History of England, *Stafford*, 1849—Poetical Compendium of the History of Russia, *ib.* 1854—Cheltenham Literary Annual, 1857—Choice Selections and Illusions, *Royston*, 1828—CHOLMELEY (ISOBEL C.) Fountain and other Poems, 1858—Child's Sacred Year, *n d.*   5 vol.
668 CHEVES (MRS E W. FOOTE) Sketches in Prose and Verse, *portrait*   *Baltimore*, 1849
669 Cheyt Sing, a Poem by a Young Lady of Fifteen 4to 1790
670 CHILD (MRS D. L.) Biographies of Lady Russell and Madame Guyon, *Boston (in America)*, 1832—Western Coronal, *Glasg* 1833—Garland of Juvenile Poems, *plate, n d*   3 vol.
671 CHILD (LYDIA MARIA) *late Francis*, Autumnal Leaves. Tales and Sketches in prose and rhyme   *New York*, 1857
672 CHILD (MISS) Spinster at Home in the Close of Salisbury, together with Tales and Ballads 4to. *Salisbury*, 1849
673 —— The same, *fourth edition*   4to. *ib.* 1849
674 —— The same, *fifth edition*   4to. *ib.* 1849

675 CHILD (MISS) Historical Appendix to the Spinster at Home, *Salisbury*, 1852—Royal Agricultural Assemblage, *ib.* 1857—Salisbury Jubilee for the Peace, *ib.* 1856 ; and Scraps, in 1 vol — Salisbury Exhibition, *ib* 1852— Annette's Birth-Day Banquet, &c. *ib. n d* 4*to* 2 vol.
676 Christian Keepsake for 1835 and 1836, 2 vol. *plates*, 1835-6 —Christian Year, *Oxf.* 1829   3 *vol.*
677 Christmas Rhymes, or, Three Nights' Revelry, by Frances and Elish, *with illustrations*   4*to*   *Belfast*, 1846
678 CHUDLEIGH (LADY MARY) Ladies Defence. or, the Bride-Woman's Counsellor Answer'd, a Poem   *folio*   1701
679 ——— Poems on Several Occasions, with the Song of the Three Children paraphras'd   1703
680 ——— The same, *second edition*   1709
681 ——— The same, *also called second edition*   1713
682 ——— Poems, 3rd and 4th Editions, 1722 and 1750—Ladies Defence, 1721   3 *vol.*
683 ——— Essays, in Prose and Verse   1710
684 CHUDLEIGH (M. ECCLESIA) Midnight Meditations and other Poems, 1854 — CHURCH (SARAH) Teachings of the Spirit, 1851   2 *vol*
685 CIBBER (MRS S) Oracle, a Comedy, 1752—Another Edition, *Dublin*, 1752—Another Edition, *portrait inserted*, 1763 —Another Edition, *Dublin*, 1772—Daphne and Amintor, *n. d* —Œconomy of the Mind, 1767   6 vol.
686 Cibber (Theophilus) Lives of the Poets of Great Britain and Ireland, 5 vol.   1753
687 CLARK (ANNIE E.) Poems   *Philadelphia*, 1866
688 CLARK (EMILY) Ermina Montrose, 3 vol. 1800—Poems and Ballads, 1810   4 *vol.*
689 CLARK (MRS R.) *of Tetbury, late Lewis of Holt*, Poems, Moral and Entertaining, *portrait*   *Bath*, 1789
690 CLARKE (ANN) Poems, Moral, Entertaining, and Religious, 2 vol 1825—Poem on a Minister in the Furnace of Affliction, *Lewes*, 1838—World an Inn, *n. d* —Christian Life a Journey, 1821   4 *vol.*
691 ——— World an Inn, 1818—Other Editions, 1820, &c — Saviour's Triumph, Heaven and Earth, *and other pieces by the same Poetess*   8 *vol.*
692 CLARKE (ANNE) Small Literary Patchwork, 1814—CLARKE (MARY COWDEN) Shakespeare Proverbs, 1848   2 *vol*
693 CLARKE (OLIVIA LADY) Irishwoman, a Comedy   1819
694 CLAUDE (M. S.) Blades and Flowers, *front* 1856—Little Poems, *numerous illustrations, n. d* —CLISSOLD (MISS E.) Meditations on Three Chapters of the Book of Canticles, *n. d.*—COBBE (FRANCES POWER) Thanksgiving, 1863   4 *vol.*

695 CLIVE (CATHERINE) Rehearsal; or, Bays in Petticoats, a Comedy 1753

696 CLIVE (HON. MRS A) IX Poems by V. 1840—I watched the Heavens, 1842—Queen's Ball, 1847—Valley of the Rea, 1851—Morlas, 1853—Poems, 1856 6 vol

698 COBBOLD (ELIZABETH) *formerly Knipe*, Sword or, Father Bertrand's History of his own Times (published when Mrs Clarke), 2 vol in 1 *Liverpool*, 1791

699 —— Mince Pye, by Carolina Petty Pasty, *portrait of Mrs Glasse, and engraved title-page* 4to 1800

700 —— Ode on the Victory of Waterloo *red morocco, g e.* *Ipswich*, 1815

701 —— Poems, with Memoir of the Author ib 1825

702 —— Poems *another copy, large paper* ib 1825

703 —— Poems, another edition, *large and thick paper, two portraits, and etchings in lithography by the Family* ib 1825

704 COCHRANE (MRS) Flights of Fancy, consisting of Poetical Pieces, Satirical, Humorous, Pathetic, &c *Arbroath*, 1844

705 COCKBURN (CATHARINE) *formerly Trotter*, Works, with Life by T Birch, 2 vol *portrait*
LARGE PAPER, *with memorandum in the autograph of Isaac Reed inserted* 1751

706 —— Fatal Friendship, a Tragedy, *portrait inserted*, 1698— Unhappy Penitent, a Tragedy, 1701 4to 2 vol

707 —— Love at a Loss; or, Most Votes carry it, a Comedy, *portrait inserted*, 1701 — Revolution of Sweden, a Tragedy, *portrait inserted*, 1706—Agnes de Castro, a Tragedy, *portrait inserted*, 1696 4to. 2 vol

708 COCKLE (MRS) Juvenile Journal; or, Tales of Truth, *frontispiece, red morocco, g. e* 1807

709 —— Simple Minstrelsy, *frontispiece presentation copy from the Authoress* 1812

710 —— Elegy to the Memory of the Princess Charlotte, 1817 —The same, *second edition, Newcastle*, 1817—The same, *third edition*, 1817—The same, *another edition, woodcut on the title page, only 20 copies printed, Newcastle*, 1817 —The same, *third edition, tinted paper*, 1817—Another copy, *different tint*, 1817—Elegy on the Death of George III *woodcut on the title-page, 20 copies only printed, Newcastle*, 1820—The same, *another edition, ib* 1820—The same, *another edition*, 1820—Reply to Lord Byron's Fare Thee Well, *woodcut on the title-page, Newcastle*, 1817—Lines to Lady Byron, *woodcut on the title-page, ib* 1817—Lines to a Boy pursuing a Butterfly, *woodcut on the title page, ib* 1826—Lines on the Death of Sir John Moore, 1810 4to in one vol

711 COCKLE (MRS.) National Triumphs, 1814 — Elegy to the Memory of the Princess Charlotte, *woodcut on the title-page, 20 copies only printed, Newcastle-on-Tyne,* 1817 —Elegy on the Death of George III. *woodcut on the title-page, 20 copies only printed, ib* 1820—Lines to a Boy pursuing a Butterfly, *woodcut on the title-page, ib* 1826—Verses on Winter, *woodcut on the title-page, ib.* 1823—Reply to Lord Byron's Fare thee Well, *woodcut on the title-page, ib* 1811—Lines to Lady Byron, *woodcut on the title-page, ib* 1817 *in one vol*

712 —— Lines to a Boy pursuing a Butterfly, *2 copies, Newcastle,* 1826—Reply to Byron's Fare thee Well, *with two title-pages, ib.* 1817-39—Lines to Lady Byron, *with two title-pages, ib* 1817-39—Elegy to the Memory of the Princess Charlotte, *with two title-pages, ib* 1817-39 —Elegy on the Death of George III *printed on one side of the paper only, with two title-pages, ib* 1820-39— Elegy on the Princess Charlotte, 1817 2 *vol*

713 COCKS (ISABELLA JEMIMA) Memoir, by Viscount Eastnor *privately printed* *Leamington,* 1838

714 COCKS (MRS S) Hymns, 1831—COKER (C.) Round Robin, 1862—COLDWELL (MRS) Poem to Queen Victoria and Prince Albert on their Marriage, 1840—COLE (M A) Days gone by, *Dublin,* 1827 4 *vol*

715 COLCHESTER (ELIZABETH SOPHIA LAW, LADY) Miscellaneous Poems, *privately printed,* 1832—Giustina, a Spanish Tale, *not published,* 1833—Views in London by an Amateur, *not published,* 1833, *white morocco, g e* *in one vol.*

716 —— Miscellaneous Poems, *another copy,* 1832—Translations of Goldsmith's Traveller and Deserted Village into Italian, 1832—Giustina, *another copy,* 1833—Thérèse de Villarejo, Roman Espagnol, *non publié, Brux. s d.* —Urge me no More, a Song set to Music for the Pianoforte, *green morocco, g. e.* *in one vol*

717 COLERIDGE (SARA) Phantasmion, *morocco, g. e Pickering,* 1837 —Lessons for Children, *four editions,* 1831-53 5 *vol*

718 Collas (A) Authors of England, a series of Medallion Portraits, with Illustrative Notices by H F Chorley, *illustrated with an autograph letter of Mrs. Hemans, &c* 4to 1838

719 Collection of Divine Hymns and Poems, by Mrs Kath Phillips, Mrs Singer and others 1707

720 —— The same, *third edition, frontispiece* 1719

721 Collection of Poems, by a Young Lady, *plate inserted* *Rochester,* 1792

722 Collection of Poems by "La Duchesse" 1862

723 COLLIER (MARY) *Washer-woman at Petersfield,* Woman's Labour an Epistle to Stephen Duck 1739

724 COLLIER (MARY) Poems, with Remarks on her Life, *plate inserted* *Winchester*, 1762
725 COLLIER (MARY, *formerly Peach*) Poetic Effusions, *Derby*, 1823—The same, *second edition, plate, ib* 1835—The same, *third edition, portrait and plate, ib* 1847—The same, *fourth edition, portrait, Leamington*, 1851 4 vol.
726 COLLING (MARY MARIA) Fables and other Pieces in Verse, with Life, &c , by Mrs Bray, *portrait* 1831
727 COLLINS (ELIZABETH) Metrical Translations, *Paris, n d*— Early Lessons in Rhyme, *ib* 1855 2 vol
728 COLLINS (ROSE EMMA) *formerly Salaman*, Poems, 1853—Morven, the Departed Spirit, and other Poems, *front* 1856 2 vol
729 COLLINS (RUTH) Friendly Writer and Register of Truth, Books II, III, IV, V, VI, and VIII. *portrait to each number, October to April* 1732-3
730 Collyer (W B) Collection of Hymns, 1812—Death of Abel, translated by Mrs COLLYER, 1807—Death of Cain, *plates*, 1810 3 vol
731 COLQUHOUN (KATHARINE) Alias, a Farce, *privately printed* 1859
732 COLQUHOUN (LADY) of Rossdhu, Works, *portrait* 1852
733 COLTHURST (MISS) Emmanuel, 1833—Life, *Cork*, 1835—Home, *ib* 1836—Futurity, *ib* 1837—Loyalty, *ib* 1838—Futurity continued *ib*. 1838—Storm and other Poems, *Liverpool*, 1840—Love and Loyalty, *Pickering*, 1851 6 vol.
734 Comic Offering; or, Ladies' Melange of Literary Mirth for 1831 to 1835, edited by Louisa Henrietta Sheridan, 5 vol. *plates and cuts by Seymour, &c* 1831-5
735 Commemorative Feelings; or, Miscellaneous Poems, 1812—Commemorative Wreath, *plate*, 1835—Common Place Book of Poetry, *portrait of Byron*, 1830 — Conder (Josiah) Hymns of Praise, &c 1856 4 vol
736 Complete Letter Writer, or, Lady's Polite Secretary, with Original Letters of Wit, a variety of Political Letters, Humorous and Pathetic, Cards of Compliment, &c By a Real Lady of Fashion, *frontispiece for S Hooper, n d*
737 Conquest of Corsica, a Tragedy, by a Lady 1771
738 Conversation, interspersed with Poems, 2 vol *Reading*, 1812-14
739 CONYNGHAM (MRS GEORGE LENOX) Dream, and other Poems, 1833—Hella, and other Poems, 1836 *in one vol*
740 —— Hella, and other Poems, 1836—Eiler and Helvig, a Danish Legend, 1863 2 vol
741 —— Horæ Poeticæ Lyrical and other Poems 1859
742 COOK (ELIZA) Lays of a Wild Harp, 1835—Melaia, and other Poems, *coloured frontispiece and vignette*, 1838 2 vol.

743 Cook (Eliza) Melaia, and other Poems, *illustrated edition*
   1840
744 ——— The same, *third edition, illustrated, no portrait* 1845
745 ——— The same, *fourth edition, illustrated* 1845
746 ——— Poems, second series, *portrait* 1845
747 ——— The same, *new edition, portrait*, 1847—Poems, vol. III, 1848 2 vol
748 ——— Poems, *fifth edition, illustrated*, 4 vol 1848-53
749 ——— The same, 4 vol *calf extra, g. e* 1851-3
750 ——— The same, *new edition in one volume, portrait and plates, blue morocco extra, g e* 1859
751 ——— The same, *illustrated by John Gilbert, J. Wolf, H Weir, J D Watson, &c &c engraved by the Brothers Dalziel*
   blue morocco extra, tooled on the sides, g. e. with autograph note of the poetess 4to 1861
752 ——— Jottings from my Journal, 1860—New Echoes, and other Poems, *portrait*, 1864 2 vol.
753 Cooke (M. A) Marion. or, The Two Crowns, *Guernsey*, 1859—Christmas Tree, *ib n d*—Beauty, a Christmas Story, *ib. n. d*—Amy's Dream, *ib.* (1859)—Exhibition Bible Stall, *ib* 1862—Santa Claus, *ib* 1863—Marie de Saint Roman, *ib.* 1865 4 vol
754 Cookson (M A) Poems, *first, second, and third editions*, 3 vol *Leith*, 1829
755 Cookson (Elizabeth) Mylecharane: the popular and most ancient Manx National Song, rendered into English Verse, *second edition, Douglas*, 1859—Legends of Manxland (second series), *ib n. d* *in one vol*
756 Coombe (Sarah Matilda) Aurestine; a Tale of Fancy
   Portsea, 1829
757 Cooper (Cecilia) Battle of Tewkesbury, a Poem
   Tewkesbury, 1820
758 Cooper (Elizabeth) Rival Widows· or, Fair Libertine, a Comedy 1735
759 ——— Muses Library, a series of English Poetry from the Saxons to the Reign of Charles II vol. I, *all published*
   1737
760 Cooper (Emily) Tales and Conversations, 1843—Countries of Europe, by a Lady, *with illustrations, n. d*—The Cowslip, *cuts* 3 vol.
761 Cooper (F. A) Address to the City of Bristol—To the Vale of C———h—The Apology, *all in verse, privately printed*
   4to (*Bristol*, 1810)
762 Cooper (Maria Susanna) *of Norwich*, Jane Shore to her Friend, a Poetical Epistle, *4to* 1776—Cooper (S) *Husband of the preceding*, Two Discourses on the Death of the eldest Daughter, with Elegies, &c *Yarmouth*, 1786 2 vol.

763 COOPER (MARY GRACE) Thamuta, the Spirit of Death, and other Poems, 1837—The same, 1839—Orletta. or, Courtly Ways and Cottage Conclusions,—1866—COOPER (FRANCES MARY) Cat's Festival, *illustrated*, Norwich, 1846   4 vol.

764 COOPER (MRS) Address to the People of Wapping and its Environs, *in verse, with notes, curious and scarce*   n d.

765 COOPER (S F) Rhyme and Reason of Country Life, *illustrations from drawings by C E Dopler*   New York, 1856

766 COPE (HARRIETT) Triumphs of Religion, 1811—The same, second edition, 1819   2 vol.

767 —— Suicide, a Poem, illustrated with notes   1815

768 —— Waterloo, a Poem, in two parts   n d

769 —— Poetical Addresses and Fragments, 1821—Monody to Thomas, Lord Erskine, 1824—Brazen Serpent, 1827   3 vol.

770 —— Death of Socrates, from the French of De Lamartine, 1828—The same, 1829   2 vol

771 CORE (ELIZA) Essays, Poems, Anecdotes, &c 2 vol   Liverpool, n d.

772 Cornelius (Elias) *of Salem, Massachusetts*, Little Osage Captive, &c *frontispiece*   York, 1824

773 CORNER (JULIA) Baronet, a Novel, 1831—Children's Own Sunday Book, 1850—Life and Memoirs of Hannah More, *portrait*, n d   3 vol

774 —— Little Plays for Little Actors, and Familiar Fables, 4 vol. *with illustrations*   1854, &c

775 CORNWALLIS (CAROLINE FRANCES) Letters, Poems, &c   1864

776 CORSTOPPHAN (WILHELMINA HENRIETTA) Poems, &c *St Andrews*, 1852—The Correspondents, a Novel, 1784—CORY (ELIZABETH) Lilies of the Valley, *second edition, Wisbech*, 1811—The same, *third edition, n d*—CORR (H) Meditations, *Bradford*, 1838   5 vol

777 COSTELLO (LOUISA STUART) Maid of the Cyprus Isle, and other Poems, *first and second editions*, 2 vol   1815

778 —— Redwald, a Tale of Mona, and other Poems, *frontispiece*   Brentford, 1819

779 —— Songs of a Stranger   1825

780 —— Specimens of the Early Poetry of France, from the time of the Troubadours and Trouveres to the reign of Henri Quatre, *plates in outline, and illuminated in gold and colours*   Pickering, 1835

781 —— Gabrielle, or Pictures of a Reign, a Novel, 3 vol   1843

782 —— Memoirs of Eminent Englishwomen, 4 vol *portraits*   1844

783 —— Rose Garden of Persia, *printed within borders and several pages illuminated in gold and colours*   1845

784 —— Lay of the Stork   4to. 1856

785 COSTELLO (L. S.) Six Songs, set to music by Lady Augusta Kennedy Erskine *folio* *n. d*
786 Country Coquet, or, Miss in her Breeches, a Ballad Opera, by a Young Lady 1755
787 Court Lady or, Coquet's Surrender, a Comedy, by a Lady, *frontispiece* 1733
788 COUSENS (MRS) *formerly Frances Upcher*, Lays of the Boudoir 1850
789 Covenant (The), with other Poems connected with the Ecclesiastical History of Scotland *Edinb* 1842
790 Cowley (A) Works, 3 vol *portraits and plates* 1707-11
791 COWLEY (MRS HANNAH) Works, Dramas, and Poems, 3 vol *portrait* 1813
792 —— Runaway, a Comedy, 1776, and two other editions 3 vol.
793 —— Albina, Countess Raimond, a Tragedy, 1779, and 4 other Editions, 1779-97 5 vol
794 —— Who's the Dupe, a Farce, 1779, and 11 other Editions, 1779-1821 12 vol.
795 —— Maid of Aragon, a Tale, part I, 1780 — Edwina, a Poem by F M. 4to *in one vol*
796 —— Belle's Stratagem, a Comedy, *two copies*, *Dublin*, 1781 —Another Edition, *ib* 1783 3 vol.
797 —— The same, *another edition, portrait inserted* 1782
798 —— The same, *second edition*, 1787, and 10 other Editions, 1806-23 11 vol.
799 —— Bold Stroke for a Husband, a Comedy, *frontispiece inserted*, *Dublin*, 1783 — The same, 1784—The same, *second edition, portrait inserted*, 1784, and other Editions, 1784-1812 8 vol.
800 —— Which is the Man? a Comedy, 1783—The same, *second edition*, 1783; & other Editions, 1783-1816 9 vol.
801 —— More Ways than One, a Comedy, 1784—The same, *second and third editions*, 1784 3 vol.
802 —— Scottish Village or, Pitcairne Green, a Poem, 4to. 1786—Poetry of Anna Matilda, 1788 2 vol
803 —— School for Greybeards, or, Mourning Bride, a Comedy, 1786 — The same, *second edition*, 1787 — The same, *Dublin*, 1787 3 vol
804 —— Fate of Sparta, or Rival Kings, a Tragedy, 1788— The same, *second edition*, 1788—The same, *Dublin*, 1788 3 vol
805 —— Day in Turkey, or Russia Slaves, a Comedy, 1792— The same, *second, third and fourth editions*, 1792— The same, *Dublin*, 1792—Airs, Duets, Choruses, &c in the same, 1791 6 vol

806 Cowley (Mrs Hannah) Town before you, a Comedy, 1795
—The same, *second edition*, 1795—The same, *Dublin*,
1795   3 vol

807 —— Siege of Acre, an Epic Poem, *4to.* 1801—The same,
another edition, 1810   2 vol.

808 Cowper (Mrs) Original Poems, revised by W. Cowper, Esq
1792—The same, *second edition, portrait inserted*, 1807
—The same, *third edition*, 1810—The same, *n d*   4 vol.

809 Cox (Frances Elizabeth) Hymns from the German, *Pickering*, 1841—The same, *2nd edition, enlarged*, 1864   2 vol

810 Craig (Isa) Poems, *Edinb* 1856—Prize Poem on the Centenary of Burns, 1859—Offering to Lancashire, 1863
—Duchess Agnes, &c 1864   4 vol

811 —— Prize Poem on the Burns Festival, *4to* 1859—Offering to Lancashire, 1863—Duchess Agnes, &c *second edition*, 1865—Craig (C P) Isidore, and other Poems, *Glasgow*, 1847 — Pursuit of Knowledge, by G L Craik, 1817   5 vol

812 Craven (E S.) Legend of Mona, a Tale   *Douglas*, 1825

813 Crawford (Margaret) Rustic Lays on the Braes of Gala Water, *Edinb* 1855 — Criswick (Margaret) Spiritual Songs, 1861—Cristall (Ann Batten) Poetical Sketches, *vignette*, 1795   3 vol

814 Crewdson (Jane) Aunt Jane's Verses for Children, *illustrated*, 1851 — Lays of the Reformation, and other Lyrics, Scriptural and Miscellaneous, 1860— A Little While, and other Poems, *Manchester, n d*   3 vol.

815 —— Aunt Jane's Verses, *second edition, illustrated*, 1855—
Another Edition, *Philadelphia*, 1859—The Singer of Eisenach, *n d*—Poems, *second edition, n. d.*   4 vol

816 Croggon (Lucy Emla) Missionary Scenes, *Bristol*, 1831—
Heavenly Themes, *ib* 1832 — Thoughts by the Way Side, *Canterbury*, 1836—Things New and Old, *Bristol*, 1839—Things Seen and Known, *ib* 1844—Attempts at Sketching, *ib* 1846—Transcripts from my Tablets, *Dublin* 1849—Selection of Hymns, *ib* 1850—Onward and Upward, *Sittingbourne*, 1853   9 vol

817 Croker (Margaret Sarah) Monody on the Death of Princess Charlotte, *4to* 1817—Nugæ Canoræ, 1818—Another Edition, 1819—Tribute to the Memory of Sir S Romilly, 1818—Monody on the Duke of Kent, 1820   1 vol

818 Crosby (Frances Jane) Blind Girl, and other Poems
    New York, 1844

819 Crosfield (Miss A) Description of the Castle-Hills (in verse), *appended to the* History of North-Allerton, in the County of York   *Northallerton*, 1791

820 —— The same Another Edition, *vignette on the title-page*   *ib* 1804

821 CROSLAND (MRS) *formerly Camilla Toulmin*. Lays and Legends illustrative of English Life, *numerous illustrations*, 4to 1845—Poems, *frontispiece*, 1846   2 vol

822 CROSS (MISS H) Christian Oracle, *Peterborough*, 1851—CROWE (CATHERINE) Cruel Kindness, a Play, 1853—Crucifixion, by a Lady, 1817—CRUIKSHANK (M. H. G) Poems, *two copies*, 1860—CRUSE (H) Small Streams, *Frome*, n d —Crystal Fount, *Glasg* 1858—CULL (MARY) Lines on the Funeral of the Duke of Wellington, and three other single Pieces, *Woolwich*, 1852-3—Poems, 1854   9 vol

823 CULLUM (MRS) Charlotte or One Thousand Seven Hundred and Seventy Three, a Play, *frontispiece*   1775

824 CUMMYNG (SUSANNA) Estelle, from the French of M. de Florian, &c 2 vol. in 1   1798

825 CUNNINGHAM (MRS JANE) Mystagogue, *Dublin*, 1851—CUNNINGHAM (MRS.) Hymns and Songs, *Lowestoft*, 1848—The same, *second edition, ib n d* —CUNNINGHAM (MRS VIRGINIA) Madelaine, *Boston (in America)* 1856—CURLING (M A.) Poetical Pieces, *Dover*, 1831—The same, *second edition, ib.* 1831   6 vol.

826 CURSHAM (MARY ANN) Martin Luther, a Poem, *portrait, Nottingham*, 1825—The same, *another edition, ib* 1828—Poems, Sacred, Dramatic, and Lyric, *ib.* 1833—Infant's Decalogue, *ib.* 1836   4 vol.

827 CURTIES (MARIANNE) Classical Pastime, in a set of Enigmas on the Planets, &c   *Reading*, 1813

828 CUSHING (MRS. E. L) Esther, a Sacred Drama, with Judith, a Poem   *Boston (in America)* 1840

829 Cyclopædia of Female Biography, edited by H G Adams, *portraits*   1857

830 —— The same, *another edition*   *Glasgow*, 1865

831 CZARNECKI (MRS L A) General Bem, and other Poems, *Glasgow*, 1852—Hero of Italy, and other Poems, *Edinb* 1861   2 vol.

832 D (A C) Affection's Souvenir, *Bath, n d* — D (A L) Aladdin and the Wonderful Lamp, *n d* — D (EMILY) Muse and Poetess, and other Poems, 1835—D (M E) Leisure Moments, or Letters and Poems, &c. *Greenwich*, 1826 — Modern Life, and other Poems, by Mrs. D. 1847   (5)

833 DACRE (BARBARINA LADY) [*Mrs Wilmot*] Ina, a Tragedy, 1815—The same, *second and third editions*, 1815 3 vol.

834 —— Dramas, Translations, and Occasional Poems, 2 vol *privately printed, with autograph note of the Poetess inserted*   1821

835 DACRE (BARBARINA LADY) [*Mrs. Wilmot*] Translations from the Italian, 150 *copies only printed for private distribution, presentation copy to Mrs R Ellice, with autograph inscription of the Poetess,* green morocco   1836
836 —— Wednesday Morning, an Interlude, written in 1827, for Private Theatricals, *only a small number printed, presentation copy to Frederica Brand, with autograph inscription of the Poetess*   *Hitchin,* n d.
837 DACRE (CHARLOTTE) [alias Rosa Matilda] Hours of Solitude, a Collection of Poems, 2 vol in 1, *portrait*   1805
838 —— The same, *second edition*, 2 vol   1806
839 D'AGUILAR (ROSE) Gortzof Berlingen, with the Iron Hand, translated from Goethe   *Liverpool* (1799)
840 DALLAS (JUSTINA D.) Original Trifles, 1832 — DALLOR (FRANCES) Duel, a Poem, 1832   2 *vol.*
841 DALTON (ELIZABETH) Memoir (by her brother, James Forbes), *head, privately printed*   1813
842 DAMER (HON. A. S) Journal of the Heart, *first and second series,* 2 vol *plates*   1830-5
843 DANA (MRS. MARY S. B) Southern Harp, consisting of Sacred and Moral Songs, adapted for the Piano Forte and Guitar   4to   *Boston (in America),* 1841
844 —— Parted Family, and other Poems   *New York,* 1842
845 —— Northern Harp   4to   *ib.* 1843
846 Dandelion Chain, by Margaret   *Glasgow,* 1837
847 D'ANOIS (COUNTESS) Diverting Works, containing all her Spanish Novels and Histories, Tales of the Fairies, &c. *second edition, plates, head line partly cut off*   1715
848 D'ANVERS (MRS ALICIA) Academia or, The Humours of the University of Oxford, in Burlesque Verse, 4to   1691
849 —— The same, *another edition*   1716
850 DARBY (ELEANOR) Sweet South, or, a Month at Algiers, &c. *frontispiece*   1854
851 —— Lays of Love and Heroism, Legends, Lyrics, and other Poems, *plates, with an autograph Poem inserted*   1855
852 —— Ruggiero Vivaldi, and other Lays of Italy, &c   1865
853 DARK (MARIANA) Sonnets and other Poems, 1818—DARNTON (ELIZA) Tendrils of the Vine, 1843—DARTON (MARGARET L.) Words in Season, 1850   3 *vol.*
854 DARWALL (ELIZABETH) Storm, with other Poems   *Birmingham,* 1810
855 DARWALL (MRS) *formerly Whateley,* Original Poems on several Occasions   *Dodsley,* 1764
856 —— The same, *second edition*   *Dublin,* 1764
857 —— The same, *another edition,* 2 vol in 1   *Walsall,* 1794
858 DASH (MARY) Sacred and Moral Pieces, *two copies*   *Brighton,* 1827

G

859 D'Asmar (Princess Maria Theresa) Prophecy and Lamentation, or a Voice from the East, an appeal to the Women of England, *portrait* 1845
860 Daughters of Eve, by a Lady *Schenectady*, 1826
861 Davidson (Lucretia Maria) Amir Khan, and other Poems, with Biographical Sketch by S. F. B. Morse *New York*, 1829
862 —— Poetical Remains, with Biography by Miss Sedgwick, *Philadelphia*, 1841—The same, *another edition, frontispiece*, 1843—The same, *another edition*, New York, 1851 3 vol.
863 Davidson (Margaret) Life and Christian Experience, with some of her Letters and Hymns, by Rev. E Smyth *Dublin*, 1782
864 Davidson (Margaret Miller) Biography and Poetical Remains, by W Irving *Philadelphia*, 1841
865 —— The same, *another edition* *ib* 1842
866 —— The same, *a new edition, revised* *ib* 1843
867 —— The same, *another edition, frontispiece*, 1843—Recollections of Margaret and Lucretia Davidson, with Poetical Remains, *n d*—Selections from the Writings of Mrs Davidson, the mother of Lucretia and Margaret, *Philadelphia*, 1843 3 vol.
868 Davie (Elizabeth) Wayside Verses, or Pilgrim Melodies, 1859—Davies (Blanche) Octavia, a Tragedy, *Doncaster*, 1832—Davidson (F. A.) Don Cæsar de Bazan and Giralda, *n. d*—Davids (Louisa) Sunday School Hymn Book, *n d* 4 vol.
869 Davies (Elizabeth) Verses to the Ivorites for their great Love of the Welsh Language, and 15 other Pieces by the same Poetess, in one vol. *Neath*, 1849-50
870 Davis (Emily) Holly-Branch: an Album for 1843, *with music and illustrations*, 4to. 1843—Davis (Jane Maria) White Chief's Urn, *portrait*, 1850—Blanche Lisle, and other Poems, by Cecil Home, *Camb.* 1860—Lilian Gray, by Cecil Home, 1864—The Olive Branch, by a Lady, *n d.* 5 vol.
871 Davis (Mary Anne) Fables in Verse from Æsop, La Fontaine, &c. 1813—Three other Editions, 1819-22—Selection from the Parables of the New Testament, *Frome*, 1836 5 vol.
872 Davison (Francis) Poetical Rhapsody, with other Poetical Pieces, with Memoirs and Notes by N. H. Nicholas, 2 vol. in 1, *facsimiles, calf gilt* *Pickering*, 1826
873 Davys (Mary) Works, consisting of Plays, Novels, Poems, and Letters, 2 vol. in 1, *a few letters torn off the corner of last leaf* 1725

874 DAVYS (MARY) Northern Heiress: or, Humours of York, a Comedy, *frontispiece* 1716
875 DAWSON (M A.) Poem on the partial burning of York Cathedral *York*, 1829
876 DAY (ELIZA) Serious Reflections on the Death of Johannes, &c by Eliza, 1789—Thoughts occasioned by the Death of Maria, also on a Beloved Friend, likewise on visiting Eusebia's Tomb, 1789—Poem on the Proclamation of Peace, *Tottenham*, 1814—Elegy on the Death of the Princess Charlotte, by T. Whitehead, *Ramsgate*, 1817—The Jubilee, a Poem (by Eliza Day), *ib* 1810 3 *vol*.
877 —— Poems on various Subjects, with several pieces on the Death of Relatives and Friends
Tottenham, printed for the Author, 1814
878 DAY (JULIA) Poems, *Pickering*, 1817—Second Series, *Romsey*, 1849
in one vol.
879 DAY (MRS.) *formerly Milnes*, and Thomas Day, Miscellaneous Productions, in Verse and Prose, &c 1805
880 DAYE (ELIZA) Poems *Liverpool*, 1798
881 DAYMAN (JULIA) Thoughts in Verse (1859)—Household Verses, *Norwich*, n. d.—Church Bells, n d —The Pearl, by Mrs Eliza Dean, 1844—Porio, a Drama, 1859—Sermon on the Death of Mrs Ann Deane, by J Chin, 1815 5 *vol*.
882 DEBENHAM (ANNA M) Hero's Child, and other Poems 1853
883 DE BURGH (EMMA MARIA) Voice of many Waters, 1858—DE CALABRELLA (BARONESS) Land of Promise, a Tale, 4to. 1844—DE CHATELAIN (MADAME) Naughty Boys and Girls, *coloured figures, two copies*, 4to n d —Joy in Departing, by J. G. Deck, 1860 5 *vol*
884 DE CRESPIGNY (CAROLINE) My Souvenir, *Heidelberg*, 1844—Enchanted Rose, translated from the German of E. Schulze, *ib* 1844—Vision of Great Men, with other Poems and Translations, *ib*. 1848 3 *vol*
885 DE CRESPIGNY (LADY CHAMPION) Monody to the Memory of Lord Collingwood 4*to* 1810
886 DE CRESPIGNY (MRS H. C) Remembrances of Friendship
Cheltenham, 1830
887 DELANY (MRS) Letters to Mrs Frances Hamilton, 1779-88, *portrait* 1820
888 —— Autobiography and Correspondence, edited by Lady Llanover, *both series*, 6 vol *portraits* 1861-2
889 Delights for the Ingenious, or Monthly Entertainment for the Curious of Both Sexes, *all the parts complete for the year 1711, blue morocco, m e* 1711
890 Dell (Henry) Select Collection of the Psalms of David, is imitated by Mrs Leapor, Mrs. Masters, Mrs Rowe, Mrs. Tollet, and others 1756

891 DENT (CAROLINE) Thoughts and Sketches in Verse, 1854—
DERENZY (MARGARET GRAVES) Whisper to a Newly-
Married Pair, *three editions, Wellington and Philadelphia,* 1825-33—Parnassian Geography, *Wellington,*
1824   5 vol.

892 DERING (MRS ROBERT) Verses from the Scriptures, 1817—
Gatherings from the Scripture, 1818—Humble Sorrows, Arno and Francisca, &c. 1819—Crystal Palace,
1851   4 vol.

893 Detached Pieces, written by a Mother, and dedicated to her
Daughter, *Canterbury,* 1808—Detached Pieces, &c. in
prose and verse, by a Lady, 1819   2 vol

894 DE VERE (FLORENCE) Eugenie: or, The Spanish Bride, 1856
—DE YOUNGE (ANNEMINA) Joy, or Dramatical Charades,
plates, n d.   2 vol.

895 DEVERELL (MRS MARY) *of Gloucestershire,* Miscellanies in
Prose and Verse, 2 vol.   1781

896 ——— Theodora and Didymus, an Heroic Poem   1784

897 ——— The same, *second edition, with Appendix of a Pindaric
Ode and Poetical Epistles*   1786

898 ——— Mary Queen of Scots, a Tragedy   1792

899 DEVERFUX (MARION) Geography in Rhyme, 1866—Dew Drops,
by a Mother, 1853—DEWHURST (MRS E H) Diadem,
1839—DEWHURST (JANE) Poems, *three editions, with
autograph letter of the Poetess inserted,* 1856-58—DEW-
SNAP (MARY LUCY) Slave Auction, 1853   6 vol.

900 DEVONSHIRE (GEORGIANA DUCHESS OF) Passage of the Mountain
of St Gothard, a Poem, *privately printed*   4to   n d

901 ——— The same, with French Translation by De Lille, *plates
in lithography*   4to. n. d.

902 ——— The same (with French Translation by De Lille), preceded by the Poem, "Dithyrambe sur l'Immortalité de
l'Ame," *frontispiece, portrait of the Duchess in mezzotint inserted, red morocco, g e.*   *Paris,* 1802

903 ——— The same, with Italian Translation by G. Polidori 1803

904 ——— The same, *another edition, beautifully printed in large
type, a portrait of the Duchess in aquatinta inserted
half morocco, g. e*   folio. 1803

905 ——— Sketch of a descriptive Journey through Switzerland,
to which is added the Passage of S Gothard, *plate and
vignette*   *Berne,* 1816

906 DICK (LAVINIA) Todtenkranze and other Poems, 1813—The
Diadem, *plates, n d*—DICKSON (E. D) Posy of Stray
Wildlings, 1853—DICKINSON (GRACE) Songs in the Night,
photograph of the author's children, Halifax, n. d.—
The same, *second edition, a different photograph of the
same, Wakefield, n. d.*   5 vol.

907 DICKINSON (ELEANOR) Pleasures of Piety, with other Poems, *Liverpool*, 1821—The Mamluk, a Poem, 1830   2 *vol.*
908 Distressed Family, a Drama, translated from Le Mercier 1787
909 Divine Poems, together with a Journal of our Lord's Gracious Dealings with the Soul of the Authoress, by Christiana, Ramsey, Huntingdonshire *St. Ives,* (1792)
910 Divine Songs of the Muggletonians, edited by Joseph and Isaac Frost, *portrait of Lodowick Muggleton*   1829
911 DIXON (CHARLOTTE) Mount of Olives, 1814—The same, *second edition,* 1815—Bread cast upon the Waters, 1830—DIXON (JANE) Sacred Lyrics, *Camb* 1813—DIXON (LUCY) Flowers from Gethsemane, 1830   5 *vol.*
912 DIXON (MRS SARAH) Poems on several occasions, *with additional Poems in Manuscript, unpublished, copied from the originals in the Poetess's handwriting*
Canterbury, by J Abree, 1740
913 —— Poems Another Copy, *the date on the title-page altered to* 1712   *ib id* ——
914 DIXON (SOPHIE) Castalian Hours, Poems, 1829—Journal of Ten Days' Excursion on the Western and Northern Borders of Dartmoor, *Plymouth,* 1830   2 *vol.*
915 Dobell (John) Selection of Evangelical Hymns (including several by Miss Eliz Scott)   *n d*
916 DODSON (MRS SUSANNA) Life of Petrarch, 2 vol *large paper, the plates ornamented with a gilt border mottled calf extra, g e*   1797
917 Doctor Dissected or Willy Cadogan in the Kitchen, by a Lady   4*to* 1771
918 DOCWRA (ANNE) Looking-Glass for the Recorder and Justices of the Peace and Grand Juries for the Town and County of Cambridge, *with various stanzas at the end*
4*to* 1682
919 —— Epistle of Love and Good Advice to my Old Friends and Fellow Sufferers in the late Times, the Old Royalists, *with various stanzas at the end*   4*to* 1683
920 —— Bugg (F) Pilgrim's Progress from Quakerism to Christianity (with verses by Anne Docwra, wrote in 1681), *portrait by F H Van Hove*   1700
921 Dodsley (J) Collection of Poems by several hands, 6 vol *old calf gilt*   1783
922 DODSWORTH (MRS) Fugitive Pieces   *Canterbury,* 1802
923 DORMOLD (MRS LETITIA) Memoirs of her Life and Death, with Poems   1790
924 DORSET (MRS) Peacock at Home and other Poems, 1809—Three other Editions of the Peacock at Home, *illustrated,* 1807-51—Lion's Masquerade, *plates,* 1807—Lioness's Rout, by a Lady, *plates, n d*—Quadrupeds' Pic Nic, by F. B. C. *Pickering,* 1810   6 *vol.*

925 DORSET (MRS.) Peacock at Home, *illustrated and illuminated with beautiful borders*   4to. 1849

926 DOUGLAS (BESSIE) Excelsior. an Ethical Poetasm, *cuts*, Dublin, 1857—DOWLING (PENELOPE) Wild Flowers, 1862—DOWSON (SUSANNA) Poems, Domestic and Miscellaneous, *privately printed, with autograph letter of the poetess inserted*, Norwich, 1844   3 vol.

927 DOWNING (HARRIET) Mary. or, Female Friendship, a Poem, *frontispiece*, 4to 1816—Child of the Tempest and other Poems, *frontispiece*, 1821—Bride of Sicily, 1830—How Fanny teaches her Children, 1836—Satan in Love, 1840   5 vol

928 Drawing Room Table Book, by the Author of Mary Powell, *plates and cuts*   4to. n. d.

929 DRAYTON (MARIAN) Ephemeris, or Leaves from her Journall, *portrait*   1592, repr. C. Whittingham, n. d

930 DRING (MARY) Infantine Poems, 1854—Child's Poetical Naturalist, n. d, and others   6 vol.

931 DRUMMOND (MARGARET) Meditations, with a Poem on Eloquence   Glasgow, 1770

932 Drummond (W. of Hawthornden) Poetical Works, edited by W. B. Turnbull (with a Commendatory Poem by Mary Oxlie), *portrait*   1856

933 DRURY (ANNA HARRIET) Annesley and other Poems *Pickering*, 1847—First of May, a new Version of a celebrated modern Ballad, ib 1852   2 vol.

934 Dryden (J) Miscellany Poems, containing variety of translations, with several Original Poems by the most Eminent Hands, 6 vol   1727

935 ——. Nine Muses: or, Poems by Nine several Ladies on the Death of John Dryden   folio. 1700

936 —— Luctus Britannici, or Tears of the British Muses for the Death of John Dryden, *portrait inserted*, 1700—Browne (T.) Poem on his Majesty's Return from Holland 1691; and other Tracts   folio in one vol

937 DU BOIS (LADY DOROTHEA) Poems on several occasions by a Lady of Quality   Dublin, 1764

938 —— Lady's Polite Secretary, or New Female Letter Writer, with variety of Poetical Letters, &c.   n d

939 —— Magnet, a Musical Entertainment   1771

940 DUCKWORTH (ELEANOR) Poems and Sketches, 2nd, 3rd, and 4th Editions, *portrait*, Edinb 1856—Dumfries Album, edited by A M Adam, 4to. Glasgow, 1857   4 vol

941 Dudley (H. a boy aged 14) Juvenile Researches, or a description of some of the principal Towns in the Western part of Sussex, and the borders of Hants, interspersed with various pieces of Poetry by a Sister, *numerous woodcuts by the author, only a very small number of copies printed for presents*   Easebourne, 1835

942 Dudley (H. a boy aged 14) Juvenile Researches, *second edition, only 50 copies privately printed by the author; from Mr Hanrott's Library*   *Easebourne,* 1835
943 Dudley (Mary) Life, with Extracts from her Letters and Poetry, edited by Elizabeth Dudley   1825
944 Dudley (M. E.) Emmett, the Irish Patriot, and other Poems, *plates*   1836
945 Duncan (Mary Lundie) Memoir, by her Mother, *frontispiece, Edinb.* 1841—The same, *second edition, ib* 1842—The same, *third edition, ib.* 1843—Rhymes for my Children, *ib. n. d.*   4 *vol.*
946 —— Memoir, *fourth edition, view of Kelso, Edinb.* 1846—The same, *another edition, New York,* 1850—The same, *sixth edition, Edinb* 1854   3 *vol.*
947 Dunch (M. E.) Leisure Moments, or Letters and Poems, &c. by a Lady, *two parts*   *Greenwich,* 1826-41
948 —— Another copy, *with extra title to the first part reprinted* 1841   *ib* 1826-41
949 Dunlop (Frances Elizabeth) Edmond of Ryedale Vale; or, the Widowed Bride, a Poem
    green morocco extra, sides tooled and gilt, joints, and g. e.
    York, printed for the author, 1822
950 Dunnett (Jane) Poems on various subjects, *Edinb* 1818—Dunn (Ann and Catharine H.) Hours of Devotion, 1857—Hymns from the German, translated by C. H. Dunn, 1867—The same, second edition, 1861   4 *vol.*
951 Dunsterville (Ann) *of Plymouth,* Poems
    Exeter, printed for the author, 1807
952 Dutton (Anne) Narration of the Wonders of Grace, in verse, in six parts, *portrait inserted*
    printed for and sold by the author, 1734
953 —— Narration, Second Edition, corrected by the author with Additions, *portrait inserted*   1734
954 —— Narration a new Edition, with Memoir by J. A Jones, 1833—Poem on the Work of the Spirit, 1818—Another Edition of the same, with Preface by W. Savory, *Brighton,* 1831   3 *vol.*
955 —— Discourse concerning the New Birth, to which are added two Poems on Salvation, and on a Believer's Safety, with Epistle by Jacob Rogers   1740
956 —— Account of the Gracious Dealings of God with a Poor, Sinful, Unworthy Creature   1750
957 —— Divine, Moral, and Historical Miscellanies, in Prose and Verse, 3 vol   (*Coventry*), 1761-3
958 Dutton (Mary) Scattered Seeds, 1860—The same, Second Edition, 1862   2 *vol.*
959 Duvard (Primogene) Poems
    Northallerton, printed for the authoress, 1842

960 DUVARD (PRIMOGENE) Poems, Second Edition, corrected and enlarged *Northallerton, printed for the authoress,* 1843
961 —— Mary Tudor, an Historical Drama *ib.* 1844
962 —— Devotional Exercises for fourteen Days *York, printed for the authoress,* 1846
963 —— Angel of Death and other Poems, *Sittingbourne,* 1862 —Poems and Hymns, *ib* 1864—Devotional Exercises, Second Edition, *ib* 1855 *in one vol*
964 Dyce (A) Specimens of British Poetesses, *morocco, m e* 1825
965 E., Stray Thoughts in Prose and Verse, *Exmouth* 1846— Poems by a Sempstress, Ode to the Memory of T Hood, and other Poems, by E L E. 1848 2 vol.
966 E (A) Rhymes, PRIVATELY PRINTED *Newry,* 1831
967 EARLE (MISS) Corinth and other Poems 1821
968 Early Blossom, or Young Inquirer: a series of Dialogues between a Child and his Mother, by Celata, *portrait,* 1852—Early Recollections, by Bertie's Mother, edited by J. B Laing, *n d.* 2 vol.
969 Early Metrical Tales; including the History of Sir Egeir, Sir Gryme, and Sir Gray-Steill, edited by D. Laing, Esq *frontispiece designed by C K. Sharpe, Esq and vignette by W. Geikie, very scarce Edinb* 1826
970 EATON (FRANCES M) Josephine, a Poem, 1842—Another copy, *Guernsey,* 1842, *both privately printed* 2 vol.
971 Eccentric Biography, or Memoirs of Remarkable Female Characters, *portraits,* 1803—EBSWORTH (MRS) Payable at Sight, *n. d*—EDGARTON (MISS S C) Flower Vase, *Boston (in America),* 1844—Language and Poetry of Flowers, *four editions,* 1850-61 7 vol.
972 ECKLEY (SOPHIA MAY) Poems, *frontispiece,* 1863—Light on Dark Days, 1863—Easter Roses, 1864 3 vol.
973 EDGAR (MISS) Tranquillity and other Poems, and Translations *Dundee,* 1810
974 —— The same, Second Edition *Edinb.* 1824
975 EDGEWORTH (MARIA) Comic Dramas, *portrait and plate, and an autograph letter of the poetess inserted,* 1817—The same, Second Edition, 1817—Little Plays for Children, *with autograph letter of the poetess inserted,* 1827 3 vol.
976 EDGWORTH (MISS TEMPLE) Metrical Tales and Romances, containing Alphonso and Clementina, Don John, Hodge's Disaster, &c. 1809—Mysterious Shriek, or Alcander and Lavinia, also Pluto and Proserpine, and Cupid's Delirium, 1809 2 vol
977 EDIS (MARY) Friendly Harp, 1852—EDGWORTH (MISS Temple) Metrical Tales and Romances, 1809 2 vol.
978 EDMOND (AMANDA M) Broken Vow and other Poems, *portrait and plates Boston (in America),* 1845

979 EDMUNDS (MARY) and John Boys, both of Margate, Trial for three Poetical Libels, *coloured caricatures* 1815
980 EDRIDGE (REBECCA) Lapse of Time, a Poem
              4to *Uxbridge,* 1803
981 —— Scrinium, 2 vol 1822
982 EDWARDS (AMELIA B) Ballads, 1865—EDWARDS (ELIZA) Flower of the Field, 1863 2 vol.
983 EDWARDS (ANNA MARIA) Enchantress, and Poems on various subjects *Dublin,* 1787
984 EDWARDS (M BEHAM) Little Bird Red and Little Bird Blue, 1861—Primrose Pilgrimage, 1865—Snow Flakes, *n d. illustrated by Macquoid and Browne* 3 vol.
985 EDWARDS (MISS) Miscellanies, in prose and verse, *Edinb* 1776—Otho and Rutha, a Dramatic Tale, *ib.* 1780 2 *vol.*
986 Effusions of the Heart, or Miscellaneous Poems, *privately printed, with autograph of the Princess Elizabeth, and numerous manuscript alterations* 4to. *n. d*
987 Elegy on the Death of Richard Reynolds, with other Poems 1818
988 ELFE (ANNE) Lays of Caruth, Bard of Dinham, and other Poems 1808
989 —— Original Poems *Chepstow,* 1809
990 Elgiva or The Monks, an Historical Poem, with some Minor Pieces 1824
991 Elizabeth (Queen) In Catilinarias Proditiones, ac Proditores Domesticos, Ode 6
 VERY RARE, *fine copy, red morocco*   Oxon. J, Barnes, 1586
992 ELIZABETH, QUEEN OF BOHEMIA, Memoirs, by one of her Ladies [Lady Frances Erskine], *privately printed, with autograph of Mary Erskine, to whom it was given by Mr Erskine of Mar, Sept 15, 1793, portrait inserted*
                 no date
993 —— Memoirs, by Miss Benger, 2 vol *portrait* 1825
994 Ellauna, a Legend of the Thirteenth Century, with notes, by Mary, dedicated to the House of Leix
 scarce   *Dublin,* 1815
995 ELLET (MRS E F) Poems, Translated and Original
              Philadelphia, 1835
996 —— Characters of Schiller *Boston,* 1812
997 ELLICE (JANE) English Idylls and other Poems *Camb* 1865
998 ELLIOT (ANNE) Heart's-Ease, *Armagh,* 1837—The same, another edition *Exeter,* 1841—Serious Thoughts, *ib.* 1841—Fancy's Wreath, by Miss Elliot, *frontispiece,* 1812 4 *vol*
999 ELLIOTT (CHARLOTTE) Hours of Sorrow, 1836—The same, 2nd, 3rd, 4th, and 5th *editions,* 1840-56—Morning and Evening Hymns for a Week, *n d*—Psalms and Hymns, selected by H. V. Elliot, 1858 7 *vol.*

H

1000 ELLIOT (MARY) *late Belson*, Simple Truths, 1816—Flowers of Instruction, 1820—Sunflower, 1822, *and other editions and pieces by the same* 13 vol
1001 Ellis (George) Specimens of the Early English Poets, 3 vol 1845
1002 ELLIS (SARAH S.) Sons of the Soil, a Poem, *with illustrations* n. d.
1003 —— The same, *second edition, portrait and cuts* n d.
1004 —— Fireside Tales of the Young, 4 vol *plates* n. d.
1005 —— Island Queen, a Poem, *portrait*, 1846—Janet one of Many, 4to 1862—William and Mary, 1865—Sacred Thoughts, by Mrs Henry Clements Ellis, 1851 4 vol.
1006 Eloise, and other Poems on several occasions, by a Young Lady *Leith*, 1815
1007 Elwood (Mrs.) Memoirs of the Literary Ladies of England from the commencement of the last Century, 2 vol, *portraits* 1843
1008 EMBURY (E. C.) Guido, a Tale, Sketches from History, and other Poems, by Ianthe *New York*, 1828
1009 EMFRY (E U.) Visit of Innocence and other Poems *privately printed* *Torquay*, 1830
1010 English Annual for 1835, 1836, 1837, 1838, 4 vol. *plates morocco, g e.* 1835-8
1011 ENGLISH (HARRIET) Conversations and Amusing Tales, *frontispiece by Bartolozzi* 4to. 1799
1012 Enigmas, Historical and Geographical, by a Clergyman's Daughter, 1831—The same, *second edition*, 1839—Enigmatical Entertainer and Mathematical Associate for 1828 to 1831, *four Nos* 1827-30 3 vol
1013 Epistle to a Clergyman, by one of his Parishioners, (a poor Woman) 1765
1014 ERSKINE (MRS. ESME STEUART) Isabel and other Poems *morocco* *Romford*, 1814
1015 —— Alcon Malanzore, a Moorish Tale *Brussels*, 1815
1016 ESLING (MRS C H W) *formerly Waterman*, Broken Bracelet and other Poems *Philadelphia*, 1850
1017 ESPENER (ISABELLA) Sentimental Poetry, Acrostics, &c *privately printed* *Hull*, 1826
1018 ESTEN (Mrs.) Epilogue to O'Keefe's World in a Village, *n. d*
1019 EVANCE (MISS S.) Poems, 1808—Essays, Poems, and Letters on various subjects, 1813—Narratives of a Parent, by Mrs Everest, 1845—Evergreen, Selections from the most Eminent American Poets, *Halifax*, 1860—Evergreen, a Selection of Religious Poetry, *n d*—Evenings abroad, *plate*, 1836 6 vol.
1020 EVANS (MRS. E. H.) Poems, with Preface by T. H. Stockton *Philadelphia*, 1851

1021 EVANS (KATHARINE) and Sarah Chevers, Relation of their Sufferings in the Inquisition in the Isle of Malta (with Hymns, Songs, Praises, &c.)
VERY RARE, *the last leaf slightly defective*   4to   1662
1022 —— History of their Voyage to the Island of Malta, and their cruel Sufferings there for near four years, with a Relation from G. Robinson of his Sufferings in his Journey to Jerusalem   1715
1023 Everest (Rev. Charles W.) Poets of Connecticut, with Biographical Sketches, *plate*   *Hartford*, 1843
1024 —— Memento a Gift of Friendship, *plates New York*, 1850
1025 EWING (BARBARA) Memoir, by her husband Greville Ewing   *Glasgow*, 1829
1026 EWING (HARRIET) Dunrie, a Poem   *Bath*, 1819
1027 Examen Miscellaneum, consisting of Verse and Prose, by the Marquis of Normanby, Lord Rochester, Mr Waller, Mrs. Wharton, Mr Wolseley, with Satires and Fables, and Translations from Anacreon   1702
1028 Expostulation, a Poem, by a Young Lady   *Bath, printed by N. Bliss, Oxford*, 1808
1029 Extraordinary Women their Girlhood and Early Life, by W. Russell, *with illustrations*   1857
1030 EYRE (MARY) Lady's Walks in the South of France in 1863, *plate*   1865
1031 —— The same, *second edition, plate*   1865

THIRD DAY'S SALE.

OCTAVO ET INFRA

UNLESS OTHERWISE EXPRESSED.

LOT
1032 F. (E.) Sketches and Souvenirs, or, Records of other Days   *Bath*, 1839
1033 Fagot of Fancies, by a Lady, *Salisbury, n d* —— Fair Crusader, an Opera, *n d* —— Fairy Tales (Two) in a Dramatic Form, by a Lady, 1851 —— Faith's Telescope and other Poems, by a Lady, *Edinb* 1830   4 vol
1034 FAIRBROTHER (MARY ANN) Poems chiefly Moral and Pastoral   *printed for the Authoress*, 1808

1035 FAIRWEATHER (MRS. MARY) Hymns and Religious Poems of a Practical Nature   *printed at the Agra Press*, 1883

1036 FAITHFUL (ANN) Verse Pictures for Cottage Walls, *Norwich, n. d* —A Welcome, Original Contributions in Poetry and Prose, *Emily Faithful*, 1863   2 vol.

1037 FALCONER (MARIA AND HARRIET) Poems, *portraits inserted* 1788

1038 —— Poetic Laurels for Characters of distinguished merit, interspersed with Poems, *plate after Cosway* 4to *printed at the Lithographic Press*, 1791

1039 FALLOW (MRS) Poetical Remains, 1833 — Familiar Account of Trees, &c 1837—Familiar Letters, 1811—Family Prayers, 1824—The same, third edition, 1832   5 vol

1040 Familiar Dialogue between Eve and Mary, concerning the Free Pardon of Sins   1757

1041 Family Picture, a Play, from the French of Diderot, with Verses, by a Lady   1781

1042 FARLEY (HARRIET) Shells from the Sea of Genius *Boston, (in America)*, 1847

1043 FARNINGHAM (MARIANNE) Lays and Lyrics of the Blessed Life, *portrait, four editions*, 1860-4—Hymns for a Week, *Northampton*, 1863   5 vol.

1044 FARQUHAR (B. H.) Poems, *Glasgow, n. d*—A Sister's Memorial, or, account of Rebecca Farrand, 1857 2 vol

1045 FARR (Edw.) Select Poetry, chiefly of the Reigns of Elizabeth and James I. 3 vol.   *Camb* 1845-7

1046 FARRELL (SARAH) Charlotte, and other Poems, *vignette* 4to. *Bath*, 1792

1047 Fate of Corsica, or, Female Politician, a Comedy, by a Lady of Quality   1732

1048 FAVGERES (MARGARETTA V) Belisarius, a Tragedy, *frontispiece*   *New York*, 1795

1049 Favart (Mons) Englishmen in Bordeaux, a Comedy, translated by a Lady, *Dublin*, 1763—The same, another edition, *G. Kearsly*, 1764   2 vol.

1050 FAWCETT (CHARLOTTE) Elijah the Tishbite, and Israel's Wanderings, *Crewkerne*, 1840 — Hymns by C. F. *Birmingham*, 1858—Memorials of Departed Love, by MRS FAULKENER, 1835   3 vol

1051 Fawcett (Joshua) Temple Offerings, or Contributions in Prose and Verse, by various Authors   1838

1052 FAY (GERDA) Poetry for Play Hours, *with eight illustrations*, 1860—Lyrics and Idylls, 1861   2 vol.

1053 FELL (ELIZABETH) *of Saffron Walden*, Fables, Odes, and Miscellaneous Poems   1771

1054 —— Poems   4to 1777

1055 FELL (MARGARET) Verses prefixed to "The Books and Divers Epistles of the Faithful Servant of the Lord Josiah Coale," *very scarce*   4to 1671

1056 FELL (MISS) *of Newcastle*, Poem on the Times, *with Manuscript Pedigrees, from the Library of T. Bell*   4to. 1774

1057 Female Forgery; or, Fatal Effects of Unlawful Love, with Elegy written by Mrs. RUDD to Mr Daniel Perreau, 1775

1058 Female Patriot, an Epistle from CHARLOTTE MACAULEY to Dr. W on her late Marriage   4to 1779

1059 Female Poets of America, with specimens of their writings, by T B Read, *portraits*   *Philadelphia*, 1857

1060 Female Poets of Great Britain, containing their choicest Poems, with Memoirs by T F Rowton   1848

1061 FENN (LADY) Dialogues and Letters, 3 vol in 1, 1816— FELLOWS (MRS. FRANK P) Poems, 1857 — FENTON (MYFANWY) Sir Howel, and other Poems, *Birmingham*, 1863   3 vol.

1062 Feud (The), a Scottish Story, in seven cantos, *Dublin*, 1814

1063 [FIFLD (MRS SUSAN)] Poems on several occasions, together with a Pastoral   (1716)

1064 FINCH (B.) Sonnets and other Poems, *frontispiece after Stothard, by Blake*   1805

1065 FINCH (CATHARINE IRENE) Juvenile Dramas, *Birmingham*, 1849—FINLAY (MRS) The Tahitians, a Dramatic Poem, *Cheltenham*, 1838—Meditations on the Canticles, 1856   3 vol.

1066 Finden's Tableaux of National Character, Beauty and Costume, 61 *plates, morocco extra, g e*   Folio, n d

1067 Finden's Gallery of the Graces, a series of Portrait Illustrations of British Poets, 36 *plates, morocco extra, g e* 1831

1068 Fine Gentleman's Etiquette, or Lord Chesterfield's Advice to his Son, versified, by a Lady, *vignette on the title-page*   4to 1776

1069 First Violet, (by a Minister's Sister) *privately printed*   *Faringdon*, 1853

1070 Fisher's Drawing Room Scrap Book for 1832 to 1850, inclusive, 19 vol. *beautiful plates*   4to. 1832-50

1071 Fisher's Juvenile Scrap Book for 1837 to 1842, 1844 to 1848, and 1850, 12 vol *beautiful plates*   1837-50

1072 FISHER (FANNY E) Lonely Hours, *Dublin*, 1864—FISHER (M) Scenes from Scripture, and other Poems, *Carlisle*, 1859—FISHER (SUSAN) Legend of the Puritans, with other Poems, *Bristol*, 1837   3 vol.

1073 FITZOSNABURGH (FRANCES A) Youth's New Monitor, patronized by the Duchess of Roxburghe   *no date*

1074 FITZ-SIMON (ELLEN) Darrynane, and other Poem *Dublin*, 1863

1075 FLETCHER (ELIZA) *formerly Dawson*, Elidure and Edward, two Dramatic Sketches, *privately printed* 1825

1076 FLETCHER (LUCY) Thoughts from a Girl's Life, *Norwich*, 1864—The same, *second edition, ib* 1865—Poems by Rev. J Fletcher and MARY FLETCHER, 1846—FLETCHER (MARY ANN P.) Poems, *two copies, Newcastle-upon-Tyne*, 1836 5 vol.

1077 FLETCHER (MARIA JANE) *formerly Jewsbury*, Phantasmagoria, or Sketches of Life and Literature, 2 vol *Leeds*, 1825

1078 —— Lays of Leisure Hours, *portrait inserted* 1829

1079 —— Letters to the Young, *third edition* 1832

1080 —— Three Histories *Derby*, 1838

1081 FLEURY (MARIA DE) Poems, occasioned by the acquittal of Lord George Gordon, *portrait*, 1781—Speech of Mr. Erskine, of Council for Lord George Gordon, 1781—Unrighteous Abuse Detected and Chastised, 1781—British Liberty Established, 1790—Henry, or the Triumph of Grace, dedicated to Lord George Gordon, 1782—Divine Poems and Essays, 1791—The same, *another edition, New York*, 1804 5 vol

1082 FLINDERS (ANNE) Naboth, the Jezreelite, and other Poems, *Bath*, 1844—Flora and Thalia, or Gems of Flowers and Poetry, by a Lady, *coloured plates* 1835—Floral Emblems, by a Lady of Title, *n. d.*—Flowers of the Forest, *Wellington*, 1828—The same, *second edition, ib* 1829 5 vol

1083 Flodden ('The Battle of) in verse, written about the time of Queen Elizabeth, with Notes by R Lambe, *frontispiece Berwick-upon-Tweed*, 1774

1084 FLOWERDEW (A) Poems, *three editions*, 1803-11—Flowers of Literature, for 1808-9, with Notes by F W Blagdon, *portraits*, 1810 4 vol

1085 Flowers of Loveliness, Thirty-six Groupes of Female Figures, Emblematic of Flowers, designed by various Artists, with Poetical Illustrations by L. E. L., the Countess of Blessington and T. H. Bayley, *coloured plates* folio. *Ackermann, n d.*

1086 Flowers of Loveliness; Forty Groups of Female Figures, with Poetical Illustrations by L. E. L, the Countess of Blessington and T. H Bayley, *beautiful plates*, folio n. d,

1087 Flowers of many hues, edited by Frederick Kempster, *illuminated title-page* 4to. *Manchester*, 1844

1088 FOLLEN (MRS) Poems, *frontispiece, Boston, (in America)* 1839

1089 —— The same, *another edition, frontispiece*, 1840—Hymns, Songs, and Fables, *plates, Boston*, 1851—Poetry Book for Children, *many engravings, New York*, 1854—Lark and Linnet, Hymns, Songs and Fables, *frontispiece*, 1854—Little Songs, illustrated with above 50 pictures, *Boston*, 1856—New Nursery Songs, 1860 6 vol.

1090 FOOT (ALICIA JULIA) Thoughts in Verse, *printed for private circulation* 1856

1091 FOOT (ROSE) Rose's Offering, *with illustrations, three editions* 4to. *Cheshunt*, 1856

1092 Foote (Sam) The Author, a Comedy (the Epilogue written by a Lady) 1782

1093 FORD (ANN) *afterwards Thicknesse*, Letter to a Person of Distinction, with a new Ballad, 1761—Letter to Miss Ford, 1761—Letter from Miss Ford, *second edition, with caricature*, 1761—Letter to Miss Ford, *second edition, with caricature*, 1761—Letter to Miss Ford, *second edition*, 1761—Maid of Bath, [Miss Ford] a Comedy, n. d. *with fac-similes inserted* in 1 vol.

1094 FORD (SARAH CAROLINE) Miscellaneous Poems *privately printed* 1831

1095 FORDYCE (HENRIETTA) Memoir containing Letters, Anecdotes, and Pieces of Poetry *Bath*, 1823

1096 Forget-me-Not, for 1823 to 1847 inclusive, 25 vol *beautiful plates* 1823-47

1097 FORREST (MARY) Women of the South distinguished in Literature, *portraits, morocco, g e* 4to *New York*, 1861

1098 FORSAYTH (FRANCES JANE) Arno's Waters and other Poems 1865

1099 FORTESCUE (LADY ELEANOR) Hymns from the German, 1843—The same, *second edition*, 1847—FORTH (JANE) Translation of the Poems God and Prayer, from the Méditations Poetiques of A. De La Martine, *Whitby*, 1839—Book of Forfeits, *frontispiece*, 1837 4 vol.

1100 FORTNUM (SOPHIA) *late King*, Poems, Legendary, Pathetic, and Descriptive
old russia, tooled and gilt on the sides, g e 1804

1101 Foscolo (Ugo) Essays on Petrarch, with Translations *Murray*, 1823

1102 Foster (C) and E. Collins, New Metrical Version of the Psalms *Hull*, 1838

1103 FOURDRINIER (HARRIET E) Our New Parish, its Privileges and Progress, *Pickering*, 1852—FOTHERBY (MARIE J. E) Poems edited by her Husband, *two copies*, 1862 3 vol.

1104 FOWKE (MARTHA) Epistles of Clio and Strephon, being a Collection of Letters that passed between an English Lady and an English Gentleman, in France, who took an Affection to each other by reading accidentally one another's Occasional Compositions *no date*

1105 —— The same, *second edition, with MS. Notes by Mr. Bindley* 1729

1106 —— The same, *third edition*, under the Title of "The Platonic Lovers," 1732

1107 Fowke (Martha) Mr. Campbell's Packet for the Entertainment of Gentlemen and Ladies, containing Verses to Mr. Campbell, by Mrs. Fowke, Mr. Philips, &c. An account of a most surprising Apparition, sent from Launceston, in Cornwall, &c. 1720

1108 Fox (Elizabeth) Wild Blossoms and Stray Leaves, *Warminster*, 1855—Fox (Sarah) Metrical Version of the Book of Job, 1852—The same, *another edition*, 1854
3 vol.

1109 Fox (Maria) *of Tottenham*, Memoirs consisting chiefly of extracts from her Journal and Correspondence 1846

1110 Fox (Lady Mary) Friendly Contributions *privately printed*   *Kensington*, 1834

1111 Francis (Ann) *of Edgefield Parsonage, Norfolk*, Poetical Translation of the Song of Solomon, with Notes, 1781—Charlotte to Werter, a Poetical Epistle, 1787—Obsequies of Demetrius Poliorcetes, a Poem, 1785
4to. 2 vol.

1112 —— Miscellaneous Poems   1790

1113 —— The same, *another edition*   1790

1114 Francis (Eliza S.) Rival Roses, or Wars of York and Lancaster, a Metrical Tale, 2 vol. in 1, 1813—Sir Wilibert de Waverley, or, the Bridal Eve, a Poem, 1815
2 vol.

1115 Francis (Miss) Santa Maura; Marion, and other Poems, 1821—Charade Dramas, by Miss Frances, n. d.—Frank (Mary) Poems and Paraphrases, 1833—Verses, Sacred and Descriptive, 1850—Glances in Palestine, and other Poems, 1860
5 vol.

1116 Frankland (Sarah) Leaves of Poesy, 1838—Affection's Token, *frontispiece*, 1851—Franklin (M.) Hours of Solitude and Sempronius, 1851
3 vol.

1117 Franklin (Lady) *formerly Eleanor Anne Porden*, The Veils, or Triumph of Constancy, a Poem   1815

1118 —— Arctic Expeditions, a Poem, *with autograph Note inserted*   1818

1119 —— Ode to Viscount B——ive, on his marriage with Lady Elizabeth Mary L——eson Gower, 1819—Ode on the Coronation of George IV 1821
in 1 vol.

1120 —— Cœur de Lion, or, The Third Crusade, a Poem, 2 vol.
1822

1121 Fraser (Janet Douglas) Poems, *portrait*, *Dumfries*, n. d.—Fraser (Mrs.) Poems, 1811—Fraser (Susan) Camilla de Florian, and other Poems, 1809—The same, *second edition*, 1809
4 vol.

1122 Freeman (Ann) Memoir, written by herself, and an account of her Death, by her husband, Henry Freeman
1826

1123 FREEMAN (ELLEN) Memorials of the Mind and Heart, *compiled and printed for private circulation, portrait*, 1858

1124 FREMONT (ANNE A.) Sacred Musings, 1843—The same, *second edition*, 1865—FRENCH (ELIZABETH WILMSHURST) Pebbles and Shells, 1858—Friendship's Memento, 1849 *4 vol.*

1125 Friendship's Offering, a Literary Album for 1824 to 1844, inclusive, 21 vol. *plates* 1824-44

1126 FRY (HENRIETTA J) Pastor's Legacy, *Bristol, n. d*—Hymns of the Reformation, 1845—Wells of Scripture, *n. d.*—Rhyming Game, 1846—Echoes of Eternity, *Bath, n d* 5 *vol.*

1127 —— Portraits in Miniature; or, Tableaux du Cœur, *portraits, green morocco* 1848

1128 Fugitive Miscellany, a Collection of Fugitive pieces in prose and verse, not in any other collection *J Almon*, 1774

1129 Fugitive Pieces (by a Lady) *privately printed* *Reading, n d*

1130 Fugitive Poems, by Emily *Pickering*, 1848

1131 Fugitive Scotish Poetry of the XVIIth Century, edited by D. Laing. Esq *curious vignette on the title-page, 72 copies only printed, very scarce Edinb* 1825

1132 FULLARTON (LADY G) The Old Highlander, the Ruins of Strata Florida, and other verses, *privately printed*, 1849

1133 FULLER (S MARGARET) Summer on the Lakes, in 1843, *plates Boston, (in America)*, 1844

1134 —— Papers on Literature and Art, *two parts, in 1 vol* 1846

1135 FURLONG (MRS W MATTHEW) Early Sketches, Prose and Poetry, *fourth edition*, 1836—The Spectre Poverty, an Allegory, *Edinb printed for the Authoress*, 1834 *2 vol*

1136 GAMMAGE (ANNE) Spring Flowers, *Liverpool*, 1843—GARLAND (ANNE) Help for Infant Minds, *Huddersfield*, 1831—Spiritual Recreations by Eliza [Carrington], 1821—GARDNER (MISS L P) Reflections in Verse, *printed for the author*, 1811—Gadsby (J) Memoirs of Hymn Writers, 1861—The Toilet, by S G. 1823—Heart's Last, by S M G. 1815 *7 vol.*

1137 GARLAND (EMMA) Ovid's Epistles in English Verse, with some Original Poems, *morocco Liverpool*, 1812

1138 GARRARD (ELIZA) Miscellanies in Verse and Prose *Bath*, 1799

1139 GARROW (THEODOSIA) Arnold of Brescia, a Tragedy, translated from Niccolini, 1846—GARROW (ANNE) Poems of Girlhood, 1843—Garden of Adonis: or, Love to no Purpose, being above 20 copies of Verses and Love Letters by a Lady, *taken from the Golden Medley*, 1720 *3 vol*

I

1140 GASCOYNE (M. A.) Ladies Hand-Book, *privately printed*, 4to. 1846—Belgravia, a Poem, 1851—The same, *second edition*, 1851—Recollections and Tales of the Crystal Palace, 1852   4 vol.

1141 GEARY (ELIZABETH) Juvenile Effusions: Moral and Religious, *privately printed*   1822

1142 GEISWEILER (MARIA) Poverty and Nobleness of Mind; a Play, translated from Kotzebue, 1799—The same, *second edition*, 1799—Johanna of Montfaucon, 1799—The Noble Lie, 1799—Crime from Ambition, 1800   2 vol.

1143 GELDART (MRS. THOMAS) Thoughts for Home, *Norwich*, 1850—Genders of the French Nouns, 1850—Gentleman's Monthly Miscellany, Nos 1 and 2, 1803—George IV. a Poem, 1822   4 vol.

1144 Gem (The) a Literary Annual for 1829 to 1832, 4 vol. *beautiful plates*   1829-32

1145 Gems from American Female Poets, *Philadelphia*, 1842—Gems from the Spirit Mine, *plate*, 1850—Gems of Thought and Flowers of Fancy, 1855—Gerard (G) Clytia, with other Poems, 1851—Grace and Remembrance, 1856   5 vol.

1146 German Christmas-Eve a Picture of Home Life in Germany, with Directions for Working Patterns for Knitting, by Madame Apolline Flohr, edited by Mrs A. Montgomery   1846

1147 GETHIN (LADY GRACE) Remains: a Collection of Choice Discourses, Pleasant Apothegms and Witty Sentences, with Funeral Sermon by Dr Birch, *portrait in mezzotinto*   4to   *printed for the author*, 1699-1700

1148 —— The same, second edition, *portrait plate of Lady Gethin on her death-bed, and another of her monument in Westminster Abbey*   4to   1700

1149 GIBBONS (MISS C. A.) Illustrated Charades   *folio*   n. d.

1150 Gibbons (Thomas) Memoirs of Pious Women, 2 vol. in 1 *portraits*   1820

1151 GIBBS (MRS. A.) Selection in Prose and Verse, with some original Pieces   *Cranbrook*, 1803

1152 Gideon and other Poems, *Sudbury*, 1829—Gift for all Seasons, *plates*, 1839—Gisborne (T) Essays, 1822—Glance at the Nations, with other Poems, *Boston (in America)*, 1835   3 vol.

1153 Gift (The), edited by Miss Leslie, for 1836, 1840, and 1843, 3 vol. *beautiful plates, that for 1843 on large paper*   *Philadelphia*, 1836-43

1154 GILBERT (ANN) *late Taylor*, Anniversary Hymns, 1827—Hymns for Infant Schools, 1827—The same, 4th edition, 1833—Seven Blessings, 1846—A Child's Walk, 1858—GILL (MARY HARVEY) Texts and Hymns, *New York*, 1861—GILPIN (ELIZABETH) Texts, 1860—GILPIN (MARGARET) Seymour Manor, *Halifax*, 1856—Wreath of Friendship, *two editions, ib* 1856-61   10 *vol.*

1155 GILCHRIST (CATHERINE) Poems, Moral and Religious *privately printed*   *Manchester*, 1839

1156 Gillian of Croydon, Pleasant and Delightful History, her Account of a Country Wedding in Kent, &c *woodcuts*   1727

1157 GILMAN (CAROLINE) Poetry of Travelling in the United States, with a Week among Autographs, by Rev S Gilman   *New York*, 1838

1158 —— Tales and Ballads   *ib.* 1839

1159 —— Stories and Poems for Children, *woodcuts*   *ib.* 1845

1160 —— Verses of a Life Time   *ib* 1849

1161 GODDARD (Mrs) Poems on several Occasions   *Dublin, printed for the author*, 1748

1162 —— The same, another copy   *ib.* 1748

1163 GODWIN (CATHARINE GRACE) *late Garnett*, Night before the Bridal, Sappho and other Poems, 1824—Wanderer's Legacy, 1829—Reproving Angel, 1835—Alicia Grey, 1847   4 *vol.*

1164 —— Poetical Works, with Life by A C Wigan, 39 *engravings*   4to 1854

1165 GOFFIN (EMMA MARY) Poems, 1845—GODFREY (Mrs HENRY) Sketches from the Bible, *Dublin*, 1852—GOM-LESALL (A) Creation, *Newport*, 1824   3 *vol.*

1166 GOMELDON (JANE) Maxims, *Newcastle*, 1779—Happiness: Characteristic Poem, *printed by Isaac Thompson, Esq.* (*Newcastle*) 1773, *very scarce*   *bd. in one vol.*

1167 GOMELDON (Mrs) Medley, consisting of Thirty-One Essays printed for the benefit of the Lying-in Hospital in Newcastle, *frontispiece*   *Newcastle*, 1766

1168 GOOCH (Mrs) [Elizabeth Sarah Villa-Real] Poems on Various Subjects, 1793—Appeal to the Public on the conduct of Mrs Gooch the wife of William Gooch, Esq, 1788   *bd.* 2 *vol.*

1169 —— Life, written by herself, 3 vol in 1   1792

1170 GOOCH (Rebecca) Original Poems   *Norwich*, 1823

1171 GOODRICK (MARIA) Great Truths in Little Stories, 1853—Poems from my Fireside, *plates*, 1854; and other pieces by the same Poetess   8 *vol.*

1172 GOODMAN (MRS) Poetical Pieces, *Worcester,* 1828—Goodrich (A. M.) Claudia, a Tale, 1853—Goodwin (G. M. Colquitt) Nothing to Do, *n. d.*—Goodwin (C. G.) Amatura and other Poems, *n. d.*—Spiders and their Homes, *Norwich, n. d.*—Goody Two Shoes, *with illustrations, n. d.* 5 vol

1173 GORDON (FRANCES) English Chronicles in Rhyme, 1862—GORDON (HENRIETTA MARIA) Bride of Siena, 1835—The same, *second edition,* 1838—GORDON (MRS) Man and the Animals, *Edinb.* 1840 4 vol.

1174 GORDON (MARGARET MARIA) *formerly Brewster,* Leaves of Healing for the Sick and Sorrowful 4to *Edinb.* 1860

1175 GORE (Mrs. C. F.) Two Broken Hearts, 1823—The Bond, 1824—Lettre de Cachet and Reign of Terror, 1827—Dacre of the South, 1840, and other pieces by the same Poetess, *with autograph letters inserted* 9 vol.

1176 Gospel Magazine for 1800, vol V. 1800—British Friend, No IV 1848, and various pamphlets, unbound
a bundle

1177 GOULD (HANNAH FLAGG) Poems, *plate*
Boston (in America), 1832

1178 —— The same, *second edition, with additions, plate*
ib 1833

1179 —— The same, *third edition* *ib* 1835

1180 —— The same, *another edition,* 2 vol. *ib* 1836

1181 —— The same, *another edition,* 3 vol *ib.* 1839-41

1182 —— Esther, a Narrative and Poem, *plate* *New York,* 1835

1183 —— Gathered Leaves, or Miscellaneous Papers
Boston, 1846

1184 —— New Poems, *illuminated title-page* *ib* 1850

1185 —— Diosma, a Perennial *ib.* 1851

1186 —— Youth's Coronal *New York,* 1851

1187 GRAHAM (GRACE) Lays for the Lyre
printed for private circulation 1865

1188 GRAHAM (ISABELLA) *of New York,* Power of Faith exemplified in her Life and Writings, *portrait* 1822

1189 —— The same, *a new edition* *New York,* 1843

1190 GRAHAME (CLEMENTINA STIRLING) Mystifications, *vignette of Duntrune on the title page* 4to. *Edinb* 1865

1191 GRANT (MRS ANN) Harp of Zion, a Selection of Hymns, *Edinb* 1832—Grant (James) Hymns and Poems, 1862 —Memoirs of Miss Grant, 1842 3 vol

1192 GRANT (DAVINA) Hymns and Verses, *only a few copies printed for presents* *Edinb* 1839

1193 GRANT (MRS) *of Laggan,* Poems on various Subjects
portrait inserted *Edinb.* 1803

1194 —— Highlanders and other Poems, *second edition* 1808

1195 —— The same, *third edition* *Edinb.* 1810

1196 GRANT (MRS) Letters from the Mountains, 1773-1807, 3 vol. 1809
1197 ——— Essays on the Superstitions of the Highlanders of Scotland, 2 vol. *Edinb.* 1811
1198 ——— Eighteen Hundred and Thirteen, a Poem *portrait inserted* *ib.* 1814
1199 ——— Memoir and Correspondence, edited by her son, J P. Grant, 3 vol *portrait* *ib* 1845
1200 GRAVES (LOUISA CAROLINA) Desultory Thoughts on various Subjects by Louisa Carolina, daughter of Sir John Colleton, Bart, wife of Rear-Admiral Richard Graves, of Hembury Fort, Devonshire, born Baroness of Fairlawn, Landgravine of Colleton, and Sovereign Proprietress of the Isles of Bahama, *both parts, very scarce*
Brussels, printed at the British Press, 1819-21
1201 GRAY (CHRISTIAN) *of Mundie, parish of Aberdalgie, Perthshire, blind from her infancy,* Tales, Letters, and other Pieces in Verse *Edinb* 1808
1202 ——— New Selection of Miscellaneous Pieces in Verse *Perth,* 1821
1203 GRAY (MARY ANN, *formerly Browne*) Mont Blanc, and other Poems, 1827—Ada, and other Poems, 1828—The same, *second edition,* 1828 3 vol
1204 ——— Ada, and other Poems, *third edition, with an autograph letter of the Poetess inserted* 1828
1205 ——— Repentance, and other Poems, 1829—The Coronal, Poems Sacred and Miscellaneous, 1833—The same, *second edition,* 1835—The same, n. d—Birth-Day Gift, 1834—The same, *second edition,* 1837—Ignatia, and other Poems, 1838—Sacred Poetry, 1840—Sketches from the Antique, and other Poems, *Cork,* 1841 9 vol.
1206 Greek Anthology, Prose and Verse, *H G Bohn,* 1854—Grecian History, in verse, by a Lady, 1832—Great Physician, an Allegory, with original Poems, *Edinb.* 1824—Green's Nursery Keepsake, 1851 4 vol
1207 GREEN (ELIZA CRAVEN) Sea Weeds and Heath Flowers, or, Memories of Mona *Douglas,* 1858
1208 GREENSTED (FRANCES) Fugitive Pieces, *Maidstone, printed for the Author by D Chalmers* 1796
1209 ——— The same, *second edition, 16 pages being all ever printed, the publication having been stopped by the death of Rev. H Jenner, of Burbage, Wilts*
1210 GREENWELL (DORA) Poems, *Pickering,* 1848—Stories that might be True, *ib* 1850—Poems by the Author of the Patience of Hope, *Edinb* 1861 3 vol.
1211 GREER (MRS S) Chained Bible, with other Poems, *Dublin,* 1852—GREVILLE (MRS) Prayer for Indifference, *in verse, taken from Effusions of Fancy,* 1766 2 vol.

1212 GREY (ROSE) Double Sight, a Poem, 4*to*. 1861—Lays of the Turf, vol. I, 1863　　　　　　　　　　　　　　2 *vol*.
1213 GRIFFITH (ELIZA) Amana, a Dramatic Poem
portrait inserted　　　　　　　　　　　　　　4*to*.　1764
1214 —— Platonic Wife, a Comedy, 1765—Double Mistake, a Comedy, *second edition*, 1766—School for Rakes, a Comedy, *second edition*, 1769—A Wife in the Right, a Comedy, 1772—Barber of Seville, a Comedy, 1776—The Times, a Comedy, 1780
portrait inserted　　　　　　　　　　　　　　*in one vol.*
1215 —— Platonic Wife, *Dublin*, 1765—Double Mistake, 1766—The same, *third edition*, 1766—School for Rakes, 1769—The same, *third edition*, 1769—The same, *Bell's edition*, 1795—A Wife in the Right, *large paper*, 1772—The Times, *Dublin*, 1780　　　　8 *vol*.
1216 GRIFFITHS (J.) Collection of Juvenile Poems on various Subjects　　4to　*Warwick, printed for the Author*, 1784
1217 GRISANI (JULIA C.) Sacred Lyrics　　　　　　1849
1218 Griswold (Rufus Wilmot) Female Poets of America
portraits　　　　　　　　　　　　　　*Philadelphia*, 1849
1219 GROTE (MRS.) Rural Œconomy of England · Collected Papers (original and reprinted) in Prose and Verse, 1842-62, *frontispiece of trees in Burnham Beeches*
　　　　　　　　　　　　　　　　　　Murray, 1862
1220 GROVE (ELIZA) Beam for Mental Darkness, 1856—The Hive, or Mental Gatherings, 1857—Little Harry's Book of Poetry, 77 *engravings*, 1854—Adventures of a Sunbeam, and other Tales, *engravings*, n d—GROVE (ELIZABETH EDEN) Simple Stories and Simple Rhymes, n d—Groves (William) Revelations, &c 1838　6 *vol*.
1221 GRUBB (SARAH) Life and Religious Labours, with Appendix containing an Account of Ackworth School, &c　1794
1222 GRYMESTON (ELIZABETH) Miscellanea · Prayers, Meditations, Memoratives, *four leaves in manuscript*　　4*to*.　1604
　⁎⁎ This edition consists of only 14 chapters
1223 —— The same, *another edition*, augmented with addition of other her Meditations
very scarce　　*by George Elde, for William Aspley, n. d.*
　⁎⁎ This edition consists of 20 chapters.
1224 —— The same, *another edition, fire copy, very scarce, from Dr Bliss's Library, half morocco, by W. Pratt*
　　　　　By Melch. Bradwood, for William Aspley, n. d
1225 GUBBINS (CHARLOTTE) One Day's Journal a Story of the Revenue Police and other Poems　　*Sligo*, 1862
1226 Guess if you can! a Collection of Enigmas and Charades in Verse, by a Lady　　　　　　　　　　1851

1227 GUINNESS (JANE LUCRETIA) Sacred Portraiture and Illustrations, *Dublin*, 1831—Sketches of Nature, *plates*, *Bristol*, 1813 2 vol.
1228 GUION (LADY, *or Madame de la Mothe*) Hymns or Songs in the Archbishop of Cambray's (Fenelon) Dissertation on Pure Love, translated by Josiah Martin 1735
1229 —— The same, *another edition* Dublin, 1739
1230 —— Poems, translated by Cowper, *portrait*, *Newport Pagnell*, 1801—The same, *second edition*, *ib.* 1802—*Third edition*, 1803—*Fourth edition*, 1811—*Another edition*, 1837 5 vol
1231 —— Life, written by herself, translated by James Gough, 2 vol. Bristol, 1772
1232 —— Life, translated from her own Account, by T. D. Brooke Dublin, 1775
1233 —— The same, *another edition, portrait added* Bristol, 1806
1234 —— Extract of the Life of Madame Guion by John Wesley 1776
1235 —— Life, Religious Opinions and Experience, by T. C. Upham, *portrait* Edinb. 1854
1236 GUNDRY (MARIA) Extracts from Letters and Memoranda *printed for private circulation* 1847
1237 GUNNING (Miss E) Wife with two Husbands, a Tragi-Comedy, translated from the French 1803
1238 GUNNING (Mrs. SUSANNAH) *formerly Minifie*, Virginius and Virginia, a Poem, *with autograph of the Poetess*
    4to   Bath, n d
1239 —— Histories of Lady Frances S and Lady Caroline S. written by the Miss Minifies, 3 vol 1763
1240 —— Letter to the Duke of Argyll, *third edition, portrait inserted*, 1791—Poem on the late Miss Catharine Gunning at Carlinstown, in the County of Westmeath, the seat of her Uncle, James Nugent, Esq Dublin, 1752
    in one vol
1241 GUPPY (Mrs) Poetical pieces in De La Garde's Essays, *Bristol*, 1800—GURNEY (PRISCILLA) Hymns from various Authors, 1822—Another Edition, 1838—GWENNAP (Mrs) Grace Manifested, with a Poem on the Death of Lewis Andrews, 1860—GWILLIAM (JANE) Primrose Hill, Queen's Jubilee, and other Metrical Effusions, 1838 5 vol.
1242 H. (E) Scripture Enigmas, with Answers, *n d* —H (H E) Musings in Sickness, *three editions*, *Staines*, 1811—H. (M A) Torquato Tasso and other Poems, 1856—Plea for the Poor Man's Holiday, 1859—H (M D) Exile of the Waters and other Poems, 1851—H. (M. J. Carodoc, *Aberystwyth*, 1815—H (Miss R) Poems, 1811 —H. (R F) Lady Ina and other Poems, 1865—H. (ROSE ELLEN) Last Rose of Summer, 1845 11 vol.

1243 HACK (MARIA) Winter Evenings, *plates, n. d.*—HADFIELD (E.) Sprays from the Hedgerows, *portrait*, 1850—Poetic Weeds, *n. d.*—HAGGARD (ELLA) Myra: or the Rose of the East, a Tale, 1857   4 vol.

1244 HALE (MRS.) Poetical Attempts, 1800—Book of Flowers, *three editions*, 1836-51   4 vol.

1245 HALE (MRS. SARAH JOSEPHA) Genius of Oblivion and other original Poems   *Concord*, 1823

1246 —— Ladies' Wreath, a selection from the Female Poetic Writers of England and America, *portrait of Mrs. Hemans*   *Boston (in America)* 1837

1247 —— Three Hours: or the Vigil of Love and other Poems   *Philadelphia*, 1848

1248 —— Harry Guy, the Widow's Son, a Story of the Sea   *Boston*, 1848

1249 —— Flora's Interpreter and Fortuna Flora, *coloured plates*   *ib.* 1850

1250 —— Poet's Offering for 1850, *portrait and plates*   *Philadelphia*, 1850

1251 —— Woman's Record or Sketches of all distinguished Women, 230 *portraits*   1853

1252 Half an Hour after Supper, an Interlude, 1st and 2nd editions, 2 vol   1789

1253 HALL (CLARA) Rhymes and Reason, *plates, n. d.*—Poetic Garland, *plates, n. d.*—Poetic Primer, *plates, n. d.*—HALL (MRS S. C.) French Refugee, and Groves of Blarney, *n. d.*   5 vol.

1254 HALL (MRS EARDLEY) Chieftain's Daughter, a Tale of Avarice, *Brighton*, 1856—Zelinda, *ib. n. d.*—St. Pierre, by Mrs S. C. Hall, *portrait*, 1837   3 vol.

1255 HALL (ELIZABETH SOPHIA) Poems on several occasions *privately printed*   1844

1256 HALL (MRS. JAMES) Plantation and other Poems, *plates*   *New York*, 1819

1257 HALL (LOUISA J.) Mariam, a Dramatick Poem   *Boston (in America)*, 1837

1258 —— The same, *second edition revised*   *ib* 1838

1259 —— The same, and Joanna of Naples, with other Pieces in verse and prose   *ib* 1850

1260 HALL (MRS. SARAH) Selections from her Writings, with Memoir   *Philadelphia*, 1833

1261 HALSE (MRS. GEORGE) Pastoral and other Poems   1859

1262 HAMILTON (ANN) Descriptive Views of the Rose of Sharon, *printed for the author*, 1837—Ezra, a Narrative of Jewish Faith and Trial, *Dublin*, 1840   2 vol.

1263 HAMILTON (ELIZA MARY) Poems
presentation copy to W Wordsworth, the poet, with his autograph   *Dublin,* 1838

1264 HAMILTON (ELIZABETH) A Friend's gift
privately printed, presentation copy to Charles Anderson, Esq with inscription in the autograph of the poetess, dated Eastfield, near Aberdeen   1839

1265 HAMILTON (ELIZABETH) Translation of the Letters of a Hindoo Rajah, 2 vol 1801—Memoirs of Mrs Elizabeth Hamilton, by Miss Benger, 2 vol. *portrait,* 1818   4 vol

1266 HAMILTON (EMMA LADY) Memoirs, with illustrative Anecdotes, *portrait*   1815

1267 HAMILTON (JANET) Poems and Essays, *Glasgow,* 1863—The same, *second edition, portrait, ib* 1863—Poems of Purpose, &c *ib* 1865   3 vol

1268 HAMILTON (SARAH) Sonnets, Tour to Matlock, Recollections of Scotland, and other Poems, by a Resident of Sherwood Forest   1825

1269 —— Art of War, translated from the German of Frederick III, King of Prussia   1826

1270 —— Liberation of Joseph and other Poems   1827

1271 —— Alfred the Great, a Drama   *Mansfield,* 1829

1272 —— The Druid and the Holy King, a Lyrical Poem, *Leamington,* 1838—The same, *another edition, ib* 1840   2 vol.

1273 HAMMOND (S) Rustic Lays, *Braintree,* 1838—The Widow's Plea, by Mrs HAMMOND, *Stourbridge,* 1837   2 vol.

1274 HANDS (ELIZABETH) Death of Amnon, a Poem, Pastorals, and other Poetical Pieces, *large paper, with enigmas in manuscript*   *Coventry,* 1789

1275 HANSFORD (LEAH M. P.) War contrasted with Peace and other Poems, *Weymouth, printed for the author,* 1810—Hannibal, a Drama, 1861   2 vol

1276 HANSON (BEULAH KLAIN) Poetical Trifles, or Thoughts in Verse, *privately printed*   *Bradford,* 1818

1277 HANSOM (MRS. GEORGE H) Beauty, Eternity, and Miscellaneous Poems   *Colchester,* 1861

1278 HANSON (HANNAH MARIA) Sacred Mountains, and other Poems   *Frome,* 1859

1279 HANSON (MARTHA) Sonnets and other Poems, 2 vol   *Uxbridge,* 1809

1280 HARBOTTLE (MRS) Via, a Tale of Coquet-Side, and other Poems, 1856—HARDCASTLE (CHARLOTTE) Poems, *Brighton,* 1865   2 vol.

1281 HARDWICKE (COUNTESS OF) Court of Oberon, or the Three Wishes, a Drama, *coloured frontispiece from a drawing by the Countess of Hardwicke, privately printed* 4to 1831

1282 Harington (Sir J) Nugæ Antiquæ: a Collection of Original Papers, in prose and verse, written in the reigns of Henry VIII, Mary, Elizabeth, James, &c 3 vol. *portraits* (Bath), 1779

1283 HARLAND (MARION) The Hidden Path, 1855—Harp of Salem, by a Lady, Edinb. 1827—Harp of the Desert, Chelmsford, 1835 3 vol

1284 HARLOW (ELIZABETH) English Tavern at Berlin, a Comedy *privately printed* 1789

1285 HARRINGTON (S) New and Elegant Amusement for the Ladies of Great Britain, by a Lady, *frontispiece and vignette on title-page* 1772

1286 HARRIS (HENRIETTA) Poems Worcester, 1805

1287 HARRISON (ELIZABETH) Miscellanies on Moral and Religious Subjects, in prose and verse, *printed for the author*, 1756

1288 HARRISON (SUSANNA) Songs in the Night, by a Young Woman under deep Afflictions, *first edition, portrait inserted* 1780

1289 —— Songs in the Night, second edition 1781

1290 —— The same, third edition, 1783—Fourth edition, Ipswich, 1788 2 vol

1291 —— The same, *eighteen other editions*, 1799-1841 18 vol.

1292 HARRISSON (A M) Gethsemane and other Poems, Bath, 1856—HARTREL (E) Poetical History of England, *portraits, morocco, g e n d* 2 vol

1293 HART (MARY KERR) Heath Blossoms or Poems written in obscurity and seclusion, *frontispiece of Lavenham Church* Ballingdon, (1830)

1294 —— The same, *second edition, portrait*, Southampton, n d —Enigmettes, or Flora's Offering to the Young, n. d—The same, second edition, n d—HARTLEY (MRS COLONEL) Chaturanga, or Game of Chess, 1841—HARTLEY (MRS) formerly Elizabeth M'Bain, Evening Thoughts, Dumbarton, 1864 5 vol

1295 HARTFORD (FRANCES COUNTESS OF) Correspondence with the Countess of Pomfret, 1738-41, 3 vol *with autograph letter of the Countess of Hartford to Mr. Dodsley inserted* 1805

1296 HARTLEY (LOUISA BYAM) Wild Flowers from the Norman Iles 4to. Jersey, 1816

1297 HARVEY (ELIZA LOUISA) Lays and Legends of Germany, translated from the German, with other Poems 1846

1298 —— Legend of the Summer Day, a Northern Dream *privately printed* 1861

1299 HARVEY (ELLA LOUISA) Christmas Offering, in aid of the Industrial School, Richmond
privately printed Richmond, 1864
1300 HARVEY (JANE) Sentimental Tour through Newcastle, by a Young Lady, *Newcastle*, 1791—Poems on various subjects, *ib.* 1797 *in one vol.*
1301 —— Castle of Tynemouth, a Tale, 2 vol. in 1, *plate and map* Newcastle-upon-Tyne, 1830
1302 —— Fugitive Pieces *ib* 1811
1303 HARVEY (MARGARET) Lay of the Minstrel's Daughter, a Poem, *frontispiece, with autograph letter of the poetess inserted* *ib.* 1814
1304 HASTINGS (LADY FLORA) Poems, edited by her Sister, *portrait inserted, calf extra, g e* *Edinb.* 1841
1305 —— The same, *second edition, portrait*, *ib.* 1842—A Dirge on the death of Lady Flora Hastings, *Dublin*, 1851 2 vol
1306 HASTINGS (MARY POOLE) Hymns for the afflicted, *Chester*, 1839—Young Child's Prayers, *ib.* 1842—Young Sunday Scholar's Texts of Scripture, *ib.* 1841 3 vol
1307 HASTINGS (SAITH) Poems, and Account of a Family Tour to the West in 1800
Lancaster, printed for the benefit of the authoress, 1808
1308 Hastings (Thomas) The Mother's Nursery Songs (including Hymns by Mrs Sigourney and Mrs Brown), *set to music* New York, 1834
1309 HATFIELD (MISS) Terra Incognita of Lincolnshire, *frontispiece* 1816
1310 HATFIELD (SIBELLA ELIZABETH), Wanderer of Scandinavia, or Sweden Delivered, 2 vol Truro, 1826
1311 HAWKE (ANNABELLA) Babylon and other Poems 1811
1312 HAWKINS (LETITIA MATILDA) Siegwart a Monastic Tale, translated from the German of J M Miller, 3 vol 1806
1313 HAWKINS (SUSANNA) Poetical Works, 9 vol in 3 with *autograph inscripton of the poetess* Dumfries, 1829-61
1314 HAWKSHAW (ANN) Dionysius, the Areopagite, with other Poems, *Salford*, 1842—Poems for my Children, *engravings, n. d.*—Sonnets on Anglo-Saxon History, 1854
3 vol
1315 HAWORTH (EUPHRASIA FANNY) St. Sylvester's Day and other Poems, *with illustrative designs by the author* 1847
1316 HAY (EMILY) Wreath of Wild Flowers, or, Simple Effusions of a Soldier's Daughter, *privately printed* Eton, 1844
1317 HAY (MRS M H) Rural Enthusiast, and other Poems, *frontispiece*, 1808— HAYNES (M S) Prayers, *Edinb* 1837 2 vol
1318 HAYS (MARY) Female Biography, or Memoirs of Illustrious and Celebrated Women, 6 vol. 1803

1319 HAYS (MARY) Letters and Essays, Moral and Miscellaneous
T. Knott, 1793
1320 HAYWOOD (MRS. ALFRED) Battles of the Crimea, with other Poems *Port Hope, Canada West*, 1855
1321 HAYWOOD (MRS. ELIZA) Works, consisting of Novels, Letters, Poems, and Plays, 4 vol. 1724
1322 —— The same, *second edition, portrait,* 4 vol. 1725
1323 —— The same, *third edition, portrait,* 4 vol. 1732
1324 —— The same, *fourth edition, portrait,* 4 vol. 1742
1325 —— Fair Captive, a Tragedy, 1721—A Wife to be Lett, a Comedy, 1724—Frederick Duke of Brunswick, a Tragedy, 1729—The Opera of Operas, or Tom Thumb the Great, 1731 *in one vol.*
1326 —— A Wife to be Lett, *second edition, frontispiece,* 1729—Another Edition, 1735—Frederick Duke of Brunswick, *Dublin,* 1729—The Husband, *imperfect, n d*—The Winter Evening's Companion, *frontispiece, imperfect, n d.* 5 vol.
1327 HEAD (FRANCES ANNE) Messiah, in English Verse, translated from Klopstock, 2 vol. in 1 1826
1328 —— The same, *without the name of the translator on the title-pages,* 2 vol. in 1 1826
1329 Heart's-Ease, or Grammar in Verse, by a Lady-Teacher *Glasgow,* 1851
1330 HEATH (ANNE) *formerly Read of Eweline, Oxfordshire,* Poems *High Wycombe,* 1816
1331 Heath's Book of Beauty, 1833-47 inclusive, 15 vol
LARGE PAPER, BEAUTIFUL PLATES, *morocco, g e.* elegantly bound 1833-47
1332 HEDGE (MARY ANN) Affection's Gift, 1821—Juvenile Poems, 1823—Affliction's Harp, by M H 1811—Death-Bed Hymns, *Bath,* 1827 4 vol.
1333 HEDGELAND (MRS) *formerly Isabella Kelly,* Collection of Poems and Fables, 1794—The same, *second edition,* 1807—Anecdotes, 1819 3 vol.
1334 HEMANS (FELICIA DOROTHEA) *late Browne,* Poems, *vignettes first edition* 4to. *Liverpool,* 1808
1335 —— Domestic Affections, and other Poems, *first edition,* 1812; and others 5 vol.
1336 —— Restoration of the Works of Art to Italy, *Oxford,* 1816—The same, *second edition, ib* 1816—Modern Greece, a Poem, 1817—Translations from Camoens, *Oxford,* 1818—The Pilgrim Fathers, *illuminated* 5 vol
1337 —— Tales and Historic Scenes in Verse, 1819—The same, *second edition,* 1824—The same, *another edition, Edinb* 1844 3 vol

1338 HEMANS (FELICIA DOROTHEA) Wallace's Invocation to Bruce, a Poem   4to. *Edinb.* 1819

1339 —— Stanzas to the Memory of the late King, 1820—The Sceptic, 1820—The same, *second edition*, 1821—The Vespers of Palermo, a Tragedy, 1823—Siege of Valencia, with other Poems, 1823   *vol.*

1340 —— Dartmoor, a Poem, *privately printed*   4to. 1821

1341 —— Forest Sanctuary, and other Poems, 1825—The same, *second edition, Edinb* 1829—*Third Edition, ib* 1835—*Another Edition, ib.* 1840   4 vol.

1342 —— League of the Alps, Siege of Valencia, Vespers of Palermo, Forest Sanctuary, Lays of many Lands, Records of Woman, and other Poems, 2 vol.
    Boston (in America), 1826-8

1343 —— Records of Woman, with other Poems, *Edinb* 1828—The same, *five other Editions,* 1828-30   6 vol.

1344 —— Records of Woman, and other Poems, *illustrated edition*   *Philadelphia,* 1853

1345 —— Songs of the Affections, with other Poems, *Edinb.* 1830—The same, 1835—The same, with National Lyrics, *ib* 1840, *and ten other editions*   13 vol

1346 —— Poetical Works, 2 vol. *plates*   *Philadelphia,* 1832

1347 —— Poetical Works, complete in one volume, *Paris,* 1836—Hymns on the Works of Nature, 1833—Scenes and Hymns of Life, *Edinb* 1834, and others   6 vol.

1348 —— National Lyrics and Songs for Music, *Dublin,* 1834—Poetical Remains, *Edinb.* 1836—Early Blossoms, 1837, and others   8 vol

1349 —— Works, with a Memoir of her Life by her Sister, 7 vol *portraits and plates*   *Edinb* 1839

1350 —— Works, complete in one volume, *portrait*
    Philadelphia, 1842

1351 —— Poems, with illustrative notes, &c. *portrait and plate*
    Edinb 1849

1352 —— Poems, 6 vol
green morocco extra, sides tooled and gilt, g. e   *ib.* 1851

1353 —— Dramatic Works, *green morocco extra, g e*   *ib* 1850

1354 —— Memoir of her Life and Writings, by her Sister, *Philadelphia,* 1839—Another Edition, *portrait and plate, Edinb* 1841—Life, with illustrations of her Literary Character, *portrait,* 1842   3 vol.

1355 HENDERSON (THULIA SUSANNAH) Olga, or Russia in the Tenth Century, *frontispiece*   1855

1356 HENDRIKS (ROSE ELLEN) Charlotte Corday, 1846—Wild Rose, with other Poems, *portrait,* 1847—Chit Chat, *portrait, n d.*   3 vol.

1357 HENNETT (MRS.) Miscellaneous Poems, *part of the list of subscribers wanting*   *Spilsby*, 1820

1358 HENRY (SARepta IRISH) Victoria, with other Poems   *Cincinnati*, 1865

1359 HERBERT (JANE EMILY) Poetical Recollections of Irish History, *Dublin*, 1842—Bride of Imael, *ib* 1847—Another Edition, *ib* 1853—Ione's Dream, *ib*. 1858—Æolian Harp, by Sarah and Mary E. Herbert, *Halifax, N. S* 1857—HERON (MATILDA) Medea, translated from the French, *New York*, 1857—Another Edition, *n. d*—HERON (MARY) Mandan Chief, *Norwich*, *n d*.   8 vol.

1360 HERON (MARY) Miscellaneous Poems, *Newcastle, printed for the author*, 1786—Sketches of Poetry, *ib*. 1786
     4to   in one vol.

1361 —— Odes, &c on various Occasions   4to. *Newcastle*, 1792

1362 HERSEE (S and E *Sisters*) My Dream, and other Poems, *morocco, g e*.   *Leamington*, 1846

1363 HERVEY (MRS I K) *formerly Eleonora Louisa Montagu*) Bard of the Sea-Kings, a Legend of Kingley-Vale, *blue morocco, with joints, Chichester*, 1833—The Landgrave, a Play, 1839—Double Claim, 1849—Pathway of the Fawn, 1852—Consumption, a Poem, 4to. 1864   5 vol.

1364 HERVEY (ROSAMOND) Duke Ernest, a Tragedy, and other Poems, 1866—The Anniversary Speaker, by Rev. Newton Heston, *Philadelphia*, 1862   2 vol.

1365 HEWITT (MRS E C) Meditations on the Covenant Names of Christ, 2 vol 1830—Scripture Emblems, 1839   3 vol

1366 HEWITT (MARY E) Songs of our Land, *Boston*, 1846—Memorial written by friends of the late Mrs Osgood, *beautiful illustrations, New York*, 1851-2   2 vol.

1367 HEWLETT (ELIZABETH) Valley of Elah, or Faith Triumphant   *Oxford*, 1822

1368 HEY (REBECCA) Moral of Flowers, *coloured plates, Leeds*, 1833—Recollections of the Lakes, *plates*, 1841   2 vol.

1369 —— Moral of Flowers, *another edition, coloured plates*, 1849—Sylvan Musings, *coloured plates*, 1849—Holy Places, and other Poems, 1859   3 vol

1370 HEYWOOD (ELIZA) Ermingarde, a Tale, Royalist Lyrics, and other Poems, *Cheltenham*, 1837—HICKS (EMMA) Church Sonnets, *Dorchester*, 1851   2 vol.

1371 HIGHLEY (HARRIET) Galatea, a Pastoral Romance from the French of M. Florian, *plates*   1804

1372 HILLS (MARY) Deluge, and other Poems, *Kidderminster*, 1828

1373 HILL (ELIZ) Poetical Monitor, 1796—The same, *twelve other editions*, 1798-1817—Sequel to the Poetical Monitor, *three editions*, 1811-22   16 vol

1374 HILL (FIDELIA S. T.) Poems and Recollections of the Past
Sydney, 1840
1375 HILL (ISABEL) Poet's Child, a Tragedy, 1820—The same, *another edition*, 1821—First of May, 1829—Brian the Probationer, 1842—Holiday Dreams, 1829—Corinne, translated from Madame de Stael, *plates*, 1817 4 vol.
1376 HILL (MRS. ROBERT) Poem sacred to Freedom, and a Poem intitled Benchee (*Dublin*), n. d.
1377 HILL (MRS. PHILIPPINA) *formerly Barton*, Portraits, Characters, Pursuits, and Amusements of the present Fashionable World, interspersed with Poetic Flights of Fancy, *printed for subscribers only, with autograph of C. L. Anstruther* n. d.
1378 Hill-Side Flowers, with Introduction by Rev Bishop Simpson, D D. *with illustrations* *New York*, 1856
1379 HILLS (FFISE) Kebu, and other Poems *Portsmouth*, 1835
1380 HINCKS (ELIZABETH) Poor Widow's Mite cast into the Lord's Treasury, wherein are contained some Reasons in the Justification of the Meetings of the Quakers, &c. *in Verse*, VERY RARE 4to. 1671
1381 HINDMARSH (ISABELLA) Cave of Hoonga, a Tongaen Tradition, and other Poems *Alnwick*, 1818
1382 HINXMAN (EMMELINE) Poems, 1856—The same, *second edition*, 1857—Hints on Education, 1821 3 vol.
1383 Historical Album, or Scenes and Sketches in British History, *plate* 4to *Leeds*, n d.
1384 History of David King of Israel, by a Lady, 1817—History of Wesleyan Methodism in the Town of Lowestoft, Suffolk, *Yarmouth*, 1843 2 vol.
1385 History of Sir Charles Grandison spiritualized, with reflections thereon, by Theophila 1760
1386 HITCHENER (ELIZABETH) Fire-Side Bagatelle, containing Enigmas on the Chief Towns of England and Wales, 1818—The Weald of Sussex, a Poem, 1822 2 vol.
1387 HOARE (SARAH) Poem on the Pleasures and Advantages of Botanical Pursuits, *Bristol*, n d.—Poems on Conchology and Botany, *plates*, ib 1831 2 vol.
1388 HOBLYN (ANNA MARGARET) Time's Changes, Pilgrims' Poems and Hymns, 1863—Hodges (R) Fragments in Verse, 1861—Waters drawn from the Well of Life, 1862—New Sunday School Hymn Book, edited by Edwin Hodder, n d 4 vol.
1389 HODGSON (Mrs) *formerly Miss Holford*, Gresford Vale, and other Poems, *view of Gresford Lodge on the title-page* 4to. 1798
1390 —— Wallace, or the Fight of Falkirk, a Metrical Romance, 4to. 1809
1391 —— The same, *second edition*, green morocco, g. e. 1810

1392 HODGSON (Mrs. MARY) Poems 1811
1393 —— Margaret of Anjou, a Poem, *frontispiece* 4to 1816
1394 —— The Past, &c. *Bath*, 1819
1395 —— Elegiac Ode *at the end of the* Memoir of the Life of Lieut. Col. Vassall, *privately printed* *Bristol*, 1819
1396 —— Neither's the Man, a Comedy, *n. d.*—The Way to Win her, *n. d.* 2 vol.
1397 HODSON (S.) *of Thrapston*, Psalms and Hymns, selected for Congregational Use 1801
1398 HOFLAND (BARBARA) *formerly Hoole*, Poems, *Sheffield* (1805) —Little Dramas, 1810—Season at Harrowgate, in a series of Poetical Epistles, *portrait inserted, Knaresborough*, 1812—The Authoress, a Tale, *frontispiece*, 1819—The Crusaders, 1826—Illustrated Alphabet, 1839—Life and Literary Remains, by T. Ramsay, *portrait*, 1819 7 vol.
1399 —— Descriptive Account of the Mansion and Gardens of White-Knights
privately printed, LARGE PAPER, INDIA PROOFS *folio.* 1819
1400 HOLBROOK (ANN CATHERINE) Dramatist, or Memoirs of the Stage, with Life of the Authoress, &c. *Birmingham*, 1809—Realities and Reflections, *frontispiece*, *Thame*, 1834 2 vol.
1401 Holcroft (Thomas) Theatrical Recorder, 2 vol. *plates*, 1805-6—Rosamond and Philip the Second, by Fanny Holcroft 4 vol.
1402 HOLDERNESS (MARY) Manual of Devotion, 1825—HOLL (LOUISA MARGARET) Indian Captive, and other Poems, *Birmingham*, 1839 2 vol.
1403 HOLMES (ANN) *of Redmire, Wensleydale*, Epic Poem on Adam and Eve, with Poetry on two Ladies in Disguise, &c. *Bedale*, 1800
1404 HOLMES (MRS. DALKEITH) Law of Rouen, a Dramatic Tale *printed for private circulation* 1837
1405 HOLMES (C.) A Mother's Offering to the Younger Members of the Church of England, *cuts*, *Bristol*, 1836—A Sister's Record, or Memoir of Mrs. Marcus H. Holmes, *ib* 1844 2 vol.
1406 HOLT (MRS.) Fairy Tale, with other Poems
old red morocco 1717
1407 HOMAN (MRS.) Address to the Jews, 1844—Home Trifles, 1841—Fairy Land, by T. and J. Hood, *with illustrations*, 1861 3 vol.
1408 Home Thoughts and Home Scenes, *engravings by the Brothers Dalziel* 4to. 1865

1409 Hood (Catherine) Remonstrance, with other Poems, 1801
—Hook (Mrs.) Sacred Hours, 2 vol. 1806   3 vol.

1410 Hook (Mrs.) Double Disguise, a Comic Opera, 1784—The
same, another edition, *Dublin*, 1784—Hooper (Mrs B.)
Poem, Sonnets and other Productions, 1818   3 vol.

1411 Hooper (Lucy) Poetical Remains, with Memoir by John
Keese   *New York*, 1842

1412 Hoper (Mrs) Queen Tragedy restor'd, a Dramatic Entertainment, 1719—Hopton's Meditations, 1717—Life, &c.
of D. Caroline Hopwood, *Leeds*, 1801   3 vol.

1413 Horace, Eight Odes translated, PRIVATELY PRINTED   1810

1414 Hornblower (Mrs. Frances) Poems, *Liverpool*, 1813—
Horsfield (Louisa A.) Cottage Lyre, *Leeds*, 1862—
Horton (A.) Winged Words, 1861—Horton (Mary L.)
Compositions, *Salem*, 1832   4 vol.

1415 Hornby (Mary) Extemporary Verses, written at the Birth
Place of Shakspeare, by people of genius, to which is
added a brief History of the Immortal Bard and
Family   (*Stratford-upon-Avon*, 1818)

1416 —— Broken Vow, a Comedy, *yellow morocco*   *ib* 1820

1417 Horsford (Mary Gardiner) Indian Legends, and other
Poems   *New York*, 1855

1418 Houghton (Jane) *aged 12 years*, Blossoms of Genius,
Liverpool, n. d.—Houghton (Mary Arnald) Emilia of
Lindinau, or Field of Leipsic, *first and second edition*,
1815—Hovenden (Sophia) Hand Unseen (*Jerusalem*,
1846)   4 vol.

1419 Houlditch (Anne) Hymns for Young Minds, *Exeter*, 1849,
and five other editions—Horwood (Miss C.) Poems,
three editions, 1818—Horwood (Miss L.) Poetry, n d—
Hours of Thought, by Annette, *morocco extra, g e n d*
    11 vol.

1420 Howe (Julia Ward) Passion Flowers, *Boston*, 1854—Words
for the Hour, *ib* 1857—World's Own, *ib* 1857   3 vol

1421 Howell (Caroline A.) Songs for the Wilderness, with
Music, 4to n. d—Howard (Lady C) Chapel Bell,
Dublin, 1854—Parlour Stories, by Caroline Howard,
n d.—Howe (Miss) Hours of Solitude, *Brighton*, 1816
    4 vol.

1422 Howitt (Mary and William) Forest Minstrel, and other
Poems, 1823—Desolation of Eyam, &c. 1827—The
same, *second edition*, 1828   3 vol.

1423 —— Seven Temptations, *portrait*, 1834—Birds and
Flowers, *portrait*, 1838—Hymns and Fire-side Verses,
1839—The same, *second edition, n. d.*   4 vol.

1424 —— The H—— Family, and other Tales, translated from
Fredrika Bremer, 2 vol in 1, *portrait*, 1844—Father
and Daughter, 1859   2 vol

1425 HOWITT (MARY and WILLIAM) Ballads and other Poems, *portrait, morocco* 1847
1426 —— The same, new edition, *portrait* *New York*, 1854
1427 —— Journal of Literature, 2 vol. *cuts* 1847
1428 —— Pictorial Calendar of the Seasons, *cuts* 1854
1429 —— Dusseldorf Artists' Album, *plates* 4to. 1854
1430 —— Otto Speckter's Fable Book—Marien's Pilgrimage, Tales in verse and prose—Sketches of Natural History, &c. *mostly with illustrations* 13 *vol.*
1431 HOWORTH (MRS.) The Poems of Baron Haller, translated into English
frontispiece and vignettes, portrait inserted 1794
1432 HOY (ELIZABETH) Poems (1863)—HOYLAND (ALICE) Hymns, 1848—Hubert, a Legend, by a Clergyman's Daughter, *Bolton-le-Moors*, 1845—HUDSON (MARY ANN) Beacon of Hope, *Ipswich* (1860) — Sabbath Lays (by Miss HUGHES), 1857—Friendly Visits from the Muse, by (Mrs. Hughes of St Luke's), 1810 6 *vol.*
1433 HUGHES (ANNE) Poems, *Dodsley*, 1784—Moral Dramas, intended for Private Representation, 1790 2 *vol.*
1434 Hulbert (C.) Poetical Bouquet, *plates and cuts, Shrewsbury, n. d.*—Sabbath Recreations, *Huddersfield*, 1850—HULL (AMELIA M.) Hymns, *n. d*—Heart Melodies, 1864—Victory, 1864—HUMBOLDT (CHARLOTTE DE) Corinth, a Tragedy, 1838 5 *vol.*
1435 HUME (ANNA) Triumphs of Love: Chastitie: Death: translated out of Petrarch
EXTREMELY RARE, *calf, g. e.* *Edinb. by E. Tyler,* 1644
1436 HUME (MARY C.) Normiton, a Dramatic Poem, 1857—Sappho, a Poem, 4to. 1862 — HUMPHREYS (ELIZA) Metrical Collects, 1856—Iscah, and other Poems, by Isabella de Paton (Miss E Hunt), 1866 4 *vol.*
1437 HUNT (ELIZA) Poems, *printed for the Authoress*, 1808—HUNTER (MRS JOHN, *formerly Anne Horne*), Poems, 1802—The same, *second edition*, 1803 3 *vol.*
1438 HUNTER (MRS. JOHN) Sports of the Genii, *plates in outline, morocco, g. e* 4to. 1804—The same, *another edition, plates,* 4to. 1816 2 *vol.*
1439 HUNTER (HARRIETT ELIZA) Gold Mine, and other Poems 1865
1440 HUNTINGDON (SELINA COUNTESS OF) Life and Times, 2 vol. *portrait* 1839
1441 —— Hymns used in her Chapels, collected by her Ladyship, with Supplement, *morocco, g. e.* *obl* 1799
1442 HUNTINGTON (MRS. SUSAN) *of Boston, Massachusets,* Memoirs, with Extracts from her Journal and Letters, by B. B. Wisner, *portrait, York,* 1828—The same, *another edition, Edinb.* 1828 2 *vol.*

1443 HUNTLEY (LYDIA) Moral Pieces in Prose and Verse
Hartford (in America) 1815
1444 Husband (The), a Poem, expressed in A Compleat Man
1710
1445 HUSKINSON (ELIZA) Song of the Spheres, *Nottingham*, 1853 — Memoirs of Col. Hutchinson (1838) — Original Poems by different hands (the daughters of William Hutchinson, of Barnard Castle), *Durham*, 1815 3 vol.
1446 HUTTON (MARY) Sheffield Manor, and other Poems, *Sheffield*, 1831—Happy Isle, and other Poems, *ib.* 1836—Cottage Tales, *ib* 1842 3 vol.
1447 HUTTON (MRS) *formerly Ann Kemble*, Poetic Trifles, by Ann, of Swansea, *Waterford*, 1811—Translations, &c. by Captain Herbert, 1808 *in one vol.*
1448 HYAMS (HELEN) Candidate for Favour, a collection of Original Poetry and Prose *Manchester*, 1844
1449 HYDE (JULIA) Summer Daydream, and other Poems, by Theta 1856
1450 Hymns of Thanksgiving to the Redeemer
printed for the Author, 1772
1451 Hymns on the Lord's Prayer, 1835—Methodist Hymns, *New York*, 1840, and other Books of Hymns 9 vol.
1452 HYNEMAN (MRS REBEKAH) Leper, and other Poems
Philadelphia, 1853
1453 Ildegonda, from the Italian of Grossi, 1859—In Memoriam, a Poem, 1861—C'est Vrai, 1861—Songs in Sorrow, by C. H. I. 1862—Prince Ahmed, by L. A. D., ILFRACOMBE, 1859 5 vol.
1454 ILIFF (MRS) Poems, *frontispiece after Chalon, by Turner*
1808
1455 —— The same, *second edition, frontispiece* *Malta*, 1818
1456 INCHBALD (MRS) Appearance is against them, 1785—I'll Tell you what, 1786—Widow's Vow, 1786—Child of Nature, 1800—Midnight Hour, 1787—Such Things are, 1805 — The Married Man, 1789 — Next Door Neighbours, 1791—Every One has his Fault, 1805—The Wedding Day, 1806—Wives as they were and Maids as they are, 1797—Lover's Vows, 1798—Wise Man of the East, 1799—To Marry or not to Marry, 1805; and others *bound in 3 vol.*
1457 —— Animal Magnetism, *Dublin*, 1789—The same, *ib. n d.*—The same, 2 copies, 1792 4 vol.
1458 —— Appearance is against Them, *Dublin*, 1786—The same, *another edition, n. d.* 2 vol.
1459 —— Child of Nature, 1788; and other editions, *portrait*
5 vol.
1460 —— Cross Partners, 1792—Another edition, *Dublin*, 1792
2 vol.

1461 INCHBALD (Mrs) Every One has his Fault, 1793; and other editions, *portrait* 9 vol.
1462 ——— I'll tell you what, 1786—Another edition, 1787 2 vol.
1463 ——— Lover's Vows, from the German of Kotzebue, 1798 —and other editions 7 vol.
1464 ——— Married Man *Dublin*, 1789
1465 ——— Midnight Hour, or War of Wits, *Dublin*, 1787—The same, *another edition, ib.* 1788—The same, *another edition*, 1788 3 vol.
1466 ——— Mogul Tale, or Descent of the Balloon (*Dublin*), 1788 —The same, *another edition*, 1796 2 vol.
1467 ——— Next Door Neighbours *Dublin*, 1791
1468 ——— Such Things are, *portrait*, 1788, and other editions 6 vol
1469 ——— To Marry or not to Marry, *portrait inserted*, 1805— another edition, *n. d.* 2 vol.
1470 ——— Wedding Day 1794
1471 ——— Widow's Vow *Dublin*, 1786
1472 ——— Wise Man of the East, 1799—The same, *another edition, Dublin*, 1800 2 vol.
1473 ——— Wives as they were and Maids as they are, 1797; and other editions 7 vol
1474 ——— Memoirs and Correspondence, edited by James Boaden, 2 vol. *illustrated by 34 additional portraits of celebrated Theatrical Characters, and an autograph letter of Mrs Inchbald, calf, m e* 1833
1475 INGELOW (JEAN) Poems, *second, third, fifth, and eighth editions*, 4 vol 1863-4
1476 INGLIS (M. M) Miscellaneous Collection of Poems *Edinb.* 1838
1477 INGLIS (MRS. RICHMOND) *daughter of Col. Gardner, who fell at the Battle of Preston*, 1745, Anna and Edgar, or Love and Ambition, a Tale 4to *Edinb.* 1781
1478 INSTONE (SARAH) Poems, inscribed to the Hon Miss Leigh *Bridgnorth*, 1797
1479 Invalid's Offering, *Bath, n. d.*—Irish Widow, *Dublin*, 1828 —Instructions for the Treatment of Negroes, &c. 1797— Infant Minstrel, *four editions*, 1816-29—Indispensable Requisites for Dandies, by a Lady, *Dublin, n. d.* 8 vol
1480 Iris (The) a Literary and Religious Offering, edited by the Rev T Dale, 2 vol. *plates* 1830-1
1481 ISAACS (MRS) Wanderings of Fancy, 1812—ISELIN (SOPHIA) My Dream Book, 1847—Israel's Journey and other Poems, *Bath*, 1860—The Island, by an Orphan, *printed for the authoress*, 1818 4 vol.

1482 Isle of Man Illustrated Guide, *plates and cuts, Douglas,*
   1836—Letters from the Isle of Man in 1846, with
   Manx Ballads, Songs, &c 1847   2 vol.
1483 Italian Bride, a Play, written for Miss Eliza Logan and
   published for private Distribution   *Savannah,* 1856
1484 J (C) Simple Lays, &c.   *Cheltenham,* 1843
1485 J. (E.) Holy War by Bunyan, versified, *with illustrations*
   4to 1859
1486 J (E C.) Poetic Thoughts   *Paris,* 1856
1487 J (E S) Poems (Count Hartfelt and Alcmena, &c.) 1799
1488 Jackson (A.) Fragments, *printed for the authoress* 1826
1489 Jackson (S. R.) Lament of Napoleon, Misplaced Love, and
   Minor Poems, &c 1819—Sketches from the Heart, by
   L J 1859—An Invalid's Pastime, *Ipswich, n d* 3 vol
1490 Jacob (Mrs) *late Miss C. Kunnison,* Poems, *Southampton,*
   1821—The Home of my Fathers, *Edinb.* 1826—Days,
   Months, and Seasons, by Maria Jacob, *with illustrations,* 2 copies, 4to. *n. d*   4 vol.
1491 James (Eliza) Hours of Leisure, *woodcut vignettes*
   Durham, printed for the author (1807)
1492 James (Maria) Wales and other Poems *New York,* 1839
1493 Jameson (Mrs) Romance of Biography, or Memoirs of
   Women Loved and Celebrated by Poets, 2 vol.
   plate   1837
1494 ———— Social Life in Germany illustrated in the Dramas of
   the Princess Amelia of Saxony, translated from the
   German, 2 vol.   1846
1495 ———— Memoirs and Essays, Illustrative of Art, &c 184,
1496 Jamieson (Frances) Cadijah, or the Black Prince, a Tragedy,
   1825—Ines, and other Poems (by Mrs Paxton Jarvis).
   1816   2 vol,
1497 Jefferies (Bradford and Harriet Anne) Widow of Nain,
   and other Poems   *Manchester, n. d*
1498 Jefferson (Joseph) Poems, Translations, and Essays
   Basingstoke, 1804
1499 Jeffreys (M. E.) Hoel the Hostage, and other Poems 1842
1500 Jemmat (Mrs. Catherine) *daughter of Admiral Yeo, of
   Plymouth,* Memoirs, written by herself   2 vol.
   printed for the author, 1765
1501 ———— The same, *another edition,* 2 vol.   1771
1502 ———— Miscellanies in Prose and Verse   4to. 1766
1503 ———— The same, *another edition*   4to. 1771
1504 ———— The same, *another copy, date altered* 4to. 1772
1505 ———— The same, *another copy, date altered* 4to. 1778
1506 Jermyn (Louisa Emily) Poetry for Youth and Childhood,
   2 vol. *Beccles,* 1851—Jephtha, a Drama, by a Lady,
   1846—Extracts from the Papers and Letters of Lucy
   Jesup, *Sudbury,* 1858   4 vol.

1507 JERVIS (LADY) Gleanings *Paris*, 1840
1508 JEVON (RACHEL) Carmen Θριαμβευτικον Regiæ Majestati Caroli II. in ejus Restaurationem, 1660—Exultationis Carmen to the King upon his Desired Return, 1660
folio. in one vol.
1509 JEVONS (MRS. THOMAS) Poems for Youth, by a Family Circle, *two parts*, 1820-1—The same, *second edition*, 1821—Poems, by one of the Authors of Poems for Youth (by JANE JEVONS), 1820—The same, *second edition*, 1821—Poems for Youth, edited by M A. Jevons, 1841—Sonnets and other Poems, *not printed for sale, Liverpool*, 1845—Clemency of Titus, from the Italian of Metastasio, by a Lady, *ib.* 1828   7 vol.
1510 —— Sacred Offering, a Poetical Offering, a Poetical Annual for 1832, 1833, 1835, 1836 (*printed at Boston, in America*), 1838, 5 vol. 1832-8—Sacred Offering, vol. I, II, and IV, *plates, Liverpool*, 1837   8 vol.
1511 JEWRY (LAURA) The Vassal, a Story of Old Normandy
1850
1512 JOBERT (F. H.) Jocelyn, an Episode, translated from the French of A. De Lamartine   *Paris*, 1837
1513 Johnson (James) Scots Musical Museum, consisting of Six Hundred Scots Songs set to Music, 6 vol in 3
scarce   *Edinb.* 1787-1803
1514 JOHNSON (MARY F.) Sonnets and other Poems, 1810—JOHNSON (SUSANNA C) Puseyite Rhymes, 1843—Monthly Wild Flowers, edited by C. A Johns, n d—Jessy's Wedding-Ring, by a Lady (MRS JOHNSON), 4*to.* 1863   4 vol.
1515 JOHNSON (ROSA VERTNER) Poems, *portrait*
Boston (in America), 1857
1516 Johnson and Walker's Dictionary of the English Language, combined by R S. Jameson, *Halifax*, 1856—Johnson's Dictionary, abridged by Chalmers, 1820
2 vol.
1517 JONES (HARRIET) Poetical Travels of Eugenius and Antonina, from the French of Madame de Genlis, 1820—Pleasing Poems for the use of Schools, 1841   2 vol.
1518 JONES (M. E M.) Waldenberg, a Poem, 1837—The same, *second edition*, 1838—Jubal, 1839—Gawyin Honor, a Tragedy, n d.   4 vol.
1519 JONES (MARY) Miscellanies in Prose and Verse
LARGE PAPER   *Oxford*, 1750
1520 JONES (MARY) Poems   *printed for the author*, 1826
1521 JONES (MARY AMELIA) Poems of Memory and Feeling, *Stafford*, 1854—Sunlight in the Shade, *ib.* 1858 2 vol.
1522 JONES (MARY ELIZABETH) Lake and other Poems
Liverpool, 1844

1523 JONES (SOPHIA) Poetical Sketches, inscribed to the Princess Charlotte *printed for the authoress,* 1808
1524 JORDAN (AGNES C.) Poems, *Leicester,* 1862—Spoil'd Child (attributed to Mrs. Jordan), 1795—Jottings for Juveniles, by Josephine, *cuts,* 1862   3 *vol.*
1525 JORDAN (JUDITH) Religious Breathings, &c.
Shrewsbury, 1809
1526 JOURDAN (M. J.) Althorp Picture Gallery and other Poetical Sketches, *Aberdeen,* 1836—Mind's Mirror, with Minor Poems, *Edinb* 1856   2 *vol.*
1527 Journey to the Highlands of Scotland, with Remarks on Dr Johnson's Tour, by a Lady, *vignette on the title-page, n. d.*—The Castles of Athlin and Dunbayne, a Highland Story, 1793   2 *vol.*
1528 JOWITT (JANE) *the poor poetess, aged* 74, Memoirs, written, by herself   *Sheffield,* 1844
1529 JOYNES (LUCY) Occasional and Miscellaneous Poems, *Nottingham,* 1820—Mental Pictures in Verse for Infants, *ib.* 1832—Original Poetry, *frontispiece, Wellington,* 1838   3 *vol.*
1530 Jubilee Hymn Book, 1852—JUDSON (EMMA) Pleasure and Profit, *frontispiece, n d* — Juvenile Wreath, *front. Wellington,* 1828—The same, *second edition, ib* 1829   4 *vol.*
1531 JUDSON (MRS EMILY C.) *Fanny Forester,* Memoir of Sarah B Judson, *plates,* 1851—Records of Alderbrook, *frontispiece,* 1853—The same, 1854—Wayside Flowers, *Edinb* 1855   4 *vol.*
1532 —— Olio of Domestic Verses, *portrait inserted*
New York, 1852
1533 ——. Alderbrook. a Collection of Fanny Forester's Village Sketches, Poems, &c by Miss Emily Chubbuck, 2 vol. *portrait*   *Boston,* 1852
1534 —— Kathayan Slave and other Papers, *Boston,* 1853—Life and Letters, by A C Kendrick, 1861   2 *vol.*
1535 Juvenile Dramas, 3 vol in 1, *plates, Exeter,* 1808—Juvenile Magazine for 1788, 2 vol *maps and plates,* 1788—Ackermann's Juvenile Forget me not, *plates,* 1830   4 *vol*
1536 Juvenile Forget me not for 1829, 1830, 1831, 1832, 1833, 1834, 1835, 1836, and 1862, edited by Mrs S. C. Hall, *beautiful plates*   9 *vol.*
1537 Juvenile Keepsake for 1829 and 1830, edited by Thomas Roscoe, 2 vol *beautiful plates*   1829-30

FOURTH DAY'S SALE.

OCTAVO ET INFRA.

UNLESS OTHERWISE EXPRESSED.

LOT
1538 K. (A) Poetic Gleanings from Modern Writers, *second edition*, 1834—The same, *third edition*, 1841—K (C M) Poetry from Life, 1856—K. (M A.) Biography for Young Ladies, *frontispiece*, 1835—Kaiserswerth Deaconesses, by a Lady, 1857—Kate's Ballads and Rhymes, *Bristol*, 1854   6 vol.

1539 KATHERINE PARR (QUEEN) Prayers or Meditacions, wherein the minde is stirred, paciently to suffre all afflictions here, to set at nought the vayne prosperitee of this worlde, and alway to longe for the everlastinge felicitee **black letter**, EXTREMELY RARE, *four leaves supplied in facsimile, dark morocco extra, g. e bound by W Pratt*
    T Berthelet, n. d

1540 —— Lamentation of a Sinner made by the most vertuous Lady Queen Katherin, bewailing the ignorance of her blinde life, first set foorth and put in Print at the instaunt desire of the right gratious Lady Katherin Duches of Suffolke, and the ernest request of the right honorable Lord William Parre, Marquesse of Northamton **black letter**, EXTREMELY RARE, *dark morocco extra, g e bound by W Pratt*   *J Alde*, 1563

1541 KAVANAGH (JULIA) English Women of Letters. Biographical Sketches, 2 vol.   1863

1542 KAY (MARY) Widow's Offering   *Keighley*, 1833
1543 —— The same, *second edition*   *ib* 1833
1544 —— The same, *third edition*   *ib* 1834
1545 —— The same, *fourth edition*   *ib.* 1837
1546 —— The same, *fifth edition*, *Wakefield*, 1841—New series, *ib.* 1849   2 vol

1547 KEATING (Miss E H.) Charade Dramas, Fairy Plays, and Pantomimes for the Drawing Room and Parlour, 2 vol and nine numbers   1859, &c

1548 KEENE (ELIZABETH CAROLINA) Miscellaneous Poems LARGE PAPER   *printed for the author*, 1762

1549 Keepsake (The) for 1828 to 1857 inclusive, 30 vol LARGE PAPER, BEAUTIFUL PLATES, *morocco, and other elegant bindings*   1828-57

1550 KELTY (MARY ANN) Fire-side Philosophy, 1842—Devotional Diary, 1854—Waters of Comfort, *Cumb.* 1856
                3 *vol.*

1551 KEMBLE (MRS. C.) Day after the Wedding, an Interlude. 1808—The same, *second edition*, 1811—Smiles and Tears, a Comedy, 1815   3 *vol.*

1552 KENLEY (MARRIANNE) Cottage of the Appenines, or Castle of Novina, a Romance, 4 vol. in 2   *Belfast*, 1806

1553 KENNEDY (JANE) Lionel Fitzgibbon and his Parrot, *plates*, 1858—Little Rhymes; and other Works, by the same
                4 *vol.*

1554 Kentish Coronal, edited by H. G. Adams, *two copies*
              Chatham, 1841

1555 KENTISH (MRS) *of St. Salvador, Brazils*, Poems, 1819—The same, *second edition*, 1821—Maid of the Village, 1835   3 *vol.*

1556 KERR (LOUISA HAY) Melodies, set to Music, *plates after Westall and Chalon*   folio. n d.

1557 Kettell (Samuel) Specimens of American Poetry, with Biographical Notices, 3 vol   *Boston*, 1829

1558 KEYNE (ADA) Spells and Voices, 1865—Life of Elizabeth Kenning, *Bradford, n. d.*—Giant of the North, by Rosina Kerslake, 1854   3 *vol.*

1559 KIDD (JANE) Poems and Hymns   *Sheffield*, 1827

1560 KILLIGREW (MRS ANNE) Poems, *portrait in mezzotinto by Beckett, with verses on the Death of the Poetess in manuscript, by E. E dated* 1685
 calf extra, g. e.   *folio.* 1686

1561 KING (CHARLOTTE AND SOPHIA) Trifles of Helicon 1798

1562 KING (MISS E) *of Croydon*, Poems and Reflections by a Young Lady   1815

1563 KING (ELIZABETH T.) Memoir, &c. *Baltimore*, 1860—The same, reprinted from the American edition 1861

1564 KING (HARRIET BARBARA) [*Mrs. Charles Gerrard*] Bridal, and other Poems, 1844—KING (MARY ADA) Poems, 1850—KING (SARAH) Poems, 1859   3 *vol*

1565 KING (HARRIOT REBECCA) Poems, *Salisbury*, 1823—Oakdale Cottage, 1829—Nuneham Park, 1831—Metrical Exercises, &c 1834—The same, *second edition*, 1834—Thoughts in Verse upon Scripture Texts, 2 vol. in 1, 1842-6—Nursery Hymns, 1843   7 *vol*

1566 KINNEY (ELIZABETH C) Felicita, a Metrical Romance, *New York*, 1855—Emerald Isle, by MISS KINSLEY, *two editions, Liverpool*, 1846   3 *vol.*

1567 KIRKLAND (MRS C. M.) Spenser and the Fairy Queen, *portrait inserted*   1847

1568 KIRKLAND (Mrs C. M) Garden Walks with the Poets
New York, 1852
1569 KITCHING (H St. A.) Moral Plays, viz, Keep your Temper,
Fate of Ivan, and Miss Betsy Bull, 1832—Monody on
the Death of the Princess Louise, 4to. 1832   2 vol.
1570 KNAPP (Samuel L) Female Biography   *New York*, 1834
1571 KNIGHT (ANN CUTHBERT) Home, a Poem, *Edinb* 1815—
A Year in Canada, and other Poems, *ib* 1816 *in* 1 *vol*
1572 KNIGHT (ANNE) School Room Lyrics, *Ipswich, n. d.*—KNOX
(ANNA) Leanord, &c *Glasgow*, 1860—Effusions from
a Sick Bed, and other Poems, *ib* 1860   3 vol
1573 KNIGHT (MRS) *of Mitcham*, Flights of Fancy, or Poetical
Effusions   1791
1574 KNIGHT (ELLIS CORNELIA) Translations from the German,
in prose and verse, VERY RARE, *only 30 copies printed
for presents, by command of Queen Charlotte
printed by E Harding, Frogmore Lodge, Windsor*, 1812
1575 ——— Prayers and Hymns, *reprinted from the preceding
edition, by permission of the Princesses Royal, with view of
Frogmore Lodge on the title-page, green morocco extra,
g e*   1832
1576 ——— Miscellaneous Poems, (by E C Knight, W R.
Spencer, Samuel Rogers, and others), *frontispiece of
Frogmore Lodge*, VERY RARE, *only a very few copies
printed for presents by command of Queen Charlotte,
red morocco, g e.*
4to *printed by E Harding, Frogmore Lodge, Windsor*, 1812
1577 ——— Sir Guy de Lusignan, a Tale of Italy, 2 vol *presentation copy from the Poetess (with inscription in her
autograph, to the Landgravine of Hesse Homburg, and her
signature on the title page*   1833
1578 ——— Autobiography, with extracts from her Journals and
Anecdote Books. 2 vol *portrait*   1861
1579 KNIPE (ELIZA) Six Narrative Poems   4to. 1787
1580 KNOWLES (MARY) Compendium of a Controversy (with Mr
Rand, a clergyman of Coventry) on Water-Baptism,
in verse, 1805, *with leaf of verses, portrait and biography*
2 vol
1581 KORTWRIGHT (FANNY) Dreams of my Youth *Pickering*, 1818
1582 Kotzebue (Aug von) Negro Slaves, 1796—Noble Lie,
1799—Memoirs of Frederick and Margaret Klopstock,
1808   3 *vol.*
1583 L (E L) Wild Flowers from the Glens, *Belfast*, 1840—
L (FANNY MARGERY) Chimes of the Heart, 1850—
L (J) Poems, 1851—L. (E) Morning of Life, *Aberdeen*, 1850—Another edition, 1851   5 vol
1584 L (J M) Sandgate, a Poem, *with illustrations*, 1847—
Hagar and Ishmael, and other Poems, 1855   2 *vol.*

LACY (FANNY ELIZA) Visitor in Grey, 1853—The same, *third edition*, 1855—Labyrinth and Path, 1856—Jehovah-Jireh, by Mrs ELIZABETH LACHLAN, 1850—Lady's Poetical Album, *Glasgow,* 1830   4 vol.

Lady's Encyclopædia, 3 vol *wanting the heads*, 1788—Ladies' Diaries and Companions, 8 vol. *wanting titles, &c* 1704-97—Ladies' Pocket Magazine, 2 vol *plates*, 1795 and 1834, *sold with all faults*—Ladies' Monthly Museum, vol. V *portraits and plates*, 1817   14 vol.

Lady's Magazine for 1776, 1778, 1800, 1801, 1803, 1804, 1805, and 1818, 8 vol *plates, sold with all faults*   1776-1818

LA FARGUE (FRANCES HARRIET) Leon, and other Poems, *plates*   1816

LAKE (CATHERINE) Use of the Senses when engaged in contemplating the External World   1848

LAMB (LADY CAROLINE) New Canto, 1819—Fugitive Pieces and Reminiscenses of Lord Byron, also some Poetry, &c of Lady Caroline Lamb, by I Nathan, *with an autograph letter of the Poetess inserted*, 1829   2 vol.

LAMB (Charles and MARY) Works, 2 vol   1818

LAMBERT (LIZA) Poetic Strains, *Derby*, 1830—LAMONT (MRS ÆNEAS) Poems and Tales, 1818—LAMONT (M M) France and Switzerland, 1811   3 vol.

LANGTON (MILLICENT) Musings of the Work-Room, *Leicester*, 1865—Memoirs of SARAH LARWORTH, with Poems, &c and account of her death by Joseph Crampin, 1861—Last Judgment, 1857—Another Edition, 1862   4 vol.

LATCHES (MRS) Poems on several occasions, by a Lady   4to *Bristol,* 1792

LATTER (MRS MARY) Miscellaneous Works in prose and verse, in three parts, *old red morocco, g e*   *Reading,* 1759

—— Miscellaneous Poetical Essay, 1761—An Unfortunate Mother's Advice to her Absent Daughters, by S Pennington, 1761   *in* 1 vol.

—— Siege of Jerusalem, a Tragedy, [and Ode on the Birth of the Prince of Wales] with Essay on Stage-Craft   1763

Laura: or Sonnets and Elegiac Quatuorzains, with Notes by Capel Lofft, 5 vol in 2   1814

LAWRENCE (ROSE) Translation of the Works of Gessner, 3 vol.   *Liverpool,* 1802

—— Last Autumn, at a favorite Residence, 1828—The same, *second edition, Liverpool,* 1829—The same, with recollections of Mrs. Hemans, *ib.* 1836   3 vol.

1602 LAWRENCE (ROSE) Cameos from the Antique, or Cabinet of Mythology, *frontispiece, Liverpool,* 1833 — *Another edition, ib* 1834—*Another edition, ib.* 1849   3 vol.

1603 LAWRENCE (SARAH) Poems, *privately printed,* 1847—LAW (ISABELLA) Winter Weavings, 1863—Lausus and Lydia, with Madam Bonso's Three Strings to her Bow, 1806 —The Laurel: Fugitive Poetry of the XIXth Century, 1830   4 vol.

1604 Lays of a Lifetime, the Record of one departed, *head of Sophia and plate*   4to. *New York,* 1857

1605 Lays of the Sanctuary, and other Poems, edited by G. Stevenson de M. Rutherford, 1859—The same, *another edition,* 1859—Lays of the Kirk and Covenant, written for Argyll Free Church, *front Glasgow,* 1847—Lays from Erin, *Belfast,* 1852   4 vol.

1606 LEAD (JANE) Heavenly Cloud Now Breaking. The Lord Christ's Ascension—Ladder sent down; To shew the way to reach the Ascension and Glorification, through the Death and Resurrection, *with verses,*
RARE, *fine copy*   4to. *printed for the Author,* 1681

1607 —— Unpremeditated Thoughts of the Knowledge of God, by Irena, *with Hymns, &c* VERY RARE, 1695—Life of T Tryon, 1705   in 1 vol.

1608 —— Fountain of Gardens, watered by the Rivers of Divine Pleasure, and springing up in all the Variety of Spiritual Plants, blown up by the Pure Breath into a Paradise, to which is prefixed a Poem, introducing to the Philadelphian Age, called Solomon's Porch, or the Beautiful Gate, to Wisdoms Temple, VERY RARE   1697

1609 —— Wars of David, and Peaceable Reign of Solomon, in two treatises, containing an Alarm to the Holy Warriors and the Glory of Sharon, &c.   1700, *repr.* 1816

1610 —— Divine Revelations and Prophecies   1700, *repr. Nottingham,* 1830

1611 LEADBEATER (MARY) Extracts and Original Anecdotes for the Improvement of Youth, *her first production*   *Dublin,* 1794

1612 —— Poems and Translation of the Thirteenth Book of the Æneid   *ib* 1808

1613 —— Cottage Biography. a collection of Lives of the Irish Peasantry   *ib* 1822

1614 —— Papers a Selection from her MSS and Correspondence, 2 vol.   1862

1615 LEAKEY (CAROLINE W) Lyra Australis, or attempts to sing in a Strange Land, *calf gilt, m e.* 1854—LEAN (MRS. E. J.) Poems, 1845—Leap Year, 1860—Leaves, 1816   4 vol.

1616 LEAPOR (MARY) *of Brackley, in Northamptonshire*, Poems, &c. 2 vol   1748-51

1617 LECKIE (MRS) Village School, *Edinb.* 1837—Power of Conscience, a Dramatic Poem, *frontispiece, ib.* 1841—Stepmother, a Dramatic Poem, *ib* 1842   3 *vol.*

1618 —— Hebrew Poem, a Dramatic Poem, *Edinb.* 1842—Power of Conscience, *ib.* 1841—Dream of the Western Shepherd, 100 *copies printed for private circulation, ib. n d.*—The Guardian, *ib* 1843   *in* 1 *vol.*

1619 LEE (ANNE ELIZABETH) Fruits of the Valley, by A. E. L. *portrait, and view of Exeter*, 1855—LEE (MRS. F. G.) Departed, and other Verses, 1865—LEE (RONA) Legend of the Three Sisters, 1853   4 *vol.*

1620 LEE (HARRIET) New Peerage, a Comedy, 1787—The same, *second edition, with Autograph Letter of the Poetess inserted*, 1787—The same, *Dublin*, 1788—Mysterious Marriage, 1798—Three Strangers, a Play, *red morocco, g. e.* 1826   5 *vol.*

1621 LEE (LEILA) Wee Wee Songs for our Little Pets, *illustrations*   *Boston, (in America)* 1859

1622 LEE (MARY ELIZABETH) Poetical Remains, with Memoir by S. Gilman, *portrait*   *Charleston, S. C* 1851

1623 LEE (REBECCA) Verses, Original and Translated
  Tynemouth, 1842

1624 LEE (SOPHIA) Chapter of Accidents, a Comedy, 1780—The same, *second edition*, 1780—Nine other editions, 1781-1823—Almeyda, Queen of Granada, a Tragedy, 1796, and two other editions   14 *vol.*

1625 —— Hermit's Tale, *with Autograph Letter of the Poetess inserted*   4*to.* 1787

1626 LEECH (MARGARET) Poems on various Subjects   4*to.* 1816

1627 LEESON (MISS) Hymns and Scenes of Childhood, *second edition*, 1848—The same, *third edition, n. d.*—Lady Ella, 1847—Songs of Christian Chivalry, &c. 1848—Chapters on Deacons, 1849—Wreath of Lilies, 1849—Margaret, (1850)   7 *vol.*

1628 LEFANU (MRS) Sons of Erin, or Modern Sentiments, a Comedy, 1812—The same, *second and third editions*, 1812—LEFANU (MISS ALICIA) Flowers, or, the Sylphid Queen, *plates*, 1809—Rosara's Chain, or the Choice of Life, *plates*, 1812—Another edition, *plates*, 1823 6 *vol.*

1629 LEFROY (MRS) *formerly Brydges*, Carmina Domestica, edited by her son, C E. Lefroy, *wood-cut vignettes by Austin, privately printed*   1812

1630 Legend Versified of the Archæological Institute of Great Britain and Ireland, held at Bristol, in 1851, 8 *pages, privately printed*   (1851)

1681 Legend of St. Bernard, a Poem, with notes, *privately printed*   *Norwich, n. d.*

1682 Legends of the Library at Lilies, by the Lord and Lady there, 2 vol. in 1   *Philadelphia,* 1833

1683 LE HARDY (ESTHER) *of Jersey,* Agabus. or the last of the Druids, a Poem   *W Pickering,* 1851

1684 LEIGH (MRS DOROTHY) Mother's Blessing, *with three pages in verse,* "Counsell to my Children," *seventh edition, title-page mended, and first sheet wrongly bound up*   1621

1635 —— The same, *tenth edition, leaves mended and torn*   1624

1636 —— The same, *another edition, wanting title-page*   1673

1637 —— The same, *another edition, some leaves wormed*   1674

1638 —— The same, *another edition*   1707

1639 —— The same, *another edition*   1718

1640 LEITH (WILLIAMINA HELEN STEWART FORBES) *of Whitehaugh, Aberdeenshire,* Whitehaugh, a Poem, *frontispiece of arms and plate, privately printed*
   4to. Boulogne sur Mer, 1848

1641 —— Prayers, dedicated to her Children, *privately printed*
   4to. Aberdeen, 1849

1642 LENIGAN (HENRIETTA JANE) Ornaments of the Mind, with a promiscuous collection of Modern Poetry, *plates, Paris,* 1842— Unlucky John, by Madame Leinstein, *coloured plates, n. d.*—Hymns, edited by Rev J. Leifchild, 1843
   3 vol.

1643 LENNOX (MRS CHARLOTTE) *formerly Ramsay,* Poems on Several Occasions, *portrait inserted*   1747

1644 —— Shakespear Illustrated: or Novels and Histories on which the Plays of Shakespear are founded, 3 vol.
   1753-4

1645 —— Philander, a Dramatic Pastoral, 1758—The Sister, a Comedy, 1769—Old City Manners, 1775, *portrait inserted*   *in 1 vol*

1646 —— The Sister, second edition, *portrait inserted,* 1769—Another edition, *Dublin,* 1769—Philander, *imperfect, ib.* 1758   *3 vol.*

1647 —— The Greek Theatre of Father Brumoy, translated, 3 vol.   *4to* 1759

1648 LE NOIR (ELIZABETH ANNE) *late Smart,* Village Anecdotes, 3 vol. *frontispiece*   *Reading,* (1807)

1649 —— Maid of La Vendee, with remarks by Dr. Burney, &c. 3 vol   *ib* 1819

1650 —— Miscellaneous Poems, 2 vol. *frontispiece, a pencil drawing*   *ib.* 1825-6

1651 LEONARD (ELIZA LUCY) Ruby Ring: or, The Transformations, *plates, olive morocco extra, g. e.*   1816

1652 —— Miller and his Golden Dream, *plates, front. partly coloured*   *Wellington, Salop,* 1822

1653 LESDERNIER (MRS. EMILY P.) Voices of Life, *beautiful frontispiece* *New York,* 1853
1654 —— The same, *another edition* *Paris,* 1762
1655 LESLIE (MARY E.) Ina, and other Poems, 1856—Sorrows, Aspirations, and Legends from India, 1858 — Heart Echoes from the East, 1861 3 vol
1656 LESLIE (MISS) Hymns for Mothers and Children, second series, *plates* *Boston, (in America)* 1866
1657 LETHBRIDGE (CAROLINE GIFFARD) Poems, 1849—Letters and Poems on several occasions, by a Lady, *printed for the Authoress,* 1835—Letters in Rhyme, *front* 1824 3 vol
1658 Letter from a Lady, [Dr Hollings daughter] to her Husband abroad [Edward second son of Sir Robert Walpole] *in verse,* 1728—The same, *second edition,* 1729 *in 1 vol.*
1659 Letters, Moral and Entertaining, in Prose and Verse, by the Author of Friendship in Death, *Part* I 1733, *Part* II. 1731—*Part* III 1733—Friendship in Death in Twenty Letters from the Dead to the Living, 1728—Letter to the heads of the University of Oxford, on a late very Remarkable Affair, 1747—Character of Queen Caroline, 1738 *in 1 vol.*
1660 LEWIS (ELIZA GABRIELLA) Poems *Brooklyn,* 1850
1661 LEWIS (EMMA) Treasures of Darkness *Philadelphia,* 1854
1662 LEWIS (ESTELLE ANNA) Records of the Heart, and other Poems, *beautifully illustrated by American Artists* *New York,* 1857
1663 —— Myths of the Minstrel *ib* 1852
1664 LEWIS (MARY) Poems and Prose, *blue morocco Stroud,* 1855
1665 LEWIS (MARY G.) Zelinda and Cardiff Castle, *portrait* 1823
1666 LEWIS (MRS SARAH ANNA) Records of the Heart *New York,* 1844
1667 —— Child of the Sea, and other Poems *ib* 1848
1668 Liberty Bell, by Friends of Freedom, *portrait of Lucretia Mott* *Boston, (in America)* 1844
1669 LICKBARROW (ISABELLA) *of Kendal,* Poetical Effusions *Kendal,* 1814
1670 —— Lament upon the Death of the Princess Charlotte, and Alfred, a Vision, *portrait inserted Liverpool,* 1818
1671 LIDDELL (MARY HANNAH) Poetry, Original and Select, *York,* 1850—LILLINGSTON (JULIANA) Glimpses of Sunlight, *Bath,* (1859)—LINDEN (LILLA) Melodies, *New York,* 1856—Lines at the Grave of Dr. Munkhouse, by Fidelia, 1811—Lines to Prince Leopold, by a Lady, *4to Colchester,* 1817 5 vol.
1672 LIDDIARD (J S ANNA) Poems, *frontispiece* *Dublin,* 1810
1673 —— The Sgelaighe, or a Tale of Old, with a second edition of Poems, and additions *Bath,* 1811

1674 LIDDIARD (J. S. ANNA) Kenilworth and Farley Castle, with other Poems, *privately printed*   *Dublin*, 1813

1675 —— Kenilworth, a Mask, *view of the Castle, Dublin*, 1815 —Mount Leinster, a Poem, descriptive of Irish Scenery, &c. 1819   *in 1 vol*

1676 —— Theodore and Laura, a Tale, and Mont St. Jean, a Poem, by W. Liddiard   1816

1677 Life of Lamenther: a true History, written by Herself, containing a just account of the many Misfortunes she underwent, occasioned by the ill-treatment of an unnatural Father   *printed for the proprietor*, 1771

1678 LINWOOD (MARY) Anglo-Cambrian, a Poem   1818

1679 —— David's First Victory, a Sacred Oratorio, with an accompaniment for the organ or pianoforte   *Folio, n. d.*

1680 LIPPINCOTT (MRS) Poems by Grace Greenwood, *portrait*   *Boston (in America)* 1851

1681 LISTER (LADY THERESA) Story of Beauty and the Beast, Dramatized, 1844—Story of Cinderella, Dramatized, *n. d.*—Literary Contributions to a Bazaar for the Infant School in Christ Church, St Marylebone, 1840—The Linnet's Life, *plates*, 1822 — Life of Miss Linnard, abridged, *n. d.*   5 vol.

1682 Literary Souvenir for 1825 to 1837, edited by Alaric A. Watts, 13 vol. *beautiful plates*, LARGE PAPER, *mostly* INDIA PROOFS, *calf, g. e*   1825-37

1683 LITTLE (CYNTHIA) Review of the First Masquerade at Brighton, 1829—The Mess Room, a Humorous Poem, 1831—Little Christian's Sunday Alphabet, by a Lady, *woodcuts*, 1849—Little Pilgrim, *n. d*—Little Derwent's Breakfast, by a Lady, *engravings,* 1839   5 vol

1684 LITTLE (JANET) the *Scotch Milkmaid*, Poetical Works   *Air*, 1792

1685 LITTLE (SOPHIA L) Birth, Last Days and Resurrection of Jesus   *Pawtucket, R I. (Rhode Island)*, 1841

1686 LIVERMORE (HARRIET) Harp of Israel to meet the loud echo in the Wilds of America, *Philadelphia*, 1835—The Model Prayer, *ib.* 1857   2 vol.

1687 LLEWELYN (MRS. PENDERLL) Hymns, translated from the Welsh, 1850—Another edition, *with Sonnet in the Autograph of the Poetess inserted*, 1857   2 vol.

1688 LLOYD (MARY) Brighton, and other Poems, *plates*, 1809— LLOYD (MARY ANN) Manual, or Defence of the Bible, *two copies*, 1820—Poems, *privately printed*, 4to. 1823 —LLOYD (SARAH MARIA) Tribute to the Princess Charlotte, *Lowestoft*, 1819—Lizzy's Poems and Pictures, *coloured plates*, 4to. 1857   6 vol,

1689 Logan (Da) Proceedings at large in the Arches Court of Canterbury, between Jacob Mendes Da Costa and Mrs Catharine Da Costa, Villa Real, relating to a Marriage Contract, *portrait, with vignette on the title-page* 1734

1690 LOGAN (MARIA) Poems on several occasions 4to. *York*, 1793

1691 —— Poems, second edition 4to. *ib.* 1793

1692 LONG (ANNE) Letters, Poems, and Tales: Amorous, Satyrical, and Gallant, found in the Cabinet of that celebrated Toast, Mrs. Anne Long, *scarce* *E. Curll*, 1718

1693 LONG (LADY CATHARINE) Midsummer Souvenir, 1846—Christmas Souvenir, 1848—Heavenly Thoughts, 1856—LORAINE (AMELIA MARY) Lays of Israel, 1847 4 *vol.*

1694 LOUD (CLARA) Violet, *Canterbury*, 1857—Woodbine, *ib.* 1861 2 *vol.*

1695 LOUD (MRS M. ST. LEON) Wayside Flowers, *portrait* *Boston, (in America)* 1851

1696 Love Intrigues or, History of the Amours of Bosvil and Galesia, written by a Young Lady, *scarce* *E Curll*, 1713

1697 Love's Repository, a collection of Valentines selected from the best British Poets, by a Lady, 1800—Kemmish's Annual and Universal Valentine Writer, 1805—Every Lady's Own Valentine Writer, *front.* 1798—Herald of Love, a choice Collection of Valentines, *front n d*—Herald of Love, another collection, *front n d in 1 vol.*

1698 LOWE (HELEN) Prophecy of Balaam, &c 1841—LOVELL (MARIA) Beginning and End, *n. d*—Ingomar, the Barbarian, *n d*—Ingomar, *New York*, *n d.*—LOVECHILD (LOUISA) Mental Amusement, *n. d.*—Aunt Jane's Tales, *cuts, n d.*—Miscellany, 1807 6 *vol.*

1699 LUBY (MISS) Spirit of the Lakes: or, Mucruss Abbey, a Poem, *green morocco extra, with joints, watered silk linings* 1822

1700 —— The same, *second edition* 1823

1701 LUMLEY (ANNE). Ford (S) Christian's Acquiescence. a Sermon at the Interment of Lady Elizabeth Langham, wife to Sir James Langham, *plate of arms, with Elegy, by Anne Lumley* 1665

1702 LUNTLY (MISS) Christmas Eve, a Ballad, *Leeds, n d*—LUSHINGTON (MRS STEPHEN) Sea Spirit, &c 1850 2 *vol*

1703 LUTTON (ANNE) Poems, *Dublin*, 1829—The same, *another edition, New York*, 1842 2 *vol.*

1704 LUTWYCHE (ELIZABETH) Broken Vase, or Scattered Flowers collected *Lyme*, 1840

1705 LUXBOROUGH (LADY) Letters to W. Shenstone, 1775—Luxurious Musings, 1817 2 *vol*

1706 LYNCH (ANNE C) Rhode Island Book. *frontispiece* *Providence*, 1845

1707 —— Poems, *with illustrations* *New York*, 1849

1708 LYNCH (ANNE C.) Poems, *another edition, with illustrations*
New York, 1852
1709 LYNCH (MRS. HENRY) Family Sepulchre, *with illustrations,
n. d.*—Maude Effingham, 1849—Lays of the Sea, and other Poems, by Personne, 1846—Another edition, 1850—Wonders of the West Indies, 1856—Songs of the Evening Land, 1861—Sabbaths of the Year, 1864 7 *vol*.
1710 LYON (EMMA) Miscellaneous Poems *Oxford*, 1812
1711 Lyra Eucharistica, with other Poems, edited by Rev O. Shipley, 1863—Lyra Messianica, with other Poems, edited by Rev. O. Shipley, 1864 2 *vol*.
1712 Lyre of Love, 2 vol. *frontispieces after Cosway and Westall, large paper* 1806
1713 LYTH (MRS. MARY) *of York*, Memorial, by her son John Lyth, 1861—Harold, by Sir Edw. Bulwer Lytton, 1866
2 *vol*.
1714 M. (A. M.) Wanda, a Dramatic Poem, translated from the Polish of Col. J. Przyiemski, *privately printed* 1863
1715 M. (E.) Maiden Queen, a Pageant, also, the Countess, a Play *Exeter*, 1829
1716 M. (E) Poems, *privately printed* 1843
1717 M. (E. J.) Poems, 1840—M. (ELEANOR) Edith of Graystock, 1833—M. (JULIA M.) Giovanni Duprés Statues, &c. *n. d*. 3 *vol*.
1718 MABERLY (MRS) Songs, Ballads, &c the Poetry by Mrs Maberly, R. Milnes, Esq Barry Cornwall and Sir E. L. Bulwer, the music by Mrs. Maberly *Folio, n. d*
1719 MACARTHUR (MRS. JAMES) Necroplis, an Elegy, *plate*
Glasgow, 1842
1720 MACAULEY (E. W.) on the Difficulties and Dangers of a Theatrical Life, *Dublin*, 1810—Poetical Effusions, 1812—Mary Stuart, 2nd and 3rd editions, 1823 4 *vol*.
1721 —— Tales of the Drama, *wood-cuts, green morocco, g e.*
1822
1722 —— Mary Stuart, *with Autograph inscription of the Poetess, two portraits inserted* 1823
1723 McCARTHY (CHARLOTTE) Fair Moralist, and Occasional Poems 1745
1724 —— The same, second edition, with a Looking-glass for the Fair Sex 1746
1725 —— Justice and Reason, Faithful Guides to Truth, and Letters, Moral and Entertaining, 1767—News from Parnassus, or Political Advice from the Nine Muses, *Dublin*, 1757 *in* 1 *vol*.
1726 M'CORD (LOUISA S.) My Dreams, *Philadelphia*, 1848—Caius Gracchus, a Tragedy, *New York*, 1851 2 *vol*.
1727 MACDERMOTT (MARY) My Early Dreams, *Belfast*, 1832—Lays of Love, *Dublin*, 1859 2 *vol*.

1728 MACDONALD (H B.) Abdul Medjid, a Lay of the Future, *Edinb.* 1854—MACDONALD (HELEN ELLIOT) Songs in the Night, *ib.* 1847   2 *vol.*

1729 MCDONALD (MRS. MARY NOEL) Poems   *New York,* 1844

1730 MCFARLANE (A.) Prayer, a Poem, 1840—Minor Poems, 1842—MCFIE (C M. E.) Stolen Hours, *Glasgow,* 1836—Magic Words, by EMILIE MACERONI, *coloured plates,* 1851   3 *vol.*

1731 MACGREGOR (HELEN) Burial of Wellington, a Dirge, 1853—Lays of the Crimea, 1855—Lays from History and Romance, 1862—MCGREGOR (JANE) Redeeming Love, and other Poems, *with autograph letter inserted, Edinb.* 1862—MACHELL (MRS) Poems and Translations, 1856   4 *vol.*

1732 MACKAY (ELIZABETH D.) *great granddaughter of the celebrated Flora Macdonald,* Poems and Hymns   *Elgin,* 1843

1733 MACKAY (MARGARET) Thoughts Redeemed, or Lays of Leisure Hours   *Edinb* 1854

1734 MACKENZIE (HANNAH) Extracts from Meditations, &c *Edinb* 1843—Cottager's Daughter, &c by M. Mackintosh, *ib.* 1836—MACLEAN (ANNA JANE) Conviction, *Dublin,* 1851   3 *vol.*

1735 MACKEY (MRS MARY) Scraps of Nature, a Poem, *portrait printed for the authoress,* 1810

1736 MACLEAN (MRS *formerly* L E. LANDON) Works, 2 vol *two portraits, one additional*   *Philadelphia,* 1838

1737 —— Poetical Works, *portrait*   *ib.* 1839

1738 —— The same, *another edition,* 4 vol *portrait and plates*   1839

1739 —— The same, *another edition, portrait Philadelphia,* 1841

1740 —— The same, *another edition,* 4 vol *plates*   1844

1741 —— The same, *another edition, pocket size,* 2 vol. in 1 *portrait*   *Philadelphia* 1845

1742 —— The same, *another edition,* 2 vol. *portraits and an autograph note of the poetess inserted calf gilt, m e*   1850

1743 —— The same, *another edition,* 2 vol. in 1, *portrait and an autograph note of the poetess inserted green morocco, g. e*   1855

1744 —— Improvisatrice, 1824 — Troubadour, &c. 1825—Golden Violet, &c. 1827—Venetian Bracelet, &c. 1829, 4 vol. *plates, green calf gilt, m. e uniform*

1745 —— Improvisatrice, *second edition, plates,* 1824 — The same, *four other editions,* 1824-25   5 *vol.*

1746 —— Easter Gift, a Religious Offering *portrait and plates*   1832

1747 —— Miscellaneous Poetical Works   1835

1748 MACLEAN (MRS. *formerly* L. E. LANDON) Troubadour, Catalogue of Pictures, and Historical Sketches, 1825, and two other editions, 1825-7—Venetian Bracelet, *Boston*, 1830—Fate of Adelaide, &c. 1821   5 *vol.*

1749 —— Birthday Tribute to the Princess Victoria on attaining her 18th year, *portrait of the Queen*   4*to.* (1837)

1750 —— Zenana, and Minor Poems, with Memoir by Emma Roberts, *portrait*, 1838—Traits and Trials of Early Life, 1839—The same, *second edition*, 1844—Characteristics of the Genius and Writings of L. E. L *portrait inserted*, 1841   4 *vol.*

1751 —— Life and Literary Remains by Laman Blanchard, 2 vol. *portrait*   1841

1752 MACLEOD (MISS JESSIE) Fifteen Designs, illustrating Tears, with descriptive Poems by MARY ELIZABETH *plates*   *folio.* 1851

1753 —— Dreamland, with illustrative lines, by MARY ELIZABETH, *plates, tinted*   4*to* 1859

1754 McMASTERS (JULIA RUSSELL) Silver Pictures, *Philadelphia*, 1856—M'LEOD (MRS. G. A. HULSE) Lines in the Life of Marshall F Chappell, *New York*, 1855   2 *vol.*

1755 M'MORINE (MARY) Poems, chiefly on Religious Subjects   *Edinb. printed for the author*, 1799

1756 M'MULLAN (MARY ANNE) Wanderings of a Goldfinch, or Characteristic Sketches in the Nineteenth Century 1816

1757 —— Naiad's Wreath   1816

1758 —— Crescent, a National Poem, to commemorate the glorious Victory at Algiers   1816

1759 —— Britain, or Fragments of Poetical Aberration   1818

1760 MACREADY (CATHERINE FRANCES B) Leaves from the Olive Mount, 1860—Cowl and Cap, and Minor Poems, 1865   2 *vol.*

1761 M'TAGGART (MRS. A) Constantia, a Tragedy, and Valville, a Drama, 1824 — Plays: Theodora, Hortensia, Villario, and a Search after Perfection, 2 vol. 1832, &c   4 *vol.*

1762 MADAN (MRS) Progress of Poetry, 4*to* 1783—Poemata a Martino Madan, *with verses on seeing some Bees at work by* MISS S MADAN, 1784   2 *vol.*

1763 MAGRATH (ANNE JANE) Blossoms of Genius, *Dublin*, 1834 —MAHONY (AGNES) Minstrel's Hours of Song, 1825— MAITLAND (ELLINOR J. S.) Poems, 1863—MAITLAND (MRS FULLER) Hymns for Private Devotion, 1827— MADDOCKS (MRS) Female Missionary Advocate, 1827 —The same, *second edition*, 1830—Cottage Similes, 1829—MALLETT (MRS.) Consolation, 1861 — Madam Tabby's Rout, by a Young Lady, *coloured plates*, 1832 —Maid of the Isle and other Poems, 1834   10 *vol.*

1764 MAJOR (ELIZABETH) Honey on the Rod, or a Comfortable Contemplation for one in Affliction, with sundry Poems on several subjects, *wants the first title-page and imperfect at the end, sold with all faults*
A VERY RARE VOLUME   1656

1765 Manchester Keepsake for 1844, edited by William Gaspey
Manchester, 1844

1766 MANGNALL (RICHMAL) Half an Hour's Lounge
Stockport, 1805

1767 MANLEY (MRS. DELARIVIER) Royal Mischief, a Tragedy
4to. 1696

1768 —— Lost Lover, or Jealous Husband, a Comedy
Roxburghe copy   4to. 1696

1769 —— Almyna· or, the Arabian Vow, a Tragedy 4to. 1707

1770 —— Secret Memoirs and Manners of Several Persons of Quality of both Sexes from the New Atalantis and Memoirs of Europe, by *Egimardus,* 3 vol.   1709-10

1771 —— Adventures of Rivella· or, History of the Author of the Atalantis   1714

1772 —— The same, *under the title of,* History of her own Life and Times, *fourth edition, frontispiece*   1725

1773 —— Lucius, the First Christian King of Britain, a Tragedy   4to. 1717

1774 —— The same, *second edition, corrected*   4to 1720

1775 —— Court Legacy, a new Ballad Opera, as acted at the European Palace   1733

1776 MANNERS (LADY) Poems, *portrait after Cosway green morocco, g e.*   4to 1793

1777 —— The same, *second edition, an additional portrait inserted*   4to. 1793

1778 —— *Another edition,* 1794—Review of Poetry, Ancient and Modern, 4to 1799   2 vol.

1779 MANNERS (LADY JOHN) Gems of German Poetry translated, *Edinb* 1865—MANNINGTON (A.) Footprints of the Holy Dead, translations from the German, 1863—Wreath of Carols from the Fatherland, 1864   3 vol.

1780 MANWARING (MISS) Slaves of Zanguebar and other Poems, *Birmingham,* 1826—MANT (MRS. RICHARD) Parents' Poetical Anthology, 1814 — Manœuvring, a Comedy, *n. d.*   3 vol.

1781 Mara, a series of Letters, *with the* "Old Maid's Wish," written by an Old Lady, a Milliner at Bath
Newcastle, 1828

1782 Maria Sophia, Grave of the Suicides, Parting Kiss, and other Poems, *front.*   1824

1783 Maria to Henric, and Henric to Maria or the Queen to the King in Holland, and his Majesty's Answer, written by a Young Lady   *folio.* 1691

1784 Marie, the Bandit's Daughter, a Poem   *New York*, 1834
1785 MARRIOTT (FRANCES SMITH) Votive Offering, *illustrations*   4to   1862
1786 MARSH (MRS. GEORGE P) Wolfe of the Knoll, and other Poems   *New York*, 1860
1787 MARSHALL (JANE) Sir Harry Gaylove, or Comedy in Embryo   *Edinb* 1772
1788 MARSHALL (LADY) Helig's Warning, a Cymric Legend, 1854—A Prince of Wales long ago, a Bardic Legend, *Chester*, 1855   2 *vol.*
1788* MARSHALL (MRS W CALDER) Poems   1843
1789 MARTIN (EMMA) Frederic and the Falcon, in English Verse, from Boccaccio   4to   1847
1790 Martin (James) Via Regia: the King's Way to Heaven, with a Memorial of Mrs Elizabeth Martin, *consisting of Poems subscribed* MARY, ANNE GREY, PENELOPE GREY, and MARY Q G. *fine copy*, VERY RARE   1615
1791 MARTIN (M K) Thoughts for quiet hours, 1860—Song of the Bell, translated by RENIPA H A. MARTIN, *Exeter*, 1849—MARTIN (SARAH) Poetical Remains, *Yarmouth*, 1844   3 *vol.*
1792 MARTINEAU (HARRIET) Addresses with Prayers and Hymns, *Norwich*, 1826—Devotional Exercises, by C. Wellbeloved, *York*, 1826, in 1 vol—Addresses, &c *second edition*, 1838—Martineau (James) Collection of Hymns, 1856—Martyr of Allahabad, 1857—Poems by EMILIE L MARZIALS, 1864   5 *vol.*
1793 MARY QUEEN OF SCOTS, Sonnet to the Earl of Bothwell 1790
1794 —— an Historical Ballad, with other Poems, by a Lady *portrait inserted*   1800
1795 —— Poetical Epistles during her Captivity in England, with other Poems by a Young Lady, 2 vol. *portraits inserted*   1822
1796 —— Memoirs by Miss Benger, 2 vol *portraits and plate inserted*   1823
1797 MASKALL (ANNE) Outline of Ancient History, *plates and cuts, n. d* —MASKELL (ELIZA) Poetical Treasury, 1842 —Moral Tales, 1847—Sacred Offering, 1849—Bible Heroes, 1852—Home Traveller, 1856—Gospel Themes, *n. d* —Poetical Musings, n d   8 *vol.*
1798 MASON (SUSANNA) Selections from her Letters and Manuscripts, with Memoir of her Life by her Daughter   *Philadelphia*, 1836
1799 MASSON (PHŒBE ANNE) Legends of the Dunbars, and other Poems by one of their Descendants   4to   1854
1800 MASTER (DORCAS) Account of the Proceedings relating to the New Meeting House in Redcross Street, with Hymns, Part I   1758

1801 MASTERS (MARY) Poems 1733
1802 —— Familar Letters and Poems 1755
1803 MATHEWS (MRS CHARLES) Poems, *with a very pleasing inscription in the autograph of Mr C Mathews, on the fly-leaf, morocco, g e* Doncaster, 1802
1804 MATURIN (E. M) Letters to a Friend, with Epitaph *privately printed* Roundwood, 1818
1805 Maurice (Peter) Choral Hymn-Book, *containing* 21 *Hymns by* MISS JANE MAURICE, n d.—MATTHEWS (ELIZABETH) Hymns and Poems, *cuts,* 1835—The Aviary, by EMMA S MATTHEWS, n d —MAXWELL (MRS) Knack and Luck, *New York,* 1850, and other pieces by Mrs Maxwell
7 *vol.*
1806 MAXWELL (ANN MARIA) *formerly Ainsle,* Letters from the Dead to the Living and Moral Letters Paisley, 1820
1807 MAXWELL (CAROLINE) Feudal Tales, a Collection of Romantic Narratives and other Poems, *coloured plates* n d
1808 MAY (CAROLINE) American Female Poets with Biographical and Critical Notices, *portraits and plates morocco extra, g e.* Philadelphia, 1848
1809 MAY (EDITH) Poems, *elegantly illustrated* ib 1852
1810 —— Poems, *second edition, elegantly illustrated morocco, g e* ib 1855
1811 MAY (EMILY JANE) Compensation and other Poems, 1865 —Spiritual Songs from the Canticles, from the German by ANNA M. MAY, 1865 — MAY (LIZZIE) Twilight Hours, *Rochford,* 1859—MAY (MARY) Rhymes for Children, *coloured cuts,* 4to. n d—A May Wreath, *Dublin,* 1857—The Wreath by S Mayes, 1836 6 *vol.*
1812 MAYER (EMILY) Week's Delight, or Games and Stories for the Parlour and Fireside New York, 1854
1813 MAYLIN (ANNE WALTER) Lays of many Hours
Philadelphia, 1847
1814 MAYNARD (CATHERINE HARRIET) Romance of the Gold and Silver Lock, and other Poems, 1862—MAYNARD (JULIA A) Poems, *portrait,* 1845—Records of Scenery and other Poems, 1843—Our Lord's Parables paraphrased, 1858—MAYNARD (MARY) Poems, 1851—Shakespeare's Dream, 1861 6 *vol.*
1815 Medley (A) of Joy and Grief a selection of pieces in prose and verse New York, 1822
1816 MEDLEY (SARAH) Original Poems Liverpool, 1807
1817 MEETKERKE (CECILIA ELIZABETH) Songs of Evening, 1863— MEDINA (MISS L H) Nick of the Woods, *Boston,* n d — Memorials of Bertie by his Mother, 1849—Meditations among the Ruins of Reading Abbey, *Reading,* 1834 4 *vol.*

1818 MELVILLE (JULIA) Poems, *privately printed Farnham, n d.*
1819 Men of the Time, Biographical Sketches of Eminent Living Characters, also of Celebrated Women of the Time 1856
1820 ——— another edition, revised by Edw Walford 1862
1821 ——— another edition, brought down to the time 1865
1822 MENTEATH (MRS. A. STUART) Lays of the Kirk and Covenant 4to. *Edinb* 1850
1823 The same, *second edition* *ib* 1852
1824 MEREDITH (MRS CHARLES) *formerly Louisa Anne Twamley,* Poems, *with illustrations by the authoress*
Birmingham, 1835
1825 ——— Romance of Nature, or the Flower-Seasons Illustrated, *beautiful coloured plates* 1836

⁂ At the end is a leaf of Extempore Lines on the Statue of a Child with Flowers, dated Birmingham, 1834

1826 ——— Romance of Nature, *second edition, coloured plates*
1836
1827 ——— The same, *third edition, coloured plates* 1839
1828 ——— Autumn Ramble by the Wye
plates after Copley Fielding, D Cox, &c 1839
1829 ——— Loved and Lost, a Story told in Gossip Verse
illustrated by Day & Sons n d.
1830 ——— Flora's Gems: or the Treasures of the Parterre
twelve beautiful coloured plates folio. n d.
1831 ——— Some of my Bush Friends in Tasmania, Native Flowers, Berries and Insects
beautifully illustrated folio 1860
1832 Merlin. a Poem, to which is added the Royal Hermitage, a Poem, both by a Lady, *frontispiece*
4to printed by Edward Cave, 1735
1833 MERRI (M A) Poems, *privately printed*
Guilden Morden, 1850
1834 MERRYWEATHER (MRS. I. A) Hermit of Eskdaleside, with other Poems *Whitby,* 1833
1835 Metrical Epistles, chiefly from Florence, 1821—The same, *second edition,* 1824—Metrical Remembrances, by a Lady, 1832 3 vol.
1836 Metrical Sketches *Birmingham,* 1810
1837 Metrical Translations from the German, by a German Lady *Hamburg,* 1852
1838 MEZIERE (MRS) *formerly Harriet Chilcot,* Elmar and Ethlinda, Adalba and Ahmora, with other pieces 1783
1839 ——— Moreton Abbey, or the Fatal Mystery, a Novel, 2 vol in 1 *Southampton, n d*
1840 Michell (Nicholas) Living Poets and Poetesses, 1832—Hymns compiled by Joseph Middleton (of Lewes), 1793—Midnight Thoughts and Musings by Eliza, 1845—Second Series, *Blackheath,* 1846 4 vol.

1841 MILBURN (Mrs. W H) Poems of Faith and Affection, *New York*, 1866—The Milkmaid, a Fable, by a Lady, *with lithographic illustrations* (1822) 2 vol.
1842 MILES (Mrs ALFRED) *late S E Hatfield*, Moments of Loneliness, *Falmouth*, 1829—Fruits of Solitude, *Plymouth*, 1831—Leisure Evenings or Records of the Past, 1859 3 vol.
1843 MILLER (LADY) Poetical Amusements at a Villa near Bath, 4 vol. in 2, *frontispiece by W Hibbart* Bath, 1775
1844 —— The same, *another edition*, 4 vol in 2 ib 1776-81
1845 —— On Novelty, and on Trifles and Triflers
4to Bath, 1778
1846 MILLIGAN (SOPHIA) Poems, with translations from Scandinavian and other Poets, 1856—Mind amongst the Spindles, a selection from the Lowell Offering, 1845—MINTON (ANN) Comedy of a Wife to be Lett, 1802
3 vol.
1847 MILLS (ELIZABETH WILLESFORD) Sibyl's Leaves Poems and Sketches Devonport, 1826
1848 MILNE (CHRISTIAN) Poems Aberdeen, 1805
1849 MINSHULL (LOUISA) Translations and Sketches of Biography 1839
1850 Miscellaneous Devotions in prose and verse, by a Convert from Infidelity 1757
1851 Miscellaneous Pieces in prose and verse, *printed for the authoress*, 1817—Miscellaneous Poems, by an Officer's Widow, *n d* 2 vol.
1852 Miscellaneous Poems, by a Young Lady Bath, 1828
1853 Miscellaneous Poems by Several Hands (Mrs C——L) and others, published by J Ralph 1729
1854 Miscellany of Original Poems, Translations, and Imitations, by LADY M W M——, MRS MANLEY &c. 1720
1855 —— The same, *second edition, portrait of Prince Frederick*, 1710—The same, 1720, *imperfect* 3 vol.
1856 Miscellany Poems, by Mrs BEHN, &c with an Essay upon Satyr 1692
1857 Missionary Annual, *plates*, 1833—Missionary Hymns, 1846—Missionary Souvenir edited by Rev T Archng, *plates*, 1850—The Missionary, by a Swedish Nightingale, 1852 4 vol.
1858 MITCHELL (ELIZABETH HARCOURT) *formerly Rolls*, First Fruits, 1857—Wild Thyme, 1861 2 vol.
1859 MITCHELL (M) Poems Yarmouth, 1796
1860 MITFORD (MARY RUSSELL) Poems 1810
1861 —— Christina, the Maid of the South Seas, *portrait inserted*, 1811—Poems, *second edition, portrait inserted*, 1811—Narrative Poems on the Female Character, &c. 1813 3 vol.

O

1862 MITFORD (MARY RUSSELL) Julian, a Tragedy, 1823—Three other editions, 1823—Foscari, a Tragedy, 1826—Two other editions, 1827—Foscari and Julian, *portrait inserted*, 1827—Rienzi, a Tragedy, 1828—Two other editions, 1828—Charles I, a Tragedy, *portrait inserted*, 1834—Sadak and Kalasrade, an Opera, *portrait inserted*, 1835 13 vol.

1863 —— Dramatic Scenes, Sonnets, and other Poems, *portrait inserted*, 1827—Dramatic Scenes, 1832 2 vol.

1864 —— Dramatic Works, 2 vol *portrait and plates* 1854

1865 —— Recollections of a Literary Life, 2 vol *portrait* 1857

1866 MOENS (E. B) Verses, *printed on single leaves, with an autograph letter of the Poetess* Birmingham, n. d.

1867 MOFFITT (MARY ANNA) Juvenile Tourist, *Philadelphia*, 1858—MITFORD (MRS.) Little Girl's Housekeeping, *cuts, n. d.*—Gottfried and Beata, translated from the German by ANNA MOLINE, 1814 3 vol

1868 MOLLINEUX (MARY) *of Liverpool*, Fruits of Retirement, or Miscellaneous Poems, Moral and Divine 1702

1869 —— The same, *third edition* 1720

1870 —— The same, *fourth edition* 1739

1871 —— The same, *fifth edition* 1761

1872 —— The same, *sixth edition* 1772

1873 —— Song of Sion, written by a citizen thereof (John Grave) whose outward Habitation is in Virginia, with an additional Postscript by MARY MOLLINEUX, *head-lines cut off and leaves mended, sold as it is morocco, g e* 4to 1662

1874 MONK (MRS) Marinda· Poems and Translations, edited by R. Molesworth 1716

1875 MONTAGU (MRS ELIZABETH) Letters, &c. 4 vol. *portrait* 1810-13

1876 Montagu (Frederic) Ages of Female Beauty, *plates* 4to 1838

1877 MONTAGU (LADY MARY WORTLEY) Court Poems, viz., The Basset Table, The Drawing Room, and The Toilet 1706

1878 —— Verses address'd to the Imitator of the First Satire of the Second Book of Horace, *n d* —Advice to Sappho, 1733—Verses to the Imitator, &c *fifth edition, n d folio in 1 vol*

1879 —— Verses to the Imitator, &c *Dublin*, 1733—A Modest Praise of Pritty Miss Smalley, *ib.* 1730 *in 1 vol*

1880 —— Six Town Eclogues, with some other Poems 4to 1747

1881 —— Letters written during her Travels, *second edition*, 3 vol 1763—Third edition, 3 vol. in 1, 1763—Other editions *together 30 vol.*

1882 MONTAGU (LADY MARY WORTLEY) Poetical Works, *first edition, wanting part of the publisher's list*   1768

1883 —— The same, *another edition*, 1781—Another edition, (*Gainsbrough*), 1785   2 vol.

1884 —— Essays on Friendship and Old Age, by the MARCHIONESS DE LAMBERT, *portrait inserted*, 1780—Moral Tales, *second edition*, 4to 1783—The same, *another edition*, 1791   3 vol

1885 —— Works, including her Correspondence, Poems and Essays, 5 vol *portraits and facsimiles*, *calf*   1803

1886 —— The same, *fifth edition*, 5 vol 1803—Sixth edition, 2 vol 1811—The same, complete in 1 vol. 1825   8 vol.

1887 —— The same, *sixth edition*, 5 vol   1817

1888 —— Letters and Works, edited by Lord Wharncliffe, 3 vol *portraits, calf gilt, m. e*   1837

1889 —— The same, *second edition*, 3 vol. *portraits calf gilt, m. e*   1837

1890 —— The same, 2 vol *half calf gilt*   *Philadelphia*, 1837

1891 —— The same, 2 vol *portrait inserted*   *Paris*, 1837

1892 —— The same, with notes by W. Moy Thomas, 2 vol *portraits*   1861

1893 MONTGOMERY (MRS ALFRED) Poems, 1816—Christian Poet, or Selections by J Montgomery, *Glasgow*, 1828—Christian Psalmist, *ib* 1837—The Months in Floral Costume by MARY EUGENIA, *Norwich, n. d.*—MOODIE (SUSANNA) *formerly Strickland*, Enthusiasm, and other Poems, 1831—Roughing it in the Bush, 1857   6 vol.

1894 Monthly Mirror reflecting Men and Manners, with Strictures on their Epitome, The Stage, vol VIII, X, XI, and XIV, *portraits*, 4 vol   1799-1802

1895 MONTOLIEU (MRS) The Gardens, translated from the French of De Lille, *vignettes by Bartolozzi*   4to 1798

1896 —— The same, *second edition plates and vignettes by Bartolozzi*   1805

1897 —— The same, *another copy* LARGE PAPER, *green morocco, g. e*   1805

1898 —— Enchanted Plants, Fables in Verse, *frontispiece by Bartolozzi, red morocco, g e*   1800

1899 —— Enchanted Plants, *another copy printed on straw-coloured paper*   1800

1900 —— The same, *second edition, plate*, 1801—The same, *third edition*, 1812—Another edition, 1822   3 vol.

1901 —— Festival of the Rose, with other Poems *vignettes by Bartolozzi*   4to 1802

1902 —— Gethsemane, a Poem, founded on the Messiah of Klopstock, 2 vol.   1823

1903 MOODY (ELIZABETH) Poetic Trifles, 1798—War, a System of Madness and Irreligion, with Anna's Complaint, written in the Isle of Thanet, 1794, by Mrs. MOODY, 1796   2 vol.

1904 Moore (Frank) Rebel Rhymes and Rhapsodies, *New York*, 1864—Songs of the Soldiers, *ib* 1864   2 vol.

1905 MOORE (JANE ELIZABETH) *of Bermondsey*, Genuine Memoirs, to which is prefixed a Poetic Index, 3 vol.
printed at the Logographic Press, n d.

1906 —— Miscellaneous Poems, *plate of the Opening of the new Docks on St. George's Day*, 1796
Dublin, printed for the author, 1796

1907 Moore (William) Sermon on the Decease of Andrew Gifford Gwennap, with Elegy, by a Lady
4to. Falmouth, 1790

1908 MORE (GERTRUDE) Spiritual Exercises: Confessiones Amantis, a Lover's Confessions, &c *part of the title supplied in manuscript*, VERY RARE   *Paris*, 1658

1909 MORE (HANNAH) Works in Prose and Verse   *Cork*, 1778
1910 —— Works, 4 vol. in 2   *Dublin*, 1803
1911 —— Works, 19 vol. *portrait, large paper*   1818-9
1912 —— Works, 11 vol. *portrait*   1830
1913 —— Works, 6 vol. *portrait and plates*   1836
1914 —— Works, 2 vol.   1840
1915 —— Works, 11 vol *portrait and plates*
half calf gilt, i. e. with autograph note of the Poetess inserted   1853

1916 —— Search after Happiness, a Pastoral Drama
portrait inserted   *4to Bristol, n. d.*
1917 —— The same, *second edition*   *Bristol*, 1773
1918 —— The same, *third edition*   *ib* 1774
1919 —— The same, *fourth edition*   *Philadelphia,* 1774
1920 —— The same, *other editions*, 1774-1818   12 vol.

1921 —— The same, *Bristol*, 1775—Inflexible Captive a Tragedy, *ib.* 1774—Percy, a Tragedy, 1778—Fatal Falsehood, a Tragedy, 1780—Search after Happiness, 1778—Sir Eldred of the Bower and the Bleeding Rock, 1778, &c.   2 vol.

1922 —— Inflexible Captive, *Bristol*, 1774 The same, *third edition, ib* 1774   2 vol.

1923 —— Sir Eldred of the Bower and the Bleeding Rock, two Legendary Tales   *4to* 1776

1924 —— Percy, a Tragedy, *Dublin*, 1778—The same, *Belfast*, 1778—The same, *second edition, Cadell*, 1778—The same, *Dublin*, 1785—Other editions, 1788-1818 10 vol.

1925 —— Fatal Falsehood, a Tragedy, 1779—The same, *third edition*, 1789   2 vol.

1926 MORE (HANNAH) Sacred Dramas, to which is added Sensibility, a Poem 1782
1927 —— The same, *second edition, portrait inserted,* 1782—Other editions, 1783-1855 39 vol
1928 —— Florio, a Tale for Fine Gentlemen and Fine Ladies, and the Bas Bleu, two Poems 4*to* 1786
1929 —— The same, *second edition,* 1787—Ode to Dragon, Mr. Garrick's House Dog at Hampton, 1777 4*to in* 1 *vol*
1930 —— The same, *second edition,* 1787—Sir Eldred of the Bower and the Bleeding Rock, 1776—Ode to Dragon, 1777 4*to in one vol*
1931 —— Slavery, a Poem 4*to.* 1788
1932 —— Bishop Bonner's Ghost, *view of Strawberry Hill on the title-page, and plate inserted* 4*to. Strawberry Hill,* 1789
1933 —— Poems, *view of a rustic building at Barley Wood, on title-page,* 1816 — Another edition, 1829 — Another edition, *portrait, Halifax,* 1814 3 *vol*
1934 —— Tragedies, *portrait inserted,* 1818—The Riot, or Half a Loaf better than no Bread, 1817—Bible Rhymes, *cuts,* 1821—The same, *second edition,* 1822—Feast of Freedom, *the vocal parts set to Music,* 1827—Tracts, Religious, Moral and Entertaining, 2 vol. *cuts,* 1830 7 *vol.*
1935 —— Life, by the Rev Sir Archibald MacSarcasm *Bristol,* 1802
1936 —— Life and Correspondence by W. Roberts, 4 vol. *portraits* 1834
1937 —— Life, with Notices of her Sisters, by H Thompson *portrait and woodcut illustrations* 1838
1938 —— Memoir, with Notices of her Works and Contemporaries, 1838—Life, with Selections from her Correspondence, 1856 2 vol
1939 —— Poetical Review of Miss H More's Strictures on Female Education, by Sappho Search, *Ipswich,* 1800 —Truths respecting Mrs H More's Meeting Houses, by Edw Spencer, *Bath,* 1802 2 *vol.*
1940 Morgan (J M) Triumph, or the Coming Age of Christianity, *plates,* 1851—Home Light, or Memoir and Letters of Rev R Bassett, of Colwinstone, and E. Bassett, Glamorganshire, *Carnarvon,* 1860—Hymn Book for Maternal Associations by ANN JANE [MORGAN], 1849—The Voice and Reply, by ELIZA F MORRIS, *Worcester, n d*—MORRIS (JANE ELIZABETH) Crocus, *plates,* 1824 5 *vol*
1941 MORGAN (LADY) *formerly Sidney Owenson,* Dramatic Scenes from Real Life, 2 vol. *portrait inserted* 1833

1942 MORGAN (LADY) *formerly Sidney Owenson*, Poems, *Dublin*, 1801—Lay of an Irish Harp, 1807—St Clair, *Philadelphia*, 1807—Lay of an Irish Harp, *New York*, 1808—St. Clair, 2 vol. 1812—Verses to Marianne Howard, &c. 1818—Fragments, 1818—Royal Progress, 1821
9 vol. and tracts

1943 —— Passages from my Autobiography *portrait and coloured plate* 1859

1944 —— Friends, Foes, and Adventures, *portrait inserted, Dublin*, 1859—Lady Morgan, her career by W. J. Fitzpatrick, *portrait inserted*, 1860 *2 vol*

1945 —— Memoirs: Autobiography, Diaries and Correspondence, 2 vol. *portraits* 1862

1946 MORGAN (MARY) Knyghte of the Golden Locks: an Ancyent Poem, *very scarce* 4to. *Wisbech*, 1799

1947 MORLEY (COUNTESS OF) Flying Burgermaster, a Legend of the Black Forest
etchings by the Countess, privately printed 1832

1948 MORTON (MRS. JAMES) Clarkson Gray, and other Poems *illustrated* *Edinb* 1866

1949 MORTON (SARAH WENTWORTH) *of Dorchester, Massachusets*, Ouabi or, the Virtues of Nature, an Indian Tale, by Philenia, a Lady of Boston, *frontispiece* *Boston*, 1790

1950 —— Beacon Hill, a Local Poem 4to. *ib* 1797

1951 —— My Mind and its Thoughts *ib* 1823

1952 Morton (W.) Woman of Shunem and Chaunts of the Family, 2 vol in 1 1850

1953 MOSS (CELIA AND MARION) Early Efforts, 1839—Second Edition, 1839—Romance of Jewish History, 3 vol 1840 *5 vol.*

1954 Moss (MARIA J.) Poetical Cook-Book *Philadelphia*, 1864

1955 Mother's (The) Fables, in verse, 1824—Another edition, *plates, Southampton, n d*—A Mother's First Thoughts, *Edinb.* 1832—A Mother's Hymns, *n. d.*—My Mother, *illustrated and printed in letters of gold, n d*—My Mother, by Comus, *coloured illustrations*, 4to 1857
7 vol.

1956 MOTHERLY (MRS) Nursery Poetry, *plates* 4to 1859

1957 MOTT (MRS. I H. R.) Sacred Melodies, 1824—MOULTON (SARAH H) Sepulchre of Lazarus, Recollections of Scotland, &c. 1842—Bible Poems and Lyrics by MRS. J. B MOULTON, 1855 *3 vol*

1958 MOWATT (ANNA CORA) Armand, a Play, 1849—Fashion, or Life in New York, a Comedy, 1850—Autobiography of an Actress, *portrait, Boston*, 1854—Plays, *ib.* 1855
4 vol.

1959 MUDIE (MISS) Poems and Fragmentary Pieces, &c
Wisbech, n. d.

1960 MULOCK (DINAH M) Poems, *plates, n. d.*—Our Year, a Child's Book, in Prose and Verse, *plates, Camb.* 1860 —The same, *another edition, plates, New York,* 1860
3 *vol.*

1961 MUMFORD (MISS) Poems by Matilda, *Richmond,* 1858, and others by the same
7 *vol.*

1962 MUNDY (F N. C.) Fall of Needwood, *with book-plate of Southey, the Poet Laureate, engraved by Bewick*
4to. *Derby,* 1808

1963 MUNRO (EMILIA) Rossale, and other Poems, *Aberdeen,* 1851 —Musings of a Pilgrim at Jacob's Well, 1857—Muston on the Perpetuation of Christian Friendship, 1831
3 *vol.*

1964 MURDEN (MRS) *formerly Eliza Crawley,* Miscellaneous Poems, by a Lady of Charleston
Charleston, South Carolina, 1826

1965 —— The same, *second edition* *New York,* 1827

1966 MURPHY (ANNA) Short Account of Trees and Plants, and Miscellaneous Poems *printed for the author,* 1808

1967 MURRAY (HANNAH L) Memoirs, by Gardiner Spring *portrait* *New York,* 1849

1968 Murray (Lindley) Biographical Sketch of Henry Tuke
York, 1815

1969 MURRY (MISS ANN) Mentoria or Young Ladies' Instructor, *plates,* 1778—The same, *another edition,* 1814—Mentorian Lectures, 1808—Poems, 4to 1779—The same, *second edition,* 4to 1779
5 *vol*

1970 Muse's Banquet, consisting of a Select Collection of pieces in the different species of Poetical Composition by the most celebrated authors, *fifth edition* *Dublin,* 1779

1971 Muse's Mercury or Monthly Miscellany, consisting of Poems, Prologues, Songs, Sonnets, Translations, and other Curious Pieces, to which is added an Account of the Stage, of the New Operas and Plays, &c 13 *numbers very scarce* 1707-8

1972 Muse's Mirrour a Collection of Poems, *second edition,* 2 vol. 1783

1973 Musse (Lady Margaret de la) Triumphs of Grace. or, her Last Words and Edifying Death, Englished by P L.
1681, *repr. Manchester,* 1795

1974 MUZZY (MRS. HARRIET) Poems, Moral and Sentimental, collected and arranged by Caroline Matilda Thayer
New York, 1821

1975 Mystical Rose, or Mary of Nazareth, the Lily of the House of David, by Marie Josephine *New York,* 1865

1976 N (C) Tears and Smiles through them *view of Belvoir Castle* *Gainsburgh, n. d.*

1977 N. (M.) *a Young Lady*, Faithful General, a Tragedy
4to. 1706
1978 NAIRNE (CAROLINE BARONESS) Lays from Strathearn, with Symphones and Accompaniments for the Pianoforte by Finlay Dun, *plates* folio. n d.
1979 NAPIER (MRS CATHERINE) City of the World, 1845—Lay of the Palace, 1852 — Narrative of the Death of Mrs. ***, *privately printed*, Bath, 1841—On the Nativity, Verses on the New Testament, *privately printed*, 1829 4 vol.
1980 NASH (CAROLINE) Sacred Bee and other Poems, 1850—Reflections on the Value of the Scriptures, 1852—NELSON (ESTHER) Island Minstrelsy, 1839 3 vol.
1981 NEAL (ALICE B.) Gossips of Rivertown, *portrait*
Philadelphia, 1850
1982 NEALDS (MRS. CHARLES) Poems 1829
1983 NEALE (A.) Biblical Sketches and Hymns 1854
1984 NEALE (M. A.) Smiles and Tears Leicester, 1834
1985 NETHERCOTT (MISS) Traveller's Dream and other Poems, Dublin, 1858—Political Pieces of Religion and Nature, *ib* 1856 2 vol.
1986 NEWCASTLE (MARGARET CAVENDISH DUCHESS OF) Philosophicall Fancies, VERY RARE 1653
1987 —— Poems and Fancies
whole length portrait, parts of the margin wanted, folio. 1653
1988 —— Poems and Fancies, *a presentation copy from the Duchess to T. Barlow, of Queen's College, Oxford,* 1653 —World's Olio, 1655 — Philosophical and Physical Opinions, 1655, *russia, g e.* folio *in one vol.*
1989 —— Poems and Fancies, *second impression, portrait by Van Schuppen, the Strawberry Hill copy* folio. 1664
1990 —— Philosophical and Physical Opinions folio. 1655
1991 —— The same, *another edition, presentation copy from the authoress,* THICK PAPER folio. 1663
1992 —— Playes, 2 vol. *portrait by Van Schuppen* folio. 1662-8
1993 —— Philosophical Letters folio. 1664
1994 —— CCXI Sociable Letters folio. 1664
1995 —— Description of a New World, called The Blazing World folio. 1666
1996 —— The same, *another edition, portrait inserted*
folio 1668
1997 —— Life of William, Duke of Newcastle folio. 1667
1998 —— The same, *another edition* 4to. 1675
1999 —— The World's Olio, *second edition, portrait by Van Schuppen* folio. 1671
2000 —— Nature's Picture, drawn by Fancies Pencil to the Life, *second edition, portrait by Van Schuppen a very fine impression* folio. 1671

2001 NEWCASTLE (MARGARET CAVENDISH DUCHESS OF) Treasure of Knowledge, or the Female Oracle, wherein is delineated The Experienced Traveller, The She Anchoret, &c. 1766
2002 —— Select Poems, edited by Sir Egerton Brydges, *25 copies only printed, the first book issued from the Lee Priory Press, yellow morocco, g e.* *Lee Priory*, 1813
2003 —— Life, with Preface by Sir E Brydges, *the impression limited to 100 copies, portrait inserted* ib 1814
2004 New Foundling Hospital for Wit, 6 vol 1784
2005 NEWMAN (SARAH) Poems *Alton*, 1811
2006 NEWNHAM (MRS) *of Farnham*, Memoir, with a Selection from her Papers and Correspondence by W. Newnham 1830
2007 New Orleans Book, edited by R G. Barnwell (contains several Poems by Ladies not likely to be met with elsewhere) *New Orleans*, 1851
2008 New Year's Gift and Juvenile Souvenir, edited by Mrs Alaric Watts, *plates*, 2 vol 1833-4
2009 New York Book of Poetry *New York*, 1837
2010 NICHOLS (ANNE SUSANNA) Journal of a Tour from Canonbury to Aldborough, through Chelmsford, Sudbury, and Ipswich, and back through Harwich, Colchester, &c *24 copies only printed*
 VERY RARE, *with an autograph letter of Mr. B. Nichols inserted* 1804
2011 Nichols (J) Collection of Poems, with Notes, 8 vol. *uncut* 1780-2
2012 NICHOLS (REBECCA S) Bernice or the Curse of Minna, and other Poems, *portrait* *Cincinnati*, 1844
2013 NOAH (ROSINA AMELIA) Henry and Rosa, 1846—NOAKES (MARY ANNE) Poems from Scripture, *Sunderland*, 1840—Night Scented Flowers, *Bath*, n d—NODDER (E. M) Gleanings for the Humble, 1852—The Name of Jesus and other verses by C. M N. *first, third, and fourth editions*, 1863-6 7 vol.
2014 NOOTH (CHARLOTTE) Original Poems and a Play *blue morocco, with joints, g e.* 1815
2015 NORTHAMPTON (MARGARET MARCHIONESS OF) Irene *privately printed* 1833
2016 Northampton (Marquis of) The Tribute a collection of Poems by various authors 1837
2017 NORTHESK (GEORGINA COUNTESS OF) Selection of Prayers and Hymns, *two parts*, 1858—The Nosegay, 1819—NOTMAN (Mrs. M) Poems *Galashiels*, 1838—NURNBERG (MRS) Blossoms of Thought, 1860 — Nursery Companion, by a Lady, *Ludlow*, 1813—The same, *another edition*, 1827 — Nursery Sunday Book, by a Lady, *coloured plates*, 1845 7 vol.

P

2018 NORTON (Hon. C. E.) *formerly Sheridan*, Sabbath Lays, set to music, *portrait* folio. n d.
2019 —— Sorrows of Rosalie, with other Poems, *presentation copy to the Duchess of Clarence, afterwards Queen Adelaide, with six stanzas of four lines each in the autograph of the authoress* 1829
2020 —— The same, *fourth edition, portrait* 1829
2021 —— Undying One, and other Poems, 2 copies, 1830— The same, *second edition, portrait*, 1830 — Another edition, *portrait inserted*, 1853
2022 —— Poems Boston (in America), 1833
2023 —— Coquette, and other Tales and Sketches in Prose and Verse, 2 vol. *portraits* 1835
2024 —— Lines on the remark attributed to Edward Oxford that this Country ought not to be governed by a Woman 1840
2025 —— Dream and other Poems, *portrait* 1840
2026 —— The same, *second edition, portrait* 1841
2027 —— Child of the Islands, a Poem, *frontispiece, portrait inserted, morocco, g e* 1845
2028 —— The same, *second edition* 1846
2029 —— Aunt Carry's Ballads for Children *illustrations by Absolon* 4to 1847
2030 —— The Martyr, a Tragedy, *portrait inserted*, 1848— Second edition, 1849—Tales and Sketches, 1850— Another edition, 1856 4 vol
2031 —— The Gossip, a Collection of Tales, Sketches, &c. 3 vol 1852
2032 —— The Lady of La Garaye, *portrait and vignette*, 1862 —The same, *second edition*, 1862—*Third edition*, 1862 —Another edition, 1862, 4 vol 8vo and 4to
2033 NORTON (Lady Frances) Memento Mori or, Meditations on Death *frontispiece of Lady Gethin on her death-bed, and large folded plate of her Monument in Westminster Abbey* 4to 1705
2034 —— Contemplations, Moral and Divine, with the Applause of Virtue, and Meditations on Death, *plates* 4to 1711
2035 NUNNEZ (Fabricia) Spinster, A Word or Two, or Architectural Hints in lines, in two parts, addressed to those Royal Academicians who are Painters, 4to 1806— Another Word or Two, on the Re-Election of Benjamin West to the President's Chair, 1807 2 vol.

FIFTH DAY'S SALE.

OCTAVO ET INFRA,

UNLESS OTHERWISE EXPRESSED.

LOT
2036 O'BRIEN (MRS MARY) Political Monitor or Regent's Friend, a Collection of Poems, *Dublin*, 1790—Fallen Patriot, a Comedy, *ib n d* 2 vol.
2037 —— Pious Incendiaries or Fanaticism Displayed, a Poem, *red morocco, g e* 1785
2038 O'CALLAGHAN (MATILDA SOPHIA) Glories of Jesus, *Dublin*, 1835 — Orange Blossoms, or Breathings of Love, *Halifax*, 1839 — The Offering, *plates*, 1834 — Odd Fellows' Offering, *New York*, 1853—Officer Pug, a Pastime of The Nineteenth Century, by a Lady, *cuts*, 1832—OKE (MRS) Sacred Poems, 1834 6 vol
2039 OGILVY (DOROTHEA and Donald) Δωροι, Poems, *Aberdeen*, 1865
2040 OGILVY (Mrs. D.) Book of Highland Minstry, *with illustrations by R. R M'Ian* 4to. 1848
2041 —— The same, another edition 4to 1860
2042 —— Traditions of Tuscany, 1851—Poems of Ten Years, 1856 2 vol
2043 OGILVY (MRS T) *formerly Bosanquet*, Hymns for Children of the Church of England, *n d* —The same, *third edition, n d*—Christian Lyrics, *n d.*—The History of our Blessed Lord, in easy verse, *plates, Oxford*, 1855—The Nun of Enzklosterle, a Legend of the Black Forest, 1861 5 vol
2044 O'KEEFE (ADELAIDE) National Characters, *plates, Lymington*, 1818—Trip to the Coast, *plates*, 1819, *and others* 10 vol
2045 —— Patriarchal Times or, The Land of Canaan, *fourth edition, presentation copy from the Poetess, with list of her Works, in her Autograph, and signed with her initials* 1826
2046 —— Original Poems for Infant Minds, by several young persons, *numerous illustrations* 1865
2047 Old Friends in a New Dress, or Select Fables of Æsop, in verse, 1826—Old Grand-Papa, and other Poems, by a Young Lady, *plates*, 1815—Old John's Fire, by a Lady, 1819—Old Stories of Switzerland, 1861—Old Semibreve Musical Instruction for young Ladies and Gentlemen, *plates, privately printed*, 4to. *n. d.* 5 vol

2048 OLDING (ANN) Sermon on her Death, with Verses by her, *first, second, and third editions*, 3 vol   1776

2049 Olive (The) and the Pine, *Boston, (in America)* 1859— The Olive Branch, *Liverpool, n. d.*   2 vol.

2050 O'NEILL (MRS FRANCES) Poetical Essays, a collection of Satirical Poems, Songs and Acrostics, *frontispiece printed for the Authoress*, 1802

2051 O'NEILL (HENRIETTA BRUCE) Nugæ Canoræ, a Collection of Poems, *calf, g e*   *Dublin*, 1847

2052 Opal (The) a Gift for all Seasons, edited by Mrs Sarah Josepha Hale, *plates*   *New York*, 1849

2053 OPIE (AMELIA) Poems, *first edition, frontispiece, portrait inserted*, 1802—The same, 2nd, 3rd, 4th, 5th, and 6th editions, 1803-11   6 vol.

2054 —— Elegy to the Memory of the Duke of Bedford, *portrait inserted*   4to 1802

2055 —— Warrior's Return, and other Poems, *frontispiece*, 1808—The same, second edition, *frontispiece*, 1808— Negro Boy's Tale, *frontispiece, Norwich*, 1824— Detraction Displayed, *ib* 1828   4 vol.

2056 —— Lays for the Dead, *frontispiece, portrait inserted*, 1834 —The same, second edition, 1840—Appearance is against Her, *n d*—Memoir of Amelia Opie, by Cecilia Lucy Brightwell *portrait, with autograph inscription by the Authoress*, 1855   4 vol.

2057 —— Memorials of her Life, by C L. Brightwell, *portrait, with autograph letter inserted*   *Norwich*, 1854

2058 OPIE (AMELIA) Father and Daughter, with Epistle from the Maid of Corinth, and other Poetical pieces   1801

2059 ORDE (ISABELLA) Poems, *with extra title page, and Charade written on Arthur's Seat, in the autograph of the Poetess*   *Portobello*, 1839

2060 Original Compositions in prose and verse, with some Vocal and Instrumental Music, *illustrated with some Lithographic Drawings*   obl 4to 1833

2061 Original Hymns and Poems, written by a Private Christian for his own use, *with commendatory verses by* LADY HUNTER BLAIR   *Edinb* 1784

2062 Original Hymns on Scripture Texts, and other Poems, by a Lady, 1840—Original Juvenile Poems, by a Lady, *n d.*—Original Poems, Translations, and Imitations, by a Lady, 1773—Original Poetry by a Lady, lately deceased, *Bath*, 1811—Original Poetry by a young Lady, *Leeds*, 1821—Original Stories and Anecdotes, *frontispiece*, 1808—Original Thinking, or Journal of the Heart, 1827—Original Valentines, by a Lady, *frontispiece, n. d.*   8 vol.

2063 Original Fables, by a Lady, *wood-cuts*, 1810—Another edition, *Louth*, 1812—Another edition, *ib.* 1815   3 vol.
2064 ORLEANS (DUCHESS OF) Life and Letters   *Bath, n. d.*
2065 ORLEBAR (MRS) Cinderella, a Fairy Tale, in Verse   *Nottingham*, 1848
2066 OPNE (CAROLINE F) Sweet Auburn and Mount Auburn, with other Poems   *Cambridge, (in America)* 1844
2067 Orphanhood, Free Will Offerings to the Fatherless, *wood-cut illustrations*   4to n d
2068 OSGOOD (FRANCES SARGENT) Wreath of Wild Flowers from New England   1838
2069 —— Poems, *plates*, presentation copy, with inscription in the *autograph of the Poetess*   *New York*, 1846
2070 —— Poems, *Illustrated edition*   *Philadelphia*, 1850
2071 OSSOLI (MARGARET FULLER) Life Without and Life Within, or, Reviews, Narratives, Essays, and Poems, *portrait*, *Boston, (in America)* 1859—Summer on the Lakes, 1861—Out-croppings, being Selections of California verse, *San Francisco*, 1866   3 vol
2072 Ovid's Epistles, translated by several hands, (with a paraphrase on the Epistle of Œnone to Paris, by Mrs A BEHN), *plates*   1688
2073 OWEN (ELLEN) *late Culley* Poems 1856—OWEN (IZABEL BERNARD) Poems, 1857, *second edition*, 1858—OWEN (JANE FRASER) Poems and Songs, 1862—Our Little Ones in Heaven, 1858   5 vol.
2074 P (L E) Here a Little and There a Little, with Prayers and Hymns, (*Norwich*, 1851)—P (M) Poems, *Leeds*, 1833—P (M A.) Sacred and Miscellaneous Poetry, 1843   3 vol
2075 P (S S) Poems to various Literary Characters, *privately printed*   *Weymouth*, 1827
2076 PACK (ELIZABETH) *of Thrapston*, Jesus Christ, a Pattern of Religious Virtue   *Oundle*, 1822
2077 Pains of Hope, and other Poems, 1817—Extracts from the Diary of Ann Palmer, *Exeter*, 1839—Another edition, *ib* 1850—PALMER (GEORGIANA MARIE) Miscellaneous Poems, *Liverpool*, 1844—Parry (J D) Guide to Woburn Abbey, *with verses by the Duchess of Devonshire*, *Woburn*, 1831   5 vol.
2078 PARDOE (JULIA) Traits and Traditions of Portugal 2 vol. 1834
2079 —— City of the Sultan, and Domestic Manners of the Turks in 1836, 2 vol. *plates*   1837
2080 —— The River and the Desert, or Recollections of the Rhone and the Chartreuse, 2 vol *plates*, 1838—The Plague, from the Italian of Sorelli, *portrait inserted*, 1834   3 vol.

2081 PARKER (ANNE) Fables and Moral Maxims, *cuts*, 1835—
The same, *second edition, cuts,* 1841—PARKER (ELIZABETH) Poems, *third edition,* 1851   3 vol.

2082 PARKER (SARAH) *the " Irish Girl,"* Opening of the Sixth
Seal, and other Poems, *Ayr,* 1846 — Miscellaneous
Poems, *second edition, Glasgow,* 1856   2 vol

2083 PARKES (BESSIE RAYNER) Poems, 1852—Summer Sketches,
and other Poems, 1854—Poems, *second edition,* 1855—
Gabriel, 1856—Ballads and Songs, 1863   5 vol.

2084 PARKINSON (MRS MARY) Giles Witherne, 1859—Parnassian
Garland, 1797—PARP (EMMA) Thoughts of Peace for
the Christian Sufferer, *seven editions,* 1840-57—
Memoirs of Mary and Hephzibah Parris, and a Memoir
of Miriam Parris, by their Sister, 1858—PARPOTT
(MARIANNE) Rough Rhymes for Farmer's Boys, 1847—
The same, *third edition,* 1858—Rough Rhymes for
Country Girls, 1854—Bible Numbers, 1848   14 vol

2085 PARMELLE (HELEN L) Poems, Religious and Miscellaneous
     New York, 1863

2086 PARMINTER (ANNE) Votive Wreath and other Poems
     printed for the Authoress, 1826

2087 PARSONS (ELIZABETH MARY) End of the Pilgrimage, and
other Poems, 1859—PARSONS (MRS LETITIA) Hymns
and Poems, 1852—Routine a Tale of the Goodwin
Sands, 1861—Parting Gift for an Emigrant Friend,
1854—Parting Gift to a Christian Friend, *five editions,*
1833-43   9 vol

2088 PARSONS (MARY) Cries out of the Depths, Poems on Sacred
Subjects   1819

2089 PARSONS (MRS.) Intrigues of a Morning   1792

2090 PARSONS (MRS LETITIA) of *Hawkhurst,* Verses, Hymns and
Poems, 1806—Second book, *Cranbrook,* 1808 *in* 1 vol

2091 —— The same, *another edition, both parts Tonbridge,* 1815

2092 PASSINGHAM (L) Wild Notes, 1857—Jaqueline Pascal, or
Convent Life at Port Royal, 1854—Patience in Tribulation a Sketch of Jessie ——, 1859—St Patrick's
Catholic Hymn Book, *Glasgow,* 1864 — PATSTON
(CAROLINE) Thoughts on the Crystal Palace, *Peterborough,* 1854   5 vol

2093 Patrick (Bp) Poems and Translations, *with two pages of
verses, in manuscript, written by a Gardener's Daughter,
of Stratford, upon the late Rebellion,* 1746   1719

2094 PATRICKSON (MARGARET) Miscellaneous Poems, 2 vol. in 1
     1806

2095 PATULLO (MARGARET) *of Perth,* Christian Psalter, a new
Version of the Psalms of David, *very scarce, the entire
impression having been bought up and destroyed*
     Edinb. 1828

2096 Peacy (Mrs M. S.) *of Newfoundland*, Convict Ship, and other Poems *Greenock*, 1850
2097 Pearch (G) Collection of Poems, 4 vol. 1770—Peacock (Lucy) Tales and Dramas, 2 vol *frontispieces, Brentford*, 1815—Peace, a Poem, by Geraldine, 1856 7 *vol.*
2098 Pearson (Agnes) Illustrious Exile of Albion, in three cantos, *frontispiece* 1815
2099 Pearson (Ann) *daughter of William Henderson, Hostman, Newcastle-upon-Tyne*, Miscellaneous Pieces, *Hexham*, 1831—Grateful Remembrance in Letters of Advice to an absent niece, *ib* 1816, *very scarce in* 1 *vol.*
2100 Pearson (Esther) Buds of Hope: Poetical Remains, with Memoir, by J Cooper, Wattisham, Suffolk, *with illustrations Ipswich*, 1855
2101 Pearson (Jane) Sketches of Piety *York*, 1817
2102 Pearson (S) Poems dedicated to the Countess Fitzwilliam 4to. *Sheffield*, 1790
2103 Piat (Anne) Poems, *eight separate pieces, with two autograph Notes of the Poetess in* 1 *vol. Edinb* 1853-61
2104 Peep (A) at the Esquimaux, or Scenes on the Ice, to which is annexed a Polar Pastoral, by a Lady, 10 *coloured plates*, 1825, *and three other editions*, 1825-33 4 *vol.*
2105 Peile (Mrs. H) Tablet of Juvenile Memory, and other Poems 1836
2106 Peirson (Lydia Jane) Forest Leaves *Philadelphia*, 1845
2107 —— Forest Minstrel, edited by Rev B S Schneck *ib* 1846
2108 Pelayo or, The Cavern of Covadonga, a Romance, by Isabel *New York*, 1836
2109 Pelham (Mary) Essays, Moral and Religious, *frontispiece*, 1807—Jingles, or Rhymes for Children, 1811—Pennington (Maryne) Poems, *Hertford*, 1847—The Pensée, by a young Lady, 1830 4 vol
2110 Pembroke (Mary Countess of) *formerly Sidney*, Antonius, a Tragedy from the French of R Garnier, *wanting the first portion, and imperfect at the end* 4to 1592
2111 —— Tragedie of Antonie, done into Englishe, *W Ponsonby*, 1595—Daniel (S) Delia and Rosamond, augmented and Cleopatra, *second edition of Delia, and first edition of Cleopatra, wants a portion of one leaf, printed for Simon Waterson*, 1594, of excessive rarity, *old russia, from the Library of Major Pearson, and purchased by Mr. Stainforth, in the Earl of Charlemont's Sale, for* £39 *in* 1 *vol.*
2112 —— Psalms, in Verse, *portraits*, 1823—Our Saviour's Passion, 1862—Works, edited by R. G. Barnwell, *port.* 1865 3 *vol.*

2113 PENNINGTON (Mrs) Letters, amongst which are interspers'd the Adventures of Alphonso, after the Destruction of Lisbon, 4 vol. 1766-7
2114 PENNY (ANNE) Anningait and Ajutt, a Greenland Tale, versified, 1761—Select Poems from Gesner's Pastorals, 1762 *4to in 1 vol*
2115 —— Poems, with a Dramatic Entertainment, *vignettes* 4to. 1771
2116 —— The same, another edition, *vignette on the title-page* 4to 1780
2117 PENNYMAN (LADY MARGARET) Miscellanies, in prose and verse, *portrait* *E Curll*, 1740
2118 PEPYS (LADY CHARLOTTE MARIA) Diary and Houres of the Ladye Adolie, a faythfulle childe, 1552
russia, top edges gilt 4to 1853
2119 —— Echoes from many minds, a collection of Sacred Poetry, 1857 — PERKINS (MISS STEELE) Flora and Pomona's Fete, *Tamworth, n d* — PERRING (MRS) Poems, 1851—PERRY (SARAH SUSANNAH) Memorials, 1857 *4 vol.*
2120 PERRING (MRS) Domestic Hours, Poems *Leeds*, 1811
2121 PERROTT (MRS. FRANCES) *of Newcastle*, Collection of Poems and Songs *Newcastle-upon-Tyne, n. d.*
2122 Peruvian (The) a Comic Opera, by a Lady, 1786—The same, *second edition*, 1786—*Another edition, Dublin*, 1789 *3 vol*
2123 PFEIFFER (MRS) Margaret, or the Motherless, 1861—PHELPS (MRS) Good Aunt, *view of North Weston House, Oxfordshire*, 1811 — The Suttee, and other Poems, *Thame*, (1831) *3 vol*
2124 PHILIPPART (MRS JOHN) Muscovy, a Poem 1813
2125 PHILIPPS (JANETTA) Poems, *blue morocco, g e.* *Oxford*, 1811
2126 PHILIPS (KATHARINE) Pompey, a Tragedy, from the French of Corneille 4to 1663
2127 —— Poems, *two portraits inserted* 1664
2128 —— Poems, to which is added M. Corneille's Pompey and Horace, with other Translations, *portrait by Faithorne, a mezzotinto by Beckett, and another portrait inserted* *folio* 1667
2129 —— The same, another edition, *portrait by Faithorne* *folio* 1669
2130 —— The same, another edition, *portrait by Faithorne, with autograph and book-plate of the Hon James Bertie, second son to James Earl of Abingdon* *folio* 1678
2131 —— The same, another edition, *portrait* 1710
2132 —— Collection of Divine Hymns and Poems, by Mrs K Philips, Philomela (Mrs. Rowe), and others 1709

2133 PHILLIPS (CATHARINE) Happy King, a Sacred Poem *privately printed, no place nor printer's name* 1794

*** At the commencement is inserted a Prayer for Wisdom, by Catherine Payton of Dudley, afterwards Phillips.

2134 —— Memoirs of her Life and Epistles 1797
2135 PHILLIPS (CHARLOTTE) Shower of Pearls *Peterborough*, 1858
2136 PHILLIPS (JOAN) Female Poems on several Occasions, written by Ephelia, *portrait* 1679
2137 —— The same, *second edition, no portrait* 1680
2138 PHILLIPSON (CAROLINE GIFFARD) Lonely Hours *two copies, portrait*, 1856—Song to the Westminster Owl, 1856—Eva, a Romance in Rhyme, 1857—Songs on Italy, 1862 *5 vol*
2139 PHILLOTT (ALICIA CATHERINE) Rectory Garden and other Poems 1866
2140 Philomela's Journal of London in different Poems, published at the desire of several Ladies and Gentlemen in North Britain, *very scarce, but imperfect at the end* 1757
2141 PHIPPS (PIMPA ANNA) Memorials of Clutha or, Pencillings on the Clyde, 12 *plates* 1842
2142 PIATT (John James and SARAH M BRYAN) Nests at Washington and other Poems *New York*, 1864
2143 PICKERING (AMELIA) Sorrows of Werter, a Poem *4to* 1788
2144 PICKERING (GILES) Charades for Acting, 1843—Proverbs for Acting, *with the Solutions printed on a single leaf*, 1844—Picture Poems, by Gertrude, *Glasgow*, 1865—The Pitt Club the Triennial Commemoration, with lines by a Young Lady sixteen years of age, 1814—PHIPSON (REBECCA) Kindness to Animals, 1862 *5 vol.*
2145 PICKERING (MRS) Poems and Poetical Sketches, by the Author and Translator of Philoton Ardene
Birmingham (1794)
2146 —— Poems, *another copy, with curious characteristic notes by Dr Parr* *ib* (1794)
2147 PICKERSGILL (MRS) Tales of the Harem 1827
2148 PIERCE (ELIZABETH) Village Pencillings in Prose and Verse, *plate of West Ashby*, 1842—Frank Merivale, or Dissolving Views from the Glass of Time, 1845—PILKINGTON (MARY) Poems, 1851 *3 vol*
2149 PIERS (LADY SARAH) George for Britain, a Poem 1716
2150 PILKINGTON (MRS LÆTITIA) Memoirs and Poems, 2 vol. 1748-9
2151 —— The same, *another edition*, 3 vol. 1749-54
2152 —— The same, *another edition*, 3 vol *Dublin*, 1776
2153 —— Jests or Cabinet of Wit and Humour, *front* 1764
2154 PILKINGTON (MRS. M.) Miscellaneous Poems, 2 vol. in 1, 1796

2155 PILKINGTON (Mrs. M.) Poems, *second edition*, 2 vol. 1799
2156 —— Obedience Rewarded and Prejudice Conquered, or History of Mortimer Lascells, *frontispiece*, 1797—Mentorial Tales, *front.* 1802—Memoirs of Female Characters, *portraits*, 1804—Poems, *portrait, with autograph Letter of the Poetess inserted*, 1811   4 vol.
2157 PINCHARD (Mrs) Dramatic Dialogues, 2 vol. *plates*   1792
2158 PINCKNEY (MARIA) Essays, Religious, Moral, Dramatic, and Poetical   *Charleston*, 1818
2159 PINKNEY (JANE VAUGHAN) Patchwork Poems, and Antediluvian Rhymes   1855
2160 PINNA Y RUIZ (DONNA TERESA) of Murcia, Heroic Epistle to Richard Twiss, *frontispiece, Dublin*, 1776 — Twiss (R.) Answer to the preceding, *ib* 1776 — Seventeen Hundred and Seventy Seven, or a Picture of the Manners and Character of the Age, *ib* 1777   *in one vol.*
2161 PIOZZI (HESTER LYNCH) *formerly Thrale*   Florence Miscellany, consisting of Poems by Mrs Piozzi, Bertie Greatheed, Robert Merry, and William Parsons
     PRIVATELY PRINTED   *Florence*, 1785
2162 —— Letters to Dr. Samuel Johnson, and Poems, 2 vol 1788
2163 —— Poetry of the World, 1788—British Album, containing the Poems of Della Crusca, Anna Matilda, &c. 2 vol in 1, *portraits*, 1790—The same, *another copy*, 2 vol. 1790 — The same, *another edition*, 2 vol. in 1, 1790—The same, *another edition, Dublin*, 1790—The same, *another edition*, 2 vol 1792—The same, *first American Edition, Boston*, 1793   9 vol.
2164 —— Piozziana· or Recollections of the late Mrs Piozzi, with Remarks by Rev. W. Maginn, 1833—Love Letters to W. A. Conway, 1843   2 vol.
2165 —— Autobiography, Letters and Literary Remains, 2 vol. *portrait and plate*   1861
2166 PIX (MRS MARY) Ibrahim the Thirteenth Emperour of the Turks, a Tragedy   4to   1696
2167 —— Spanish Wives, a Farce   4to.   1696
2168 —— Innocent Mistress, a Comedy   4to   1697
2169 —— Queen Catharine· or, the Ruines of Love, a Tragedy   4to   1698
2170 —— Deceiver Deceived, a Comedy, *wants part of last leaf*, 1698—Beau Defeated, or Lucky Younger Brother, a Comedy, *last page in manuscript*, n d.—False Friend, *wants the Epilogue*, 1702   4to. 3 vol.
2171 —— False Friend, or Fate of Disobedience, a Tragedy   4to.   1699
2172 —— Double Distress, a Tragedy   4to   1701
2173 —— Czar of Muscovy, a Tragedy   4to.   1701
2174 —— False Friend, a Comedy   4to.   1702

2175 Pix (Mrs. Mary) Violenta, or the Rewards of Virtue, from Boccace 1704
2176 —— Conquest of Spain, a Tragedy 4to. 1705
2177 —— Different Widows; or, Intrigue All-A-Mode, a Comedy 4to. n. d.
2178 —— Adventures in Madrid, a Comedy 4to (1709)
2179 Pizey (Susanna) *of Bury St Edmunds*, Poems *printed for the Authoress*, 1817
2180 Planché (Mrs J. R.) Welsh Girl, 1834, and other Plays by the same, in one vol.; and six other volumes of Plays 7 vol.
2181 Plato (Ann) *a Negress*, Essays and Miscellaneous Pieces in Prose and Poetry *Hartford, printed for the Author*, 1841
2182 Pleasants (Miss Julia) and Thomas Bibb Bradley, Apheila and other Poems *New York*, 1854
2183 Plomley (Mary Ann) Rural Lays, *front Cranbrook*, 1826
2184 Plowden (Mrs F.) Virginia, an Opera 1800
2185 Plumptre (Anne) Natural Son, a Play from the German of Kotzebue, 1798 — Other Editions and Plays from the German of Kotzebue 5 vol
2186 —— Count of Burgundy, a Play from the German of Kotzebue, 1798 — Three other Editions, 1798-99 4 vol.
2187 —— Letters from various parts of the Continent, from the German of Frederick Matthisson 1799
2188 —— Pizarro; the Spaniards in Peru, or Death of Rolla, a Tragedy, from the German of Kotzebue, *four editions*, 1799 — La Peyrouse, a Drama, from the German of Kotzebue, *Dublin*, 1799 — Virgin of the Sun, a Play, *three editions*, 1799 — Force of Calumny, a Play, *Dublin*, 1799 9 vol
2189 —— Sketch of the Life and Literary Career of Kotzebue, with Tour to Paris in 1790, *portrait* 1800
2190 Plumptre (Bell) Foresters, a Play, from the German of W A Iffland 1799
2191 Plunkett (Anna H.) Beatrice of Ferrara, a Tragic Drama, 1837
2192 Pocket Magazine of Classic and Polite Literature, *plates and woodcuts illustrative of the Works of Scott, Campbell, and Shakspeare*, vol II, III, and IV, *new series* 1825-6
2193 Poem sacred to the Immortal Memory of Queen Anne, by a Lady of Quality, *very scarce* 1715
2194 Poems [*not published*] *Bradbury and Evans, printers, n d.*
2195 Poems *printed by Frank Dutton*, 1824
2196 Poems *Derby, printed in aid of the funds for rebuilding the Parish Church of Saint Alkmund*, 1848

2197 Poems addressed to several persons, by a Lady residing in Newcastle *Newcastle, printed for the Authoress,* 1829
2198 Poems and Fugitive Pieces, by Eliza, *frontispiece* 1796
2199 Poems and Hymns, by a Lady *Dublin,* 1816
2200 Poems and Translations, by a Lady, *privately printed* 1811
2201 Poems by a Lady, *frontispiece after Cipriani, presentation copy from the Poetess to Germain Lavie, Esq* 4to. 1781
2202 Poems by a Lady 1798
2203 Poems by a Lady 1818
2204 Poems by a Lady [*price 7 Rupees*] *Calcutta,* 1828
2205 Poems by a Lady, *second edition* *Carlisle,* 1851
2206 Poems by Eminent Ladies, 2 vol. 1755
2207 Poems by Eminent Ladies, 2 vol. *Dublin,* 1756-7
2208 Poems by Eminent Ladies, 2 vol. *printed by W Stafford, n.d.*
2209 Poems by Firola *Belfast,* 1851
2210 Poems by Fritz and Liolett 1849
2211 Poems by Lily *Dorking,* (1860)
2212 Poems by Rose and De Rupe *Belfast,* 1856
2213 Poems by Susanna 4to. 1789
2214 Poems by Three Sisters 1864
2215 Poems, chiefly Dramatic, edited by Thomas Hill-Lowe Dean of Exeter *Pickering,* 1840
2216 Poems founded on the Events of the War in the Peninsula, by the Wife of an Officer, *privately printed* *Hythe,* 1819
2217 Poems, Moral and Entertaining, by a Lady, *Doncaster,* 1808
2218 Poems of Anna Maria [*price one Gold Mohur*] or 32s. *Calcutta,* 1793
2219 Poems on Slavery, by Longfellow, Whittier, Southey, H. B. Stowe, &c 1853
2220 Poems on various Subjects, by a Lady *printed for the Author,* 1798
2221 Poems on various Subjects, by a Young Lady *Margate* (1819)
2222 Poems Original and Select, by a Lady 1815
2223 Poems suggested by a Journey to Italy, by a Lady *privately printed* *Maidstone,* 1847
2224 Poetical Effusions, by a Young Lady *Bath,* 1821
2225 ——— The same, *second edition* *ib.* 1824
2226 Poetical Epistle from Mrs. Elizabeth Williams, with Apology in her particular Case 4to. 1783
2227 Poetical Keepsake, containing Poems of Eliza Cook, Mrs. Hemans, L. E. L. &c *frontispiece, n.d*—Poetical Picture of America, by a Lady, 1809—Poetic Gleanings, by a Governess, *front* 1827—Poetic Melodies, by Aunt Charlotte, *front n.d*—Poetic Thoughts, by a Factory Girl, *Derby,* 1853—Poetic Scraps, *mounted in a volume,* 1865, &c. 6 *vol.*

2228 Poetical Register and Repository of Fugitive Poetry for 1801-11, 8 vol. 1815, &c.

2229 Poetical Scrap Book, a very curious and unique Volume of Effusions, printed on single leaves, mostly of modern date, but including a few old pieces, including an Elegy on Dr. John Gill, 1771; Elegy on the Death of the Duke of Cumberland, 1765—The Neuter or a Modest Satire on the Poets of the Age, by a Lady, 1733—On the Death of Lady Oxenden, by Mrs. RANDOLPH, n d—Divine Poem, by MARY WELLS, *in 24 four-line stanzas, arranged in alphabetical order according to the first letter of each*, 1690, &c &c. *folio*

2230 Poetical Thoughts. the Offspring and Alleviation of Solitary Hours, *russia, with joints, g e* Holt, 1826

2231 Poetic Fugitives, by a Young Lady, 1827—Poetic Prism, edited by R N Greville, *Edinb* 1818—Poetry for Home and Day Schools, by a Lady, n. d.—Poetry of Flowers, 1841—Poetry without Fiction, by a Mother, 1823 5 vol

2232 Poetic Works of a Weird, *woodcut vignettes, Newcastle*, 1827

2233 Poetry and Prose, a collection of original compositions, edited by Rev. J Boyle
privately printed 4to Edinb. 1844

2234 Poets of the West, a selection of favourite American Poems, with Memoirs of their Authors, *illustrated by Darley and others* 4to. 1859

2235 POINTON (MRS PRISCILLA) *of Lichfield*, Poems *very scarce* Birmingham, 1770

2236 POLGLASE (ANN CATO.) Shipwreck, a Tale of Arabia, 1827

2237 Political Priest. or Propagation with a Vengeance, a Satire by a Married Woman 4to 1781

2238 PONSONBY (CATHERINE) Lays of the Lakes, *Edinb* 1850—Minstrel's Home Leaving, *ib n d*—PONSONBY (EMILY) Mary Gray, and other Tales, 1852—POLLEY (ESTHER) God's Love to his Saints, 1849—Reed (I) Sermon on the Death of Mrs CHARLOTTE POPE, with Verses by her, 1819 5 vol.

2239 Pope (A) Additions to his Works, containing many Poems of cotemporary Writers, 2 vol *portrait inserted* 1776

2240 Porch and Academy opened, or Epictetus's Manual and Cebes's Table, in English Verse, by a Lady 1707

2241 Portal (Ab) Poems containing Cynthia, an Elegy, written by a Lady, *vignette on the title page*
thick paper *printed for the author*, 1781

2242 PORTER (ANNA MARIA) Original Poems on various subjects, by a Young Lady Eighteen Years of Age 4to. n. d.

2243 PORTER (ANNA MARIA) Ballad Romances, and other Poems, *frontispiece, two portraits inserted*, 1811—The same, another edition, *Philadelphia*, 1816—Don Sebastian, an Historical Romance, *plate*, 1838—Lake of Killarney, a Novel, *plates*, 1839   4 vol.

2244 Portraits of Female Poets, *a very interesting and unique collection, 370 in number, some very scarce, including a fine impression of the whole-length figure of the Duchess of Newcastle by Van Schuppen, a drawing of the Newcastle Family, private plates, proofs, &c and several interesting autograph letters*, in 3 large vol half morocco   folio

2245 POSTLETHWAITE (MRS) Home Songs and School Songs *privately printed*   n d

2246 Posy for Youth, *sixth edition*   Birmingham, 1833

2247 POTTER (M. A) Catholic Hymns, 1847—POTTS (ANNA H) Sketches of Character, *Camb* 1849—Simple Poems, *ib* 1852   3 vol

2248 POTTER (MISS) Poetry of Nature, comprising a selection of the most sublime and beautiful Apostrophes, Histories, Songs, Elegies, &c from the Works of the Caledonian Bards   4to. 1789

2249 —— The same, another copy, *with an additional list of subscribers*   4to   n d

2250 POTTS (ETHELINDA MARGARETTA) Moonshine, 2 vol   1814

2251 —— The same, *second edition*, 5 vol. *portraits and plates*   1832-6

2252 —— Visit to Bonaparte in Plymouth Sound, with another Piece descriptive of Stoke   Dock, 1815

2253 POULTER (LOUISA FRANCES) Imagination, *with lines in manuscript, 3½ pages, to Lady Charlotte Bury*   1820

2254 —— The same, another edition, with other Poems   1841

2255 POWELL (ANNE) Clifton and other Pieces, *Bristol*, 1821—POWER (MARGUERITE A) Virginia's Hand, 1860—POYNDER (MRS M) Pensive Lyrics, 1866   3 vol.

2256 POYNTZ (ANNE B) Je ne scai quoi a Collection of Letters, Odes, &c. *the dedication printed in red*   1769

2257 Praise of London, a Poem   Leicester, 1804

2258 PRATT (ANNE) Flowers and their Associations, *frontispiece*, 1840—PRATT (MRS HENRY F A) *late Harriet Agatha Lethbridge*, Poems, 1843—PRENTICE (EMILY) Dew Drops for Spring Flowers, *n. d.*—PRESCOTT (HENRIETTA) Poems, written in Newfoundland, 1839   4 vol.

2259 PRICE (EMMA) Moral Muse, 1830—The same, *second edition*, 1837—Sacred Harp, 1844—PRICHARD (MRS) Siege of Pembroke, 1851—PRIDEAUX (MRS. FREDERICK) Claudia, 1865   5 vol.

2260 Preston (William) Posthumous Poems (with Verses to his Memory by Miss Stewart), *portrait*   Dublin, 1809
2261 Primrose (Lady Diana) Chaine of Pearle or, A Memoriall of the peerles Graces and Heroick Vertues of Queene Elizabeth, of Glorious Memory
     excessively rare, *orange morocco, g e, from Mr Heber's Library*   4to   1630
2262 Prince (Mrs) Sacred Lays from a Baxterian Harp, Leominster, n d—Primrose Hill, the Queen's Jubilee, and other Metrical Effusions, 1838—Memoir of W Butler, with Stanzas by Miss Maria Prior, *portrait*, 1826   3 vol
2263 Prisoner (The) or Nature's Complaint to Justice, a Poem by a Lady in Confinement   4to   1758
2264 Procter (Adelaide Anne) Legends and Lyrics, 1858—Another edition, *morocco, g e* 1861—Another edition, 1864—Legends and Lyrics, 2nd vol 1861   4 vol
2265 —— Legends and Lyrics, 2 vol *morocco, g. e.*   1860-1
2266 —— The same, 2 vol *morocco, g e*   1863
2267 —— The same, *illustrated edition*   4to   1866
2268 —— Victoria Regia contributions in Poetry and Prose, *gilt cloth*, 1861—Chaplet of Verses, *two editions*, 1861-2   3 vol
2269 Proctor (Edna Dean) Poems   New York, 1866
2270 Protestant Annual, 1811, edited by Charlotte Elizabeth, *plates*, 1811—Protestant Lays, by a Lady, 1850—Protestant Remembrancer, *two copies*, 1851   4 vol
2271 Prowse (Anne) Of the Markes of the Children of God, translated from the French of J. Taffin
     rare   *by T L for Thomas Man*, 1608
2272 Prowse (Mrs I S) Poems, 1830—Poems by a Father and Daughter (Miss Plowett), 1815—Prodigal's Return, by a Lady, 1852—Psalms and Hymns for Female Orphans, 1801—Psalms and Hymns from Dr. Watts and others, 1826   5 vol
2273 Psalms, selected by Rev G H Drummond, 1795—Hymns and Psalms (including one by the Hon. Martha Venables Vernon), n d   in one vol
2274 Pugh (Christiana E) Exile and other Poems, 1851—Public Characters of 1805, *portraits*, 1805—Christmas Plays for Children, by Theresa Pulszky, *coloured illustrations*, 1858   3 vol
2275 Pullen (Mrs) Book of Riddles, 1855—Two other editions (1855)—Putnam (M L) Bondmaid, translated from the Swedish, 1844—Pyer (Kate) Peace Stories, n d—Wild Flowers, 1844—Dialogues for Recitation, 1861—Touching Incidents, 1857   8 vol
2276 Pye (Mrs Hampden) Poems, by a Lady   1771
2277 —— Poems, *second edition*   1772

2278 Pike (Sarah Leigh) Israel, a Juvenile Poem, by Serena, 2 vol. in 1, *Bath*, 1795—Triumph of Messiah, *Exeter*, 1812—Eighty Village Hymns, *Taunton*, 1832—Pye (Miss) Poems, n d—Pym (Edith E) Fairy Tales, 1860—Tales for my Grandchildren, 1861—Piper (Mary) Select Pieces *Edinb.* 1817—Hebrew Children, Poetic Illustrations of Biblical Character, *ib* 1858   8 vol.

2279 Quarles (Mrs Virginia) Poems, *New York*, 1861—Queen and her Ladies, by Jane Incognita, n d—Quiet Hours, by a Brother and Sister, *Abingdon*, 1853   3 vol

2280 Quigley (Catharine) Microscope, or Village Flies, with other Poems
    Monaghan, printed by Nathaniel Greacen, 1819

2281 R. (A) Select Contemplations and Meditations, Divine Poems, &c   1739

2282 —— The same, *second edition*   1761

2283 R (E) Poetical and other pieces, *Plymouth*, 1837—The same, another edition, *Bath*, n d—R. (M C) Fragments, original and translated, 1857—Radcliff (Ann) Poems, 1816—Another edition, 1845—Radcliffe (Mira M) Ina and other Poems, *Liverpool*, 1841   6 vol

2284 Radcliffe (Anne) Posthumous Works, comprising Gaston de Blondeville, St Alban's Abbey, with some Poetical pieces, and Memoir of the Authoress, 4 vol
half morocco   1826

2285 —— The same, another edition, 4 vol.   1833

2286 —— Poetical Works, 2 vol   1834

2287 Raine (Rosa) Queen's Isle, Chapters on the Isle of Wight, n d—The same, *second edition*, 1861—Florent Ecclesia, a Manual of Church Poesy, 1851—Verses for Church Schools, 1861   4 vol.

2288 Ramsay (Mrs C H) Translations of the Inferno and Purgatorio of Dante, in metre, 2 vol   1862

2289 Ramsay (Martha Laurens) *who died in Charleston, S C* Life, by D Ramsay   *Glasgow*, 1818

2290 Randolph (Mrs Charles) Chaplet of Pearls, Rhymes and Fragments of Ancient and Modern Verse, *beautifully illuminated*   4to 1852

2291 Rathbone (Hannah Mary) Selection from the Poets, *frontispiece*, 1810—Strawberry Girl, 1858—Niebelungen Treasure, a Tragedy, by Ernest Raupach, translated from the German, 1817—Rawlins (C. A) Famine in Ireland, 1847   4 vol

2292 Realities of Life, by a Country Parson's Daughter, *Bristol*, 1838—Recollections of Childhood, by Primogenita, *Canterbury*, 1810—Recollections of Youth, by a Young Lady of Manchester, 1838—Reculver (The) or Two Sisters of Thanet, 1855—Remembrancer (The) *plates*, 1830   6 vol.

2293 READ (HARRIETTE FANNING) Dramatic Poems
Boston (in America), 1818

2294 REDDEN (LAURA C.) Idyls of Battle and Poems of the Rebellion
New York, 1865

2295 REES (CHARLOTTE) Sermons, *with verses written at the age of 12*   *Bristol,* 1796

2296 REES (MARY ISABELLA IRWIN) Forest House and other Poems   1850

2297 REEVE (CLARA) Poems, *portrait inserted*   4to   1769

2298 REEVE (MARY ANNE) Lays from the West, *Oldham,* 1865—REEVE (MRS.) Flowers at Court, 1809—Holiday Annals, *Norwich, n. d.*—Christmas Trifles, *ib.* 1826—The same, another edition, *ib.* 1827   5 vol.

2299 REEVES (ELIZA) Poems on various subjects
4to   *printed for the author,* 1780

2300 Reflections on Spring, by a Lady   4to   *Lewes, n. d.*

2301 RENDALL (SOPHIA) Village Minstrel, or Simple Lays, 1808—RENNIE (ELIZA) Poems, 1828   2 vol.

2302 RENNEW (ANN) Pious and Holy Breathings, a Treatise of Choice and Precious Hymns
VERY RARE   *printed for and sold by the author,* 1711

   *** The first Hymns sung at the Church at Burwell were composed by this female poet, a blind maid, born at Empington, not far from Cambridge, formerly a member of the Congregational Church of Christ at Cottenham, but afterwards at Cambridge

2303 RENO (LYDIA M.) Early Buds   *Boston (in America),* 1853

2304 RENOU (SARAH) Temple of Truth, *Edinb.* 1821—Another edition, *with autograph of the Princess Elizabeth,* 1822—Ionian (The) or Woman in the Nineteenth Century, 3 vol. in 1, 1824   3 vol.

2305 REVELL (RACHEL) Winter Evening Pastimes, 1825—REVELL (S.) Five Worlds of Enjoyment and other Poems, *Sudbury,* 1847—Review of Home Enjoyments, by a Lady, 1838—Retrospection, a Poem, 1805   4 vol.

2306 RHOADS (Mrs. RACHEL) Poems, a series of Tales in verse
Philadelphia, 1863

2307 RHODES (HENRIETTA) Poems and Miscellaneous Essays
Brentford, 1814

2308 Rhymes without Reason with Reasons for Rhyming, *plates,* 4to, 1823—Rhymes for my Children, by a Mother, 1835—Second edition, 1840—Rhymes for the Nursery, 1818—Rhyming River Geography, *Tenby, n. d.*—Memoir of Mrs. P. E. Richards, 1853   6 vol.

2309 RIBBANS (REBECCA) Lavenham Church, a Poem, *plate inserted*   4to.   *Ipswich,* 1822

2310 ——— Effusions of Genius, *frontispiece*   *ib.* 1829

2311 RICHARDSON (CHARLOTTE) Poems, with Memoir by Catharine Cappe, *York*, 1806—The same, *second and third editions, ib.* 1806-9—Poems, vol. II, *ib* 1809   3 vol

2312 RICHARDSON (CHARLOTTE CAROLINE) Waterloo, a Poem, *n d.*—Isaac and Rebecca, *plates*, 1817—Harvest, with other Poetical Pieces, *plate*, 1818—Ludolph, 1823   4 *vol*

2313 RICHARDSON (C. E. [*Mrs G G*]) Poems, *Dumfries*, 1828—The same, *second and third editions, ib* 1828-9—Poems, second series, 1834   4 vol

2314 RICHARDSON (ELIZABETH) *formerly Beaumont, then Ashburnham*, A Ladies Legacie to her Daughters, composed of Prayers and Meditations [at the end my owne Prayer in Meeter, or to be sung as a Hymne], &c
VERY RARE, *old blue morocco, with initials H B. on the sides, intended as a present to her brother Sir Henry Beaumont (who died in 1646), with manuscript notes and corrections in the autograph of the authoress*
                       by Tho Harper, 1645

2315 RICHARDSON (ELIZABETH) *formerly " Betty Smales,"* Poems, *two copies*, 1846—RICHARDSON (MARGARET) Buds of Hope, a collection of Miscellaneous Poems, 1839—RICHARDSON (MARIAN) Welcome to Alexandra, &c 1863—RICHARDSON (MARIAN) *formerly Straker*, Talk of the Household, 1865   5 vol

2316 RICHARDSON (SARAH) Poems for the Instruction of Youth, 1808—Ethelred, a Legendary Drama, *n d*—The same, *second edition, n d*—Gertrude, a Tragic Drama, *n d*   4 vol

2317 Rich Old Bachelor: a Domestic Tale, in the style of Dr Syntax, by a Lady   *Canterbury*, 1824

2318 RICHTER (Mrs H W) Nun, and other Poems   *Hull*, 1811

2319 RICKEY (ANNA S) Forest Flowers of the West
portrait   *Philadelphia*, 1851

2320 RICORD (MRS ELIZABETH) Zamba, or the Insurrection, a Dramatic Poem   *Cambridge (in America)*, 1842

2321 RIDDELL (MARIA) Metrical Miscellany, 1802—Second edition, 1803   2 vol

2322 Riego, Romancero, with Translations, &c. *portraits* 1842 6

2323 RILEY (ANNA TERMINIA) Poetical Clavis, for the use of her pupils at Albion House, Epsom, 1815—RIMMERT (JANE) Recollections and Poems, 1825—RITCHIE (MARIA KATE) Love and Hatred, and other Poems, *Edinb* 1865   3 vol

2324 RITSON (ANN) Poetical Chain, 1811—Classical Enigmas, *woodcuts*, 1811—The same, *a new edition*, 1815—Exercises for the Memory, new Improving Enigmas, 1814—Another edition, *front.* 1818   5 vol.

2325 ROBE (J.) Fatal Legacy, a Tragedy, *dedicated to T. Coke, of Norfolk*   - 1723

2326 ROBERTS (ELIZABETH PIDDOCKE) Miscellaneous Poems
Birmingham, 1845
2327 ROBERTS (ELLEN) Heathen Fables in Christian Verse, 1860
—Verses by the Wayside, 1864—ROBERTS (HARRIET
ALICIA) Forest Thoughts, 2 vol. *fronts.* 1852—ROBERTS
(L J) Thou God seest me, *Philadelphia*, 1861—
ROBERTS (M. A.) Poems, 1830 6 vol.
2328 ROBERTS (EMMA) Tancred, a Tale, 1819—The same, *second
edition*, 1820—Conrad and the Kinsmen of Naples, 1821
—Oriental Scenes, Dramatic Sketches and Tales, *Calcutta*, 1830—The same, *another edition, with autograph
letter of the authoress inserted*, 1832 5 vol.
2329 ROBERTS (MARGARET) Duty, a Novel interspersed with
Poetry, with Character, by MRS OPIE, 3 vol. in 1, 1814
—Rose and Emily, *front* 1815—ROBERTS (MRS. MARTYN) Spiritual Creation, a Poem, *two copies*, 1843 4 vol
2330 ROBERTS (MARY) Conchologist's Companion, *coloured front
and woodcuts*, 1834—Ruins and Old Trees, *illustrations
by Gilbert*, n d—Flowers of the Matin and Even Song,
coloured plates, 1845 3 vol.
2331 ROBERTS (MISS) Dartmoor Legends, and other Poems
Exeter, 1857
2332 ROBERTS (MISS R) Malcolm, a Tragedy
printed for the author, 1779
2333 —— Albert, Edward and Laura, and the Hermit of Priestland, three Legendary Tales 4to 1783
2334 ROBERTSON (ELIZA F) *of Blackheath*, Life and Memoirs,
1802—Who are the Swindlers? (1801)—Dividends of
Immense Value, 1801—Consolatory Verses, with Life
of the Authoress, *front.* 1808 2 vol.
2335 ROBINSON (ELLEN) Poem on the Death of Rev T Spencer,
portrait, Liverpool, 1811—Funeral Discourse on the
same by W Roby, *Manchester*, 1811 *in one vol.*
2336 —— Tribute of Sorrow and Affection to the Memory of a
Beloved Son Drowned in the Mersey
woodcuts by T Robinson *Liverpool*, 1821
2337 ROBINSON (EMMA) Richelieu in Love, 1844—Revolt of
Flanders, 1848—Christmas at Old Court, 1864 3 vol.
2338 ROBINSON (MARIA ELIZABETH) Shrine of Bertha, a Novel,
2 vol in 1, 1796—Wild Wreath, *cuts*, 1804 2 vol
2339 ROBINSON (MRS MARY) Poems, *frontispiece, very scarce*, 1775
2340 —— Captivity, a Poem, and Celadon and Lydia, a Tale,
vignette on title-page, portrait inserted 4to 1777
2341 —— Illusions of Love, being the Amorous Correspondence between the Amiable Florizel and the Enchanting Perdita *n. d.*

2342 ROBINSON (Mrs. MARY) Poetical Epistle from Florizel to Perdita, with Perdita's Answer, *illustrated with portraits including one of Sarah Gurney, as the "Fair Quaker," published in 1718, Caricature Prints, &c.*
                4to   n d.

2343 —— Memoirs of Perdita, with Anecdotes *scarce and curious*   1784

2344 —— Monody to the Memory of Sir Joshua Reynolds, 1792 —Modern Manners (by Horace Juvenal), 1793—Sight, the Cavern of Woe, and Solitude, 1793—Monody to the Memory of the late Queen of France, 1793, &c.
               4to. *in one vol.*

2345 —— Poems, *new edition, portrait*   n. d.
2346 —— Poems, 2 vol. *portrait, blue morocco, g e*   1791-3
2347 —— Poetical Works, 3 vol *portrait*   1806
2348 —— The same, 3 vol *complete in one, portrait*   1824
2349 —— Beauties selected and arranged from her Poetical Works   1791
2350 —— Vancenza, or Dangers of Credulity, Fifth Edition, with additions, 2 vol in 1, *blue morocco, g e.*   1791
2351 —— Sicilian Lover, a Tragedy, *portrait inserted*   1796
2352 —— Sappho and Phaon, Sonnets and Anecdotes, *head of Sappho*   1796
2353 —— The same, *new edition*   1813
2354 —— Lyrical Tales, *portrait inserted*   Bristol, 1800
2355 —— Walsingham, or the Pupil of Nature, a Domestic Story, *second edition*, 4 vol   1805
2356 —— Memoirs, with some Posthumous Pieces, 4 vol   1801
2357 —— Memoirs, 2 vol *portrait*   1803
2358 —— Memoirs, *portrait*, 1826 — Life of Mrs Charlotte Charke, 1827   *in 1 vol.*

2359 ROBINSON (RACHEL) Belgium in 1830, with a Supplement, a Poem, *printed for the author*, 1831 — Geographical Opusculum for the Use of Schools, 1857   2 vol

2360 ROBINSON (S) *chambermaid at an inn in Bath*, Cælia's Revenge in answer to the Lady's Dressing Room by Dean Swift   1744

2361 Robinson (Thomas Romney) Juvenile Poems (with a pathetic address by Miss Jessy Stewart)   Belfast, 1806

2362 ROBY (MARY K) Story of a Household, and other Poems, *Camb* 1862—Children and their Thoughts, 1862—Original Poems for the Young, *second edition*, 1865
                 3 *vol.*

2363 ROE (A. M.) Poems on several occasions, 2 vol in 1
              Birmingham, 1807

2364 Rogers (Charles) Sacred Minstrel a Collection of Spiritual Songs, with Biographical Sketches of the Authors, *Edinb.* 1860—Festive Wreath, edited by John Bolton Rogerson, *frontispiece, Manchester*, 1842—Roman Vagaries, with Legend of a Wreck, by Cromleach, *Dublin*, 1851 3 vol.

2365 Rogers (Eliza) Poems, 1857—Thoughts on a Future State, occasioned by the Death of Mrs H. A. Rogers, by a Young Lady, *Birmingham*, 1795 — Another edition, *Bristol*, 1796—Life and Journal of Mrs H A Rogers, 1816—Rogers (Mary Eliza) My Vis-a-Vis, and other Poems, 1865—Rogerson (E A) Wife at Home, *Leeds*, 1864 6 vol

2366 Rolfe (Mrs Ann) *late Mrs Plumb*, Miscellaneous Poems for a Winter's Evening, *Colchester, n. d*—Choice and No Choice or, the First of May, 2 vol in 1, 1825—Rolls (Mrs Henry) Sacred Sketches, 1815 3 vol

2367 Rolls (Mrs Hs) Sacred Sketches, 1815—Moscow, 1816—Poetical Address to Lord Byron, 1816—Home of Love, 2 copies, 1817—Legends of the North, or the Feudal Christmas, 1825, *with autograph note of the poetess inserted* 3 vol.

2368 Rolt (Elizabeth) *of Chesham in Bucks*, Miscellaneous Poems, *very scarce* *printed for the author*, 1768

2369 Ross (A) Poems on several occasions *Glasgow*, 1791

2370 Rossetti (Christina) Goblin Market and other Poems, 1862—The same, *second edition*, 1865—Prince's Progress, and other Poems, 1866 3 vol

2371 Rossetti (Christina G) Verses dedicated to her Mother, *privately printed at the press of G Polidori, the maternal grandfather of the authoress* 1847

⁎ Bound in the same vol are The Wild Flowers of Dover and its Neighbourhood, *Dover*, 1853, and Day and Night Songs by William Allingham, 1854

2372 Romilly (Mrs) *formerly Mary C Hume*, Bridesmaid, Count Stephen, and other Poems, 1853—Rose Buds by Hairietti, *New York, n d*—Round Church of Little Maplestead, Essex (by a Lady), 1850 3 vol.

2373 Rouse (Miss T) *of Cley* Poems, *Holt*, 1810—Naomi, a Dramatic Poem, and other Pieces, *Norwich, n d* 2 vol.

2374 Rowan (Frederick) Meditations on Death and Eternity, translated from the German 1862

2375 Rowden (Frances Arabella) Poetical Introduction to the Study of Botany, *plates*
LARGE PAPER, *some additional engravings added, and 30 specimens of flowers, &c in their natural colours, beautifully drawn on the margins by Mrs Dallaway*
russia, g e. royal 8vo. 1801

2376 ROWDEN (FRANCES ARABELLA) Poetical Introduction to the Study of Botany, *second edition, plates*, 1812—Third edition, *plates, some inserted*, 1818 — Pleasures of Friendship, a Poem, 1810—The same, *second edition, plates*, 1811—The same, *third edition, front.* 1818
    5 *vol.*

2377 ROWE (ELIZABETH) Poems on several occasions, by Philomela   1696

2378 —— Divine Hymns and Poems, by Philomela and others   1704

2379 —— The same, *fourth edition, n. d*—Poems on several occasions, *port.* 1759—Another edition, *port.* 1767—Another edition, 1778; and 2 others   6 *vol.*

2380 —— Friendship in Death, in Twenty Letters from the Dead to the Living, to which are added Thoughts on Death, *second edition*, 1729—Letters in Prose and Verse, 1729—Letters Moral and Entertaining, Part Second, 1731—The same, *other editions*, 1733-45   8 *vol.*

2381 —— The same, *other editions*, 1746-76   14 *vol.*

2382 —— The same, *other editions*, 1750-1816   6 *vol.*

2383 —— The same, *other editions*, 1776-1808   15 *vol.*

2384 —— History of Joseph, a Poem, *frontispiece in eight compartments*   1736

2385 —— The same, *second edition, front.* 1737—Devout Exercises of the Heart, 1738—Woman not Inferior to Man, by Sophia, a Person of Quality, 1739—Other editions of the History of Joseph, 1741-59   7 *vol.*

2386 —— Devout Exercises of the Heart in Meditation and Soliloquy, Prayer and Praise, 1738—Devout Exercises, *other editions*, 1761-1814   11 *vol.*

2387 —— Miscellaneous Works in Prose and Verse, 2 vol. *ports.* 1739—Friendship in Death, *leaf defective*, 1740   3 *vol.*

2388 —— Miscellaneous Works, *second edition*, 2 vol. 1749—Third edition, 2 vol 1750—Fourth edition, 2 vol 1756—Fifth edition, 2 vol *port* 1772—Friendship in Death, 2 vol. 1774   10 *vol.*

2389 —— Works, 4 vol. (*Edinb*) 1796—Another edition, vol. I-III, *ib.* 1770   7 *vol.*

2390 —— Life, with Elegies on her Death, *portrait inserted*, 1769—History of Joseph, in prose by T Herbert, *portrait and plates, n d*—Devout Exercises of the Heart in blank verse, by Rev E Smyth, *front. n d*   3 *vol.*

2391 ROWE (HANNAH) Pindaric Poem, consisting of Versified Selections from the Revelation of St John
    4to. Rochester, 1789

2392 ROWLAND (CATHERINE ANN) Happy Hours : or, Affection's Whispers   *Bristol*, 1861

2393 ROWLES (CHARLOTTE AND MARTHA) Nadaber, a Tradition, with other Poems, 1829—Eastern Scenes in Early Ages, 1835—ROWSE (MRS) Outlines of English History in verse, 1808—The same, *three other editions*, 1811-33   6 vol.

2394 ROWSON (SUSAN) Miscellaneous Poems, *Boston (in America)*, 1804—Mentoria, or Young Lady's Friend, 2 vol in 1, *n. d*   2 vol.

2395 Royal Scottish Minstrelsy · a collection of Loyal Effusions on the Visit of George IV to Scotland, Aug 15, 1822   *Leith*, 1824

2396 RUMSEY (MARY C) Midsummer Night, or Shakespeare and the Fairies, from the German of L Tieck (edited by S. W Singer), *only a few copies printed for presents* 1854

2397 Russell.—Dewdrop and Glorio, or the Sleeping Beauty in the Wood, written and dedicated to Lord John Russell by G W R. Illustrated by the Honourable Mrs. Drummond Acted at Pembroke Lodge, December 23 and 28, 1858, *plates in outline*

    PRIVATELY PRINTED   4to. (1858)

2398 RUTHERFORD (ELIZA) Maternal Sketches, with other Poems, 1832—The Ruby, a Juvenile Forget me not, *two copies, plates, n d*—Prose and Poetry, with the History of Orenzo and Sarah, by Mrs Rueful, *Bristol* (1796)—RYAN (MRS) Poems, *Dublin*, 1816   5 vol.

2399 Ryan (Richard) Poetry and Poets a Collection of Anecdotes relative to the Poets of every age and nation, *3 vol portraits and cuts*   1826

2400 RYVES (ELIZA) Ode to Rev. Mr Mason, *n d*—Epistle to Lord John Cavendish, 1784— Dialogue in the Elysian Fields between Cæsar and Cato, 1784—Ode to Lord Melton, *privately printed*, 1787, *with corrections by the authoress, and a long autograph letter inserted*

    4to. *in one vol.*

2401 RYVES (ELIZABETH) Poems on several occasions

    printed for the author, 1777

2402 RYVES (F) *of Ryves Castle*, Cumbrian Legends, or Tales of other Times   *Edinb printed for the author*, 1812

2403 S (C A) Meditations for a Month, 1860—Poetry and Prose by Elizabeth [E F S.] *Doncaster*, 1821—S (E N) Sacred and Moral Poems, 1851—S. (E P) Young Cottager, and other Stories in Rhyme, 1865—S (F) Minor Poems, 1835   5 vol.

2404 S (F M) Songs in the Shade, *privately printed* 1844

2405 S (H J) Bunch of Violets, or Poetry of the Heart, 1860—S (J E) Hopes and Fears, 1843—Another edition, 1844—S. (S C) Sketches from Nature, *Chelmsford*, 1837   4 vol.

2406 S. (S S) Life and other Poems, 1814—Child's In-Door Companion, or Stories for Rainy Days, 1852   2 vol

2407 SABINE (Charles and Mary Elizabeth) Wild Thyme, 1857—Laurel and Flowers, by M E. J S. *Brighton*, 1846—Sabbath Bells, n d—Sacred Iris, *plates, n. d*—Sacred Meditations, written by a Female, 1824   5 vol.

2408 SAFFERY (Maria Grace) Poems on Sacred Subjects, 1834—Memoirs of Rev Joseph Horsey, with Elegy by Mrs Saffery, *Portsea*, 1803   2 vol

2409 ST. AUBYN (Mary) The Deformed, Jessy Bell, and other Poems   1812

2410 ST GERMANS (Jemima Countess of) Gleanings of Verse, edited by G. E H. Vernon, *privately printed*   1847

2411 ST. JEAN (Madame la Vicomtesse de Saigl) Sketches and Extracts from a Travelling Journal, *plates*, 1813—The Cave of the Huguenots, and other Poems, *plates, Bath, n d*   2 vol

2412 ST. JOHN (Mrs) Voice from the East, or Scriptural Meditations   1851

2413 ST. MAUR (Lady Jane Wilhelmina) Sacred Songs for the School at Teignmace, *privately printed*   1836

2414 ——— Sacred Songs for British Seamen *privately printed*   1836

2415 ——— The same, *another edition, frontispiece*   1837

2416 SALTER (Harriet) Miscellaneous Poems   *Crewkerne*, 1850

2417 SAMPSON (Mrs Theophilus Graham) Christian Virtues, edited by Dr J. R Major   1860

2418 SANDBACH (Mrs Henry R) Poems, 1840—Giuliano de' Medici, a Drama, with other Poems, 1842—The Amidei, a Tragedy, 1845—Aurora, & other Poems, 1850   4 vol

2419 SANDERS (Charlotte) Little Family, 1800—Holidays at Home, *front* 1812—SANDERS (Maria R) Original Rhymes, 1833—Another Edition, 1851   4 vol

2420 SANDERS (Charlotte Fitz) Poems on various Subjects, *frontispiece*   *printed at the Logographic Press*, 1787

2421 SANDERSON (A) Poems on various Subjects, *North Shields*, 1819—Poem to Her Majesty, *ib* 1820—Letter and Poem on the War in the West, *ib* 1819   (3)

2422 SANDYS (M. A) *of Miserden, Gloucestershire*, The Decalogue, the Belief, and the Lord's Prayer Versified   *Pickering*, 1849

2423 SARGANT (Jane Alice) Sonnets and other Poems, *Hackney*, 1817—The same, *second edition, ib* 1818—Joan of Arc, a Play, 1840—Christian's Sunday Companion, 1843   4 vol.

2424 SARGEANT (ANNE MARIA) Isle of Wight, and other Poems, 1832—Holly Wreath, *plates*, 1853—SARGEANT (CHARLOTTE ELIZA) Book for Mothers, 1850 — SARGEANT (EMMA LOUISA) Co-operation, 1832—SARGENT (George E. and MYRA) Holly Tree, *plates*, 1850   5 vol.

2425 SATCHELL (AGNES F.) Miscellaneous Poems *privately printed*   *Antigua*, 1852

2426 —— Reminiscences of Missionary Life in the Caribbean Islands   *Loughborough*, 1858

2427 Saul, a Tragedy, and Jephtha's Daughter, by a Lady, 1821

2428 SAUNDERS (John and MARY) Songs, Sonnets, and Miscellaneous Poems   1838

2429 SAVAGE (Miss ANNA) Angel Visits Poems   1815

2430 SAVAGE (Mrs) Poems, 2 vol.   *printed for C. Parker in New Bond Street*, 1777

2431 SAVORY (Mrs) Life's Vicissitudes, or Winter's Tears, Original Poems, *frontispiece*   1809

2432 SAWTELL (M LETHIND) Mourner's Tribute, or Effusions of Melancholy Hours   *Montreal*, 1840

2433 SAWYER (ANNA) Poems, with Notes, Historical and Explanatory, *vignette of Chedder Cliffs on the title-page*   *Birmingham*, 1801

2434 SAYER (S) Garland, or, Poems on various Subjects, dedicated to the Princess of Wales   1808

2435 SCAIFE (Miss ELIZABETH) *of Liverpool*, Poems *morocco, with joints*   1816

2436 SCANNEL (FLORENCE) Miscellany   *Cork*, 1848

2437 SCHIMMELPENNICK (MARY ANNE) Life, edited by Christiana C Hankin, 2 vol *portrait*, 1858—Asaph, or the Herrnhutters, 1822   3 vol

2438 School of Instruction a Present, by a Lady, *two copies*, 1817—School-Room Lyrics, *Ipswich*, 1846 — Scraps from the Mountains, by Christabel, *Dublin*, 1840—Scientific Receptacle, 2 vol *plates*, 1795—SCOONES (Mrs EMILY) Poem on Spurgeon, 1858   7 vol.

2439 SCOT (ELIZABETH) *of Edinburgh*, Alonzo and Cora, with other Poems, 1801—Memoir of Mrs JULIA H SCOTT, with her Poems, &c *portrait*, *Boston (in America)* 1853—SCOTT (Mrs JOHN) Thoughts in Verse, 1846—SCOTT (Miss) Old Oak Chest, *two editions*, n d   5 vol

2440 SCOTT (ELIZABETH) Specimens of British Poetry, *Edn* 1823

2441 SCOTT (MARY) Female Advocate, a Poem, 1771— Another Edition, 1775—Messiah, a Poem, *Bath*, 1788 *4to* 3 vol

2442 Scriptural Enigmas, *plates in outline*, *4to* 1829—Scripture Truths, in Verse, 1844—SCROOBY (Mrs.) Poetical Stories, *front* 1821— SEARLE (ELIZABETH) Pathway of Providence, *Bonmahon*, 1855—SEDGWICK (Miss) Pearls of Thought strung in Rhyme, 1862 — Another Edition, 1863—Model Nurseries, 1866   7 vol.

2443 Select Collection of Love Letters, to which are subjoin'd Poems by Eminent Ladies, particularly Mrs. BARBER, Mrs. BEHN, &c. 1755

2444 Select Collection of Poems from admired Authors and scarce Miscellanies *North Shields*, 1790

2445 Select Female Biography, *frontispiece* 1829

2446 Selection of Poems from the Manuscripts of a Young Lady *privately printed, morocco, g e* *Edinb.* 1838

2447 Selections from the Poetical Literature of the West, *Cincinnati*, 1841—Selection of Hymns and Poetry, 1853—Selection of Psalms and Hymns, 1832 3 *vol.*

2448 SELLON (MARTHA ANN) Individuality or the Causes of Reciprocal Misapprehension, 1844—Hymns of the Holy Feast, *n d.*—Selwood Wreath, edited by C Bayly, 1841—The Seven Churches, and other Poems, by Annie and Ellen Amelia, *Winchester*, 1847 4 *vol.*

2449 SELWYN (MRS.) Journal of Excursions through parts of England, Wales, and Scotland, 1819-23
PRIVATELY PRINTED 1823

2450 SEMPLE (MRS.) *of Doncaster*, Elegiac Verses to the Memory of Lady Elizabeth Loftus, PRIVATELY PRINTED 1811

2451 Sentimental Tales, &c. including The Faithful Negro, by CHARLOTTE BEVERLEY, *woodcut frontispiece of Harley's Visit to Bedlam, by Bewick, and vignettes*
VERY RARE, *not mentioned by Mr Hugo in his Catalogue of the Works of Bewick* *Newcastle upon Tyne*, 1804

2452 Seraph (The) a Collection of Divine Hymns and Poems from the best Authors *Edinb.* 1754

2453 SERGEANT (MRS. R) Souvenirs of a Tour on the Continent by Adeline, *privately printed* 1827

2454 —— Ernald, or The Martyr of the Alps and other Poems, *two copies*, 1843—Missionary Lays, 1848—Edward Travers, 1849—Scenes in the West Indies, 1849—The same, *third edition*, 1860—Stray Leaves, Poetry and Prose, *Leeds*, 1855 7 *vol.*

2455 SERRES (OLIVIA WILMOT) Flights of Fancy, *portrait, with autograph letter inserted*, 1805—Correspondence with the Earl of Brooke and Warwick, with Poems, &c 1819—The Princess of Cumberland's Statement to the English Nation, *with autograph of "The Princess Olive," portrait inserted*, 1822 3 *vol.*

2456 Seventeen Hundred and Seventy-Seven, or a Picture of the Manners and Character of the Age, in a Poetical Epistle from a Lady of Quality (to Omiah at Otaheite)
4*to.* 1777

2457 SEWARD (ANNA) Elegy on Captain Cook, to which is added an Ode to the Sun, 1780—Three other Editions, 1780-4 *4to. 4 vol.*

2458 —— Monody on Major André, *first and second editions, Lichfield,* 1781 *4to. 2 vol.*

2459 —— Poem to the Memory of Lady Miller *4to.* 1782

2460 —— Louisa, a Poetical Novel, *Lichfield,* 1784—The same, *second, third, and fourth editions, ib* 1784; *fifth edition,* 1792—Florio and Bas Bleu, by Hannah More, 1787 *4to. 5 vol.*

2461 —— Ode on General Eliott's Return from Gibraltar, *portrait inserted* *4to.* 1787

2462 —— Llangollen Vale, with other Poems, *vignette on the title page,* 1796—The same, *third edition,* 1796—Sonnets and Odes, *three editions,* 1799 *4to. 4 vol.*

2463 —— Monumental Inscriptions in Ashbourn Church, Derbyshire, written by Sir Brooke Boothby and Miss Seward, PRIVATELY PRINTED *Ashbourn* (1805)

2464 —— Blindness, a Poem, VERY RARE *4to. Sheffield,* 1806

⁎ One of the few books printed by the Poet James Montgomery

2465 —— Memoirs of Dr Darwin, 1804—Monody on the Death of Major André, 1808—The same, *another edition, plates, Bury* 1817 *5 vol.*

2466 —— Poetical Works, with extracts from her Literary Correspondence, edited by Sir W Scott, 3 vol *Edinb* 1810 —Letters, 1784-1807, 6 vol *portraits, ib.* 1811 *9 vol.*

2467 —— Beauties, alphabetically arranged under appropriate heads, by W C Oulton 1813—The same *another edition* 1822 *2 vol*

2468 SEWELL (MARY) relict of Rev Geo Sewell, Poems, *frontispiece, blue mor. cco, q e Chertsey,* 1803—The same, *second edition, frontispiece, ib.* 1803 *2 vol*

2469 —— Poems and Essays, 3 vol *frontispiece* *Egham and Chertsey,* 1805-9

2470 —— The same, *second edition* 3 vol *front Chertsey* 1816

2471 —— Homely Ballads for the Working Man's Fireside, *the edition printed for private circulation* 1858

2472 —— The same, *another edition,* 1859—Stories in Verse, 1861—Isabel Gray, 1864—Little Forester and his Friend, and other Works by the same Authoress *12 vol*

2473 SHACKLETON (MRS) *formerly Jane Atkinson,* Facts and Fancies by Jenny Wren *Keighley,* 1864

2474 SHAW (LOUISA) Zuleika, and other Poems, *Birmingham,* 1816

2475 —— Isle of the Deathless, with minor Poems, also Spare Moments *Herald* 1830

2476 SHEIL (R) Bellamira, or, the Fall of Tunis, a Tragedy, 1818

2477 SHELLOCK (SARAH) Voice from a Cottage, or Thoughts in Verse *Ipswich*, 1858

2478 SHENSTON (MARY) Memoir and Select Remains, by her Brother and Sister *Finsbury*, 1823

2479 SHEPHERD (MRS.) Poems, 1807—SHEPPARD (S.) Illustrations of Scripture, &c. *Northampton*, 1837—SHEPPARD (MRS. G. W.) Sunshine in the Workhouse, *Frome*, 1858   3 *vol.*

2480 SHERIDAN (FRANCES) Discovery, a Comedy, 1763—Other Editions, 1763-1810   6 *vol.*

2481 —— Dupe, a Comedy, 1764—Illusion, or the Trances of Nourjahad, an Oriental Romance, 1813—Memoirs of her Life and Writings, by Alicia Lefanu, *with additional portraits*, 1824   3 *vol.*

2482 SHERIDAN (LOUISA H.) Diadem, a Book for the Boudoir, *plates*   folio. *n. d.*

2483 She Ventures and He Wins, a Comedy, written by a Young Lady   4to   1696

2484 SHIPTON (ANNA) *formerly Savage*, Whispers in the Palms, Hymns and Meditations, 1855—The same, *third edition*, 1865—Precious Gems, 1862—The Book in the Way, 1864—Little Golden Harp, *n. d.*   5 *vol.*

2485 Shipton (Mother) Life and Death, with her Prophesies, with Preface by R. Head, *cuts*   4to   1687, *repr. n. d.*

2486 SHORE (A. and L.) War Lyrics, 1855—A Short Story interspersed with Poetry, by a Young Lady, 2 vol in 1, 1800   2 *vol.*

2487 SHORT (C.) Dramas for the use of Young Ladies, *vignette on the title-page*   *Birmingham*, 1792

2488 SIDDONS (SARAH) Story of our First Parents, selected from Milton's Paradise Lost, *portrait inserted*, 1822—Siege of Mansoul, a Drama, by a Lady, *Bristol*, 1801   2 *vol.*

2489 SIGOURNEY (MRS. L. H.) Traits of the Aborigines of America, a Poem   *Cambridge* (in *America*) 1822

2490 —— Poems   *Philadelphia*, 1834

2491 —— Lays from the West, *Andover*, 1834—Lays of the Heart, *n. d.*—Simple Tales, *cuts, n. d.*—Girl's Reading Book, *New York*, 1838—Pleasant Memories of Pleasant Lands (1842)—Scenes in my Native Land, 1845—The Coronal, 1848—Poetical Works, 1850   8 *vol*

2492 —— Zinzendorff, and other Poems, *New York*, 1837—Pocahontas, and other Poems, 1841—Poems, Religious and Elegiac, 1841—Pleasant Memories of Pleasant Lands, *Boston*, 1844—Scenes in my Native Land, *Boston*, 1845—Poems for the Sea, *cuts, Hartford*, 1850—Voices of Home, *cuts, ib.* 1852—Sayings of Little Ones, and Poems for Mothers, *front. Buffalo*, 1855 8 *vol.*

2493 —— Poems, *Illustrated Edition*   *Philadelphia*, 1853

2494 SIGOURNEY (MRS. L. H.) Scenes in my Native Land, 1852
—The Coronal or, Tales and Pencilings, *plates*, 1850—
Poetical Works, 1854—Another edition, 1857—Mary
Rice, and other Tales, *plates*, 1855—Olive Leaves,
plates, New York, 1857   6 vol

2495 ——— Faded Hope, 1852—Past Meridian, *New York*, 1854
—Western Home, and other Poems, *port. Philadelphia*,
1854—Sayings of the Little Ones, and Poems for their
Mothers, *front Buffalo*, 1855   4 vol.

2496 SIKES (MRS S) Hymns and Poems, 1815—The same, *second edition*, 1815   2 vol

2497 SIMON (BARBARA ANNE) Hope of Israel Presumptive Evidence that the Aborigines of the Western Hemisphere are descended from the Ten Missing Tribes of Israel   1829

2498 SIMPSON (L. C.) Rhymes for the Young   *Launceston*, 1838

2499 SIMPSON (MRS JANE CROSS) *formerly Bell*, April Hours, by Gertrude   *Glasgow*, 1858

2500 ——— Linda, or Beauty and Genius, a Metrical Romance
     ib 1859

2501 SINCLAIR (CATHERINE) Scotch Courtiers and the Court, *Edinb* 1842

2502 SISSON (FRANCES KOSTER) Country Musings *Cirencester*, 1838

2503 SKELTON (SOPHIA) Saul, a Dramatic Poem, *Dover*, 1864—
Bride of the Nile, *ib* 1865   2 vol

2504 SKENE (FELICIA M. F.) Isles of Greece, and other Poems
     Edinb 1843

2505 Sketches of Wales and the Welsh, by Amy   *Bristol*, 1847

2506 Slade (J.) Memoirs of celebrated Female Characters
     Barnstaple, 1836

2507 SLEIGH (MRS) Poems, Moral and Religious, with a few sketches of her History and Character by her Husband
     Barnstaple, 1819

2508* Small Literary Patchwork, a collection of Miscellaneous Pieces in Prose and Verse, by a Country-Woman
     Shipston, 1805

2509 SMALLPIECE (ANNA MARIA) Sonnets and other Poems, 1805
—Smart (Martin) Female Class Book, *Weybridge*, 1813
—SMEDLEY (M) Story of Queen Isabel and other Verses,
1863—Lays and Ballads from English History, &c by
S M n d   4 vol.

2510 SMITH (CHARLOTTE) *of Bignor Park, Sussex*, Elegiac Sonnets and other Essays, *first edition, portrait inserted*
     4to 1784

2511 ——— The same, *second edition, portrait inserted*
     4to. *Chichester*, 1784

2512 ——— The same, *third edition, with signature of the poetess*
     4to. **n. d.**

2513 SMITH (CHARLOTTE) Sonnets, *fourth edition, with signature of the poetess, portrait inserted* 4to. 1786

2514 —— The same, *fifth edition, plates,* 1789—Elegiac Sonnets, vol II, *portrait and plates,* 1797 *in 1 vol.*

2515 —— The same, *sixth edition,* Dublin, 1790 — Another edition, *port and plates,* 1792 2 vol.

2516 —— The same, *seventh edition,* with other Poems, 2 vol. *port and plates* 1795 7

2517 —— The same, *eighth edition,* 2 vol. *port. and plates* 1797-1800

2518 —— The same, *ninth edition,* 2 vol *port and plates, morocco, g e* 1800— Another edition, 2 vol in 1, 1811 —Another edition, 1827 4 vol.

2519 —— Emigrants, a Poem, *portrait and autograph letter of the poetess inserted* 4to. 1793

2520 —— What is she? a Comedy, 1799—Another edition, *Dublin,* 1799—Three other editions, 1799-1800—Minor Morals, *front Dub* 1800—Conversations introducing Poetry, 2 vol 1804—Another edition, 2 vol in 1, 1819 —Beachy Head, with other Poems, 1807 — Natural History of Birds, 2 vol in 1, *plates,* 1807 11 vol

2521 SMITH (ELIZABETH) Life Review d, a Poem, founded on Reflections upon the silent Inhabitants of the Church-Yard of Truro, in the County of Cornwall
 4to Exeter, 1780

2522 —— The same, *another edition* 4to. ib 1781

2523 —— The same, *another edition* Ilminster, 1781

2524 —— The same, *another edition* Glocester, 1783

2525 —— The same, *sixth edition* Birmingham, 1783

2526 —— Brethren, a Poem ib 1787

2527 —— Israel, a Poem, *tree marbled calf* ib. 1789

2528 —— Fragments in Prose and Verse, *port* Bath, 1808— Other editions, 1808-42 10 vol

2529 —— The same, 2 vol *port* Bath, 1809—Other editions, 2 vol 1810-24 9 vol

2530 —— The same, *another edition,* 2 vol
 green morocco extra, g e 1818

2531 —— Book of Job translated from the Hebrew, *Bath,* 1810 —Second edition, ib 1810—Poems on Malvern, &c Worcester, 1829— Second edition, ib 1831 4 vol

2532 SMITH (ELIZABETH OAKES) Sinless Child and other Poems, edited by John Keese, *New York,* 1843— Poems, *second edition,* ib 1846—Bertha and Lily, or the Parsonage of Beech Glen, 1854—SMITH (MRS E FRANCIS) Wellington Lyrics, 1852—SMITH (EMILY) Attilius Regulus, from the Italian of Metastasio, 1847 5 vol

2533 SMITH (JANE) Admonitory Epistles Birmingham, 1824

2534 Smith (Joseph) Descriptive Catalogue of Friends' Books, with Biographical Notices, 3 parts in 12 Nos. A to Bar
1863-5

2535 Smith (Lucy) Convict's Grave, &c. *Shrewsbury*, 1853— Smith (Lady B.) Songs of Granada and the Alhambra, 1836—Bianca and other Poems, *Bath*, 1858—Smith (Mary) Poems, 1860 4 vol.

2536 Smith (M.) *formerly Aikman*, Miscellanies in Prose and Verse, *front* 1822—Smith (Mary Elizabeth) Moscha Lamberti, a Romance, 1819—Sappho, a Tragedy, translated by Lucy Caroline Cumming, afterwards Mrs Smith, *Edinb* 1855 3 vol

2537 Smith (Mrs) *formerly Savory*, Poetical Tales, founded on facts 1808

2538 —— Another copy, *wanting the title-page, which was destroyed and the volume suppressed by the authoress*
(1808)

2539 —— Pathetic Tales, another copy with a new title-page, *front* 1813

2540 Smith (Rev Mr) Great Duty of Contentment and Resignation to the Will of God recommended, *with Midnight Hymn by a Lady*, 1758—The same, *sixth edition*, 1764
2 vol

2541 Smith (S Louisa P.) Poems *Providence*, 1829

2542 Smith (Sophia Mary) *formerly Bigsby*, Imilda de'Lambertazzi and other Poems, 1830—Eastern Princess and other Poems *Nottingham*, 1844 2 vol.

2543 Smith (Mrs S S.) Amaranth Blooms a collection of Embodied Poetical Thoughts *Utica* 1853

2544 Smith (Mrs Agnes) Religion of the Heart delineated, *with Elegies by Mrs Kendall and Mrs Dorothea King, of Dublin*, 1758—Christian's Triumph, 1783 2 vol.

2545 Smyth (Charles Metcalfe) Memorial of a Beloved Son, containing Extracts from a Mother's Diary, *front*
printed for private circulation, 1841

2546 Smythies (Mrs Yorick) Prince and People, a Poem, 4to 1854—Sebastopol, a Poem, 1854 2 vol.

SIXTH DAY'S SALE.

OCTAVO ET INFRA

UNLESS OTHERWISE EXPRESSED.

LOT

2547 Snatches of Sacred Song, 1854—Snow-Drop, or Fraternal Offering, n d — Snowdrop, by a Lady, *coloured plates*, n d — SNOW (ELIZA R) Poems, vol I, *Liverpool*, 1856   4 vol.

2548 SNOW (ELIZABETH) Bouquet of Wild Flowers, *with illustrations* 4to   *printed by Private Subscription*, 1843

2549 SNOWDEN (ELEANOR) Moorish Queen, a Record of Pompeii, and other Poems, *Dover*, 1831—Maid of Scio, a Tale of Modern Greece, *ib* 1832—SOLTAU (MISS H W) Hymns for Boys and Girls, n d.   3 vol

2550 SOMERS (MRS B) Selections from the Modern Poets of France translated into English Verse   *Dublin*, 1846

2551 Songs and Ballads of Cumberland, edited by Sidney Gilpin, *portrait of Susanna Blamire*   *Carlisle*, 1866

2552 Songs in the Wilderness, by a Blind Lady, 1866—Songs of Freedom, 1849—Song of Mercy, *Southampton*, 1850—Sonnets and Verses, by Rehtira, *Birmingham*, 1856   4 vol

2553 Songs of the Soul, derived from the writings of British, Continental and Transatlantic Authors   1860

2554 SOTHEBY (MISS) Patient Griselda, a Tale from Boccaccio, *Bristol*, 1798—Another copy, *with a Ballad of Patient Grissel, &c bound up at the end, ib* 1798   4to   2 vol

2555 SOUDER (MRS EDMUND A) Leaves from the Battle-field of Gettysburg, *front.*   *Philadelphia*, 1864

2556 SOUTHALL (ELIZA) Diary and Remains, *privately printed, Birmingham*, 1855 — The same, *another edition, Philadelphia*, 1862   2 vol

2557 South Briton, a Comedy, written by a Lady   1774

2558 SOUTHCOTT (JOANNA) Prophecies and other Works, *an extensive and curious collection, bound in 9 vol*   v y.

2559 —— Hymn Book for the Sealed Number, or the Millenium-Church, 1804—Hymns on the Millennium, by Pullen, 1809—The Holy of Holies Unveiled, n d—Life of Joanna Southcott, 1814—History of all Religions, with Life of Joanna Southcott, n. d.   4 vol,

2560 SOUTHEY (CAROLINE) *formerly Bowles*, Ellen Fitzarthur, a Metrical Tale, 1820—The same, *second edition*, 1822—The Widow's Tale, and other Poems, *morocco, g. e.* 1822—Solitary Hours, *Edinb* 1826—The same, *second edition, ib* 1839—Tales of the Factories, *ib.* 1833—Birth-Day and Occasional Verses, *ib* 1836   7 vol.

2561 —— and Robert Southey, Robin Hood, with other Fragments and Poems   1847

2562 Southwell (Robert) Mary Magdalen's Funeral Tears (with Verses to the Memory of Alphonso Brown, who died Oct. 14, 1769, by Mrs CHARLOTTE MCCARTHY)   1772

2563 Souvenir of Modern Minstrelsy, 1860—SOUTHWELL (MARY) Flowers of the Wilderness, *cuts, n d*   2 vol.

2564 SPAULDING (MRS. ANNA MARIE) Poems   *New York*, 1866

2565 SPENCE (ELIZABETH ISABELLA) Sketches of Manners, Customs and Scenery of Scotland, 2 vol in 1   1811

2566 SPENCE (SARAH) Poems and Miscellaneous Pieces
     Bury St Edmunds, 1795

2567 SPENCE (SARAH) Widow of George Spence, Poems ('The Millennium), and a Meditation   *Colchester*, 1821

2568 SPENCER (MRS.) *late Miss Jackson, from Manchester*, Poetical Trifles   1781

2569 SPENCER (MRS CANNING) Early and Late Recollections, *published for the authoress*, 1853 (*misprinted* 1653)—SPENCER (MRS) Commemorative Feelings, 1812—SPENCER (HARRIET) Handful from a Wheat-field, 1861—Letters on the Doctrines of Latter-Day Saints, by Orson Spencer, 1852   1 vol

2570 Spenser (Edm) Faerie Queen, Shepheard's Calendar, and other Works (containing an Epitaph on Sir Philip Sidney, supposed to be written by MARY COUNTESS OF PEMBROKE), *with copious Manuscript Notes by Mr. Park*   1611-17

2571 SPICER (ISABELLA) Gem of Christian Peace, and other Poems, 1836—Spice Islands passed in the Sea of Reading, 1859—SPRATT (MRS G) Language of Birds, *coloured plates*, 1837—Spring Blossoms, *plates*, 1831—SPROAT (MRS. N) Village Poems, *front New York, n d*—SPROULE (HARRIET LETITIA) Poems, &c *n d*—STURGEON (ELIZABETH GEORGIANA) Evergreens, *n d*   7 vol

2572 SQUIRRELL (ELIZABETH) Autobiography and Selections from her writings, 1853—Selection of Scriptural Poetry, by Lovell Squire, 1818—Tributes of Esteem to the Departed, by C C STAMMERS, *Colchester, n d*—STANLEY (LOUISA) Juvenile Story-Book, *woodcuts, n d*—Stanzas on the Death of Rev T Coke, by a Young Lady, 1811—STAPLETON (Miss) Apricot Golding of Sunnyside, 1866   6 vol

2573 STANHOPE (LOUISA SIDNEY) Treachery or, The Grave of Antoinette, a Romance, interspersed with Poetry, 1 vol. 1815

2574 STARKE (MARIANA) Sword of Peace, or Voyage of Love, a Comedy, 1789—Another Edition, *Dublin*, 1789—Another Edition, 1792—Widow of Malabar, a Tragedy, 1791—The same, *another edition, Dublin,* 1791—Third Edition, 1791—Tournament, a Tragedy, 1800—Beauties of Carlo-Maria Maggi paraphrased, *Exeter,* 1811
8 vol

2575 STEEL (MRS) Pathetic and Religious Poems, *Saxmundham*, 1831—The same, *fourth edition, Romford,* 1836, and others by the same Authoress—STEEL (ELIZABETH ANNE) Fireside Musings, *Bury St Edmunds,* 1857—STEELE (MARY) Miscellany, *Croydon,* 1825—STEELE (SARAH) Eva, with some Lyric Poems, *Dublin,* 1816   8 vol.

2576 STEELE (ANNE) Danebury, or, the Power of Friendship, a Tale   4to *Bristol, n d*

2577 —— Poems on Subjects chiefly Devotional, by Theodosia, 2 vol *fronts*   1760

2578 —— The same, with Miscellaneous Pieces, *a new edition,* 3 vol. *fronts*   *Bristol,* 1780

2579 —— The same, *another edition,* 2 vol *Boston (in America),* 1808—Poems, chiefly Devotional, 1818—Hymns, Psalms, and Poems, *front* 1863   4 vol.

2580 STEERS (FANNY) Ant Prince, a Rhyme, 1847—STEINBERG (MADAME) Oswald the Enthusiast, Caiphas in London, &c. 1852—Stella, a Poem of the Day, *Dublin,* 1845   3 vol

2581 Stenhouse (W) Illustrations of the Lyric Poetry and Music of Scotland   *Edinb* 1853

2582 STERNE (G M) Strong Will and a Fair Tide a Novel, 3 vol 1860—Mamma's Stories in Rhyme, *Wycombe, n d*—Palace of Truth, *n d*—STEVENSON (S. G) Golden Quiver, or Poems for Children, *front n d*—STEWART (ELIZABETH) Anaya, 1838—STEWART (ELIZABETH M) Sketches of Sacred Biography, 1834—Poetry for Young Persons, 1816—STEWART (MRS COL) Don Quixote, a Comic Opera, 1834   12 vol

2583 STIRLING (CATHERINE MARY) Prince Arthur and Tales by the Flowers, by Caroline B Templer, *coloured plates, n d*—STOCKLY (HARRIET E) Conversations with Theodore and his Sister, *Philadelphia,* 1860   2 vol

2584 STOCKDALE (MARY R) Effusions of the Heart, *frontispiece,* 1798—Family Book, *frontispiece,* 1798—The same, second edition, *frontispiece,* 1799—Mirror of the Mind, 2 vol *portrait,* 1810—The same, another edition, 2 vol 1817—Widow and her Orphan Family, 1812—Shroud for Sir Samuel Romilly, 1818   9 vol.

2585 STODART (M. A.) Every Day Duties, 1840—Third edition, 1845—Scriptural Poems for Children, 1840—National Ballads, 1841—The same, another edition, 1851—Female Writers, 1842   6 vol

2586 —— Epitaphs, from the Greek Anthology, translated by Major R G Macgregor (containing 118 Christian Epigrams by Miss Stodart)   n. d.

2587 STOKES (CATHERINE) *of Damerham*, Poems, Religious, Moral, &c.   *Salisbury*, 1818

2588 STONE (ANNE) Features of the Youthful Mind, *Margate*, 1802

2589 STOPFORD (OCTAVIA) Sketches in Verse and other Poems *privately printed*   *Hull*, 1826

2590 STORR (CECILIA GRANTHAM) Robert's Rhymes, 1851—Minnows from Brenchley Brook, 1861—STOPPS (S A.) Thoughts and Sketches in Rhyme, 1857—STOTT (E A) Sunday Memorials, 1850—Guide to Laurel Hill Cemetery (with a Poem by Mrs Z Barton Stour), *Philadelphia*, 1854   5 vol.

2591 STOW (MARIA MARGARET) The Types, in verse and prose, 1836—STOW (John) A Hermit's Narrative of Opinions (with Verses by Mrs Stow) 1861   2 vol.

2592 STOWE (H B) Tales and Sketches of New England Life, 1855—Christian Slave, dramatised, 1856—STOWELL (MRS) Memoirs by Rev H Stowell of Ballaugh, Isle of Man, *Wellington*, 1817—STRAFFORD (ELIZABETH) Hymns for the Collects, 1857 and 1858—STRAFFORD (E H) Lizzie and Florence n d—STRANGE (LADY) Sacred Mountains and Waters *three copies*, 1841   9 vol

2593 STRATHMORE (MARY ELEANOR BOWES COUNTESS OF) Siege of Jerusalem, PRIVATELY PRINTED VERY RARE   1774

2594 —— Confessions, written by herself, *very scarce*   1793

2595 —— Trial of Andrew Robinson Bowes, when the Countess of Strathmore obtained a Divorce, *frontispiece very scarce*   1789

2596 —— Lives of A R Bowes and the Countess of Strathmore, by Jesse Foot, *portrait, &c*   n d

2597 STRETTELL (MISS) The Doris, a Drama   *Edinb* 1835

2598 STRICKLAND (AGNES) Worcester Field, or the Cavalier, n d—Seven Ages of Woman and other Poems, *Bungay*, 1827—Demetrius, with other Poems, 1833—Floral Sketches, Fables and other Poems, *plates*, 1836—The same, another edition, *coloured plates, n. d.*   5 vol.

2599 —— Historic Scenes and Poetic Fancies, *portrait, with an autograph letter of the poetess inserted*, 1850—Floral Sketches, *coloured plates, n d*   2 vol

2600 —— Sea-Side Offering *privately printed, 4to Edinb* 1856—Juvenile Scrap Book, by Agnes Strickland and Bernard Barton, *plates*, 1837   2 vol.

2601 STRINGER (MRS.) Chain of Affection, a Moral Poem, and other Pieces, *privately printed*   Richmond, (1830

2602 STRUTT (ELIZABETH) Wreath for the Altar of the New Church, *privately printed*   n d.

2603 —— Domestic Residence in Switzerland, 2 vol. *plates* 1842

2604 —— Story of Psyche, *plates in outline from designs by J. Gibson*   folio. n d.

2605 STURGE (H.) Texts and Hymns selected for Children, *Birmingham*, 1857—Summer Excursion, by a Lady, *coloured plates, n. d.*—Sunbeams for Little Children, *Edinb.* 1855—Sunday Reading, 1827—Sunday Sunshine, by a Lady, 1858   5 vol.

2606 SUTCLIFF (ANN) Poems
PRIVATELY PRINTED   Iris Office, Sheffield, 1800

2607 SUTCLIFFE (ALICE) Meditations of Man's Mortalitie, *in prose and verse, second edition, rare, russia, g e*   1634

2608 SUTCLIFFE (FRANCES MARY) Long Tom, otherwise Thomas Long, *Bungay*, 1836—Mount Pleasant and Pleasant Row, *ib.* 1838—The Squire and his Man, 1839
in one vol.

2609 SWALLOW (JANE) Memoirs, with Extracts from her Diary and Correspondence, *Liverpool*, 1860—The Swan Lake and other Poems, 1862   2 vol.

2610 SWANWICK (ANNA) Selections from the Dramas of Goethe and Schiller, translated   Murray, 1843

2611 —— Dramatic Works of Goethe, translated, and Goetz von Berlichingen, by Sir Walter Scott, *plate*, 1850—The Agamemnon, Choephori, and Eumenides of Æschylus, translated, 1865   2 vol

2612 SWANWICK (CATHERINE) Poems, by L *three series*, 1858-60 —St. Bernardine, a Dramatic Poem, 1862—The Talisman, a Drama, 1864   5 vol.

2613 SWARBRECK (MRS. SAMUEL DUKINFIELD) Valencia, a Tragedy *privately printed*   Richmond, Yorkshire, 1830

2614 —— Valencia, a Tragedy, and Who could believe it? a Comedy, *privately printed*   ib. 1830

2615 Sylvan Sketches, by the Author of Flora Domestica 1825

2616 —— The same, another edition, *frontispiece*   1831

2617 Sylvia's Revenge, or a Satyr against Man, in Answer to the Satyr against Woman   4to. 1688

2618 —— The same, second edition   4to. 1697

2619 —— The same, eleventh edition   4to. 1707

2620 —— Complaint of her Sexes Unhappiness a Poem, being the second part of Sylvia's Revenge   4to. 1692

2621 —— The Poetess, a Satyr, being a reply to the Female Author of a Poem call'd Silvia's Revenge   4to. 1707

2622 SYMMONS (CAROLINE) Memoir, with a few Poetical Productions, edited by F. Wrangham, 1804—Another copy of the latter portion only of the volume, *plate of a bust*, 1804—Poems, by Caroline and Charles Symmons, 1812 3 *vol.*

2623 T (E) Meditations, in verse
PRIVATELY PRINTED *Maidstone*, 1839

2624 T. (E M.) Wayside Gatherings, edited by a Lady, 1857—Wild Flowers, and other Poems, by A S T. 1841 2 *vol.*

2625 T. (L A) Poems, with illustrations by the authoress
PRIVATELY PRINTED *Birmingham*, 1834

2626 TAGGART (CYNTHIA) Poems, *first edition* *Providence*, 1834

2627 —— The same, *second edition, plate* *Cambridge*, 1834

2628 —— The same, *third edition* *New York*, 1848

2629 Tahiti, or The Voice of Truth, by a Lady *Brighton*, 1843

2630 TALBOT (Mrs. CATHERINE) Essays on various subjects, 2 vol 1772

2631 —— The same, second edition, 2 vol in 1, *portrait inserted*, 1772—Works, *portrait inserted*, 1780—Works, another edition, *portrait inserted*, 1795—Reflections, 1820—Essays, 1820; and 3 others 7 *vol.*

2632 —— Works, seventh edition, with Life, by Rev M. Pennington, *portrait inserted*, 1809—The same, eighth edition, *portrait*, 1812—The same, ninth edition, *portrait*, 1819 3 vol

2633 Tale of the Hamlet and other Poems, by a Scottish Dame *presentation copy from the authoress* *Glasgow*, 1844

2634 Tales, Original and Translated from the Spanish, by a Lady, *frontispiece and other woodcut illustrations*, 1810

2635 Talisman (The) or Bouquet of Literature and the Fine Arts, *plates*, 1831—The same, for another year, *plates*, n d. 2 *vol.*

2636 TALLANT (Miss ANNE) Octavia Elphinstone, a Manx Story, and Lois, a Drama, 2 vol 1834

2637 TALMAGE (Mrs ANN) *late Heath, of Chichester, Sussex*, Descriptive Pieces, *privately printed* *Oxford*, 1836

2638 TANNER (Mrs) *formerly Clara Coulthard*, Rhymes for an Hour, *Bath*, 1842—Poems, *ib* 1842—Prayers and Hymns, 1845—Vision of the Blue Isle, *Bath*, n d 4 *vol.*

2639 TANNER (Mrs) *formerly Selina Ann Jones of Fairford, Gloucestershire*, Living Epistle, or Life and Last Illness, *portrait* 1855

2640 Tasso, Night Thoughts, translated by Mrs *****, *Paris*, 1828—Tassoni, Memoirs, with Notices of his Literary Contemporaries, edited by S. Walker, *portrait*, 1815

2641 TATHAM (EMMA) Dream of Pythagoras and other Poems, second edition, *Bath, n. d*—The same, third edition, *portrait*, 1858—The same, fourth edition, with Memoir by Rev B Gregory, abridged, *portrait*, 1864—Memoir by Gregory, with the Angels' Spell, &c. *portrait*, 1859—Etchings and Pearls, or, a Flower for the Grave of Emma Tatham, by Mrs. J. Cooke Westbrook, 1857   5 vol.

2642 TATLOCK (ELEANOR) Poems, 2 vol *with a Solemn Appeal to Great Britain, printed separately, inserted*   1811

2643 TAYLOR (ANN and JANE) Associate Minstrels, 1810—The same, second edition, *Edinb.* 1813   2 vol.

2644 —— Hymns for Infant Minds and Rhymes for the Nursery, *various editions*   18 vol.

2645 Taylor (Daniel) *of Bridport in Dorsetshire*, Remains (with Verses by ELIZABETH NICHOLLS)   1715

2646 TAYLOR (ELLEN) The Irish Cottager, Poems, *scarce* 4to. (*Dublin*), 1792

2647 TAYLOR (EMILY) Vision of Las Casas, 1825—Poetical Illustrations of Passages of Scripture, *Wellington*, 1826—Sabbath Recreations, *ib* 1829; and other editions 7 vol

2648 TAYLOR (HANNAH) Memoir, extracted from her own Memorandums   *York*, 1820

2649 TAYLOR (JANE) Wedding among the Flowers, *plates*, 1808—Essays in Rhyme, 1816—The same, other editions, 1816-40—Hymns for Infant Minds, *n d*   8 vol.

2650 —— Memoirs and Poetical Remains, with Extracts from her Correspondence, by Isaac Taylor, 2 vol *Oxford*, 1825—Other editions, 1826-33   8 vol.

2651 —— Contributions of Q Q to a Periodical, 2 vol second edition, *Oxford*, 1826—Display, a Tale, *frontispiece*, 1827   3 vol

2652 TAYLOR (MISS CLARE) Hymns on the Sufferings of Christ, *privately printed*, 18 —The same, another edition, 1865   2 vol.

2653 TAYLOR (MRS.) *of Ongar*, Present of a Mistress to a Young Servant, *frontispiece*, 1816—Maternal Solicitude, *frontispiece, n d*—TAYLOR (MRS) Hebrew Captivity, *Bury*, 1851—TAYLOR (MRS ELIZABETH) Memoir and Poems, *printed for the author*, 1819—The same, *fifth edition, Woodbridge*, 1857—TAYLOR (MRS SARAH LOUISA) Memoir, by Lot Jones, *portrait, Glasgow*, 1839   6 vol.

2654 TEFT (ELIZABETH) *of Lincoln*, Orinthia's Miscellanies, a Collection of Poems   1717

2655 TELFORD (SARAH) Miscellaneous Poems, with Introduction by Rev. T Ebdon   *Durham*, 1818

2656 TEMPLE (ANNA CHAMBER COUNTESS) Poems, *vignette on the title page, portrait inserted*
 morocco, with joints, g. e. 4to *Strawberry Hill*, 1764
2657 TEMPLE (LAURA SOPHIA) Poems, *portrait inserted* 1805
2658 —— Lyric and other Poems, *portrait inserted, Bristol*, 1808
2659 —— Siege of Zaragoza and other Poems 1812
2660 TEMPLE (ROSE ELLEN) Poets' Souvenir of Amateur Artists, *portrait inserted* 1856
2661 TERRY (ROSE) Poems, *Boston (in America)*, 1861—THUPON (H MARY) Fruits of the Valley, n. d. 2 vol.
2662 Thanks to Eliza, a Poetical Epistle from the Comic Muse to the Countess of D——, in which various eminent Dramatic and Political Characters are displayed 1798
2663 THAYER (CAROLINE MATILDA) Religion recommended to Youth, and Poems, *Dublin*, 1819—The same, *another edition, York*, 1826—The same, *another edition, New York*, 1840—Thank Offering, 1850—THISTLETHWAYTE (GRACE) Hymns, 1840 5 vol.
2664 Theodorick, King of Denmark, a Tragedy, by a Young Gentlewoman *Dublin, printed on Cork Hill*, 1752
2665 Thespian Dictionary, or, Dramatic Biography, *ports* 1805
2666 THOMAS (ELIZABETH) Miscellany Poems on several Subjects 1722
2667 —— The same, *second edition* 1727
2668 —— Pylades and Corinna, or, Memoirs of the Lives of Richard Gwinnett, of Great Shurdington in Gloucestershire, and Elizabeth Thomas, of Great Russel Street, Bloomsbury, to which is added the Life of Corinna, *written by herself, 2 vol. portraits* 1731-2
2669 THOMAS (ELIZABETH) Dramatick Pastoral, occasioned by the Collection at Gloucester on the Coronation Day for portioning Young Women of virtuous Characters
 4to *Gloucester*, 1762
2670 THOMAS (ELIZABETH) Purity of Heart, or the Ancient Costume, 1817—Confession, or, The Novice of St Clare, 1818—Georgian, or, Moor of Tripoli, and other Poems, *Gloucester*, 1817 3 vol.
2671 THOMAS (LADY) Faithful Hound, *second edition, coloured plates* 1863
2672 THOMAS (MRS.) Convert, a Tale of Real Life
 privately printed n. d.
2673 —— Serious Poems, &c. 1834—Poems, 1816 2 vol.
2674 THOMAS (MRS EDWARD) Tranquil Hours, 1838—Sir Redmond, a Metrical Romance, 1839—Merchant's Daughter of London, 1855—Autumnal Leaves, 1860—Primroses by a River's Brim, *portrait*, 1865 5 vol.
2675 THOMSON (ELIZA) Poems on various Subjects 4to. 1787

2676 Thompson (Henry) Original Ballads by Living Authors (some Female) *woodcut vignettes* 1850
2677 Thompson (Mrs J. Bowen) *née Elizabeth Maria Lloyd*, Scripture Portions, 1858—Thomson (Mrs.) Recollections of Literary Characters, &c 2 vol 1851 3 vol.
2678 Thorne (J) Farewell to Mawbey — Adieu to Mawbey, by E. H. T.—Mawbey-Goodbye, by I. T.—Recollections of Mawbey, by R. T. T., *on four sheets of note paper privately printed* Southern Hill, 1860
2679 Thornton (Lewis M) Sacred Poems (with Tributary Verses by Mary Collier), *second edition, port* Leeds, n d.
2680 Thornwell (Emily) Rainbow around the Tomb New York, 1860
2681 Threlfall (Miss J) Woodsorrel, or leaves from a Retired Home, 1856—Thornton (Miss) Solace in Sickness and Sorrow, 1856—Thoughts for the Sea, *n. d* —Thoughts and Meditations, in verse, by a Young Lady of the Hebrew Faith, *Pickering*, 1848 — Three Bachelors, translated from the German by a Young Lady, 1862—Selection of Fables, by Theresa Tidy, 1837 6 vol.
2682 Throckmorton (Ann) *Verses in the* "Discourse upon the Life and Death of Mr. G Throckmorton" (her brother) *very scarce* Printed in the year 1706
2683 Tiernan (Mary Ann) Monody on the Death of the Princess Charlotte 1818
2684 Tighe (Mrs. Henry) Psyche, or, The Legend of Love First edition, very rare, *100 copies only printed for presents, with autograph inscription,* To Camilla Blackford, *by the Poetess, portrait inserted, blue morocco, with joints, g e* 1805
2685 ——— Psyche, with other Poems, *portrait morocco, g. e.* 4to 1811
2686 ——— The same, *third edition, portrait* 1811
2687 ——— The same, *fourth edition, portrait, an additional one inserted* Edinb 1812
2688 ——— The same, *another edition, port.* Philadelphia, 1812
2689 ——— The same, *fifth edition, portrait* 1816
2690 ——— The same, *another copy*, LARGE PAPER, *port.* 1816
2691 ——— The same, *another copy*, LARGE PAPER, *port* 1816
2692 ——— The same, *other editions*, 1813-52—The same, with a Translation of Apuleius, 1853 5 vol
2693 Tillotson (J) Lives of Illustrious Women of England, *portraits* n d
2694 Tilt (Julia) Poems and Ballads, 1847—Arundel Castle, and other Poems, 1849—Lays of Alma, and other Poems, 1856 3 vol.
2695 ——— Poems and Ballads, 2nd, 3rd, 4th, 5th, 6th and 7th editions, 1847-53 6 vol.

2696 TIMBURY (JANE) Story of Le Fevre, from the Works of Sterne, put into Verse 1787
2697 —— History of Tobit, with other Poems 1787
2698 Time's Telescope for 1833 and 1834, with Sketches of Contemporary Biography, &c. 2 vol. *numerous engravings* 1833-4
2699 Timpson (T.) British Female Biography 1816
2700 TINDAL (Mrs. ACTON) Lines and Leaves, 1850 — TINSLEY (Mrs. CHARLES) Lays, 1848 — Hints of Talent from many pencils, edited by G. M. Busey, 1837 — Titus before Jerusalem, and other Poems, *Bath* (1851) 4 vol.
2701 TIPPER (ELIZABETH) Pilgrim's Viaticum: or, the Destitute, but not Forlorn. being a Divine Poem, digested from Meditations upon the Holy Scripture *very scarce, old morocco, g. e.* 1698
2702 Tixall Letters: or Correspondence of the Ashton Family, with Notes and Illustrations by Arthur Clifford. 2 vol. *Edinb.* 1815
2703 Tixall Poetry, with Notes and Illustrations by Arthur Clifford, *frontispiece of the Ruins of Tixa'l It.* ib. 1813
2704 TODD (Mrs. SUSAN HILL) Occasional Poems *Boston (in America),* 1851
2705 TOLLET (Mrs. ELIZABETH) Poems on several occasions, with Anne Boleyn to King Henry VIII, an Epistle 1755
2706 —— The same, *second edition* *in T. Land, n. d.*
2707 TOMLINS (ELIZABETH SOPHIA) Tributes of Affection, with the Slave, and other Poems 1797
2708 TONGE (ELIZA) Poetical Trifles *Cheltenham, n. d.*
2709 TONNA (CHARLOTTE ELIZABETH) Osric, a Missionary Tale, with the Garden, and other Poems *front. on India paper,* 1826 — Izram, a Mexican Tale, and other Poems, *portrait inserted,* 1826, *blue morocco, g. e.* 2 vol.
2710 —— Letters from Ireland, 1838 — Personal Recollections, 1841 — Osric, &c. *portrait inserted, Dublin, n. d.* — The same, *third edition,* 1841 — Zebra, 1847 — Posthumous and other Poems, 1846 4 vol.
2711 —— Convent Bell, and other Poems *New York,* 1845 — Osric, ib. 1847 — Izram, ib. 1847 — Conformity, ib. 1851, &c. 5 vol.
2712 —— Minor Poems, 90 in a dozen, *Dublin, n. d.,* and others by the same Poetess 11
2713 TOOGOOD (Mrs.) Summer Lake, a collection of Poems, 1852 — The Offering, a selection from the Poems of a Minister's Daughter (Miss TOOGOOD) *Edinb.* 1851 — TOVANI (Mrs. ELIZABETH) Stray Thoughts, n. d. — TOWNSEND (HANNAH) History of England, in verse *Philadelphia,* 1852 4 vol.

2714 TOOTH (ELIZA T.) Memorial of Mrs. Camplin
privately printed *Hoxton,* 1833

2715 Tousey (Geo. Phil.) Flights to Helicon: or, Petites Pieces, in verse, (including five the productions of a Young Lady of the Author's acquaintance) *front.* 1768—Town and Country Magazine, vol. II, *plates,* 1817-18—Tobin (J.) Curfew (the Prologue by a Lady, and the Epilogue by Mrs. Opie) 1807 3 vol.

2716 TOWNLEY (CHARLOTTE) Memoir, by C. G. Townley, *Limerick,* 1839—TOVANI (MRS ELIZABETH) Stray Thoughts, *front. n. d.* 2 vol.

2717 TOWNSEND (ELIZABETH W.) White Dove and other Poems for Children, *with illustrations, New York,* 1855—TOWNSEND (HANNAH) History of England, in Verse, *Philadelphia,* 1852 2 vol.

2718 Translations in verse from various German Authors
4to 1818

2719 Translator (The) by a Mother and her Sons [the Honble — Trevor] *three numbers for Sept. Oct. and Nov.* 1825, *no title-page, evidently privately printed, and having a few corrections in manuscript* 1825

2720 TRAPNEL (ANNA) Cry of a Stone, or Relation of something spoken in Whitehall, uttered in Prayers and Spiritual Songs, by an Inspiration extraordinary, and full of Wonder, VERY RARE, *but a few words and letters cut off the top margins, a copy of the scarce print inserted*
4to 1654

2721 TRAVERS (REBECCA) This is for all or any of those that resist the Spirit, &c   Also

Things to come are here declared
but blind men cannot see·
But as the World draws to an end,
some shall remember me

VERY RARE, *fine copy*   4to   *Printed in the Year* 1664

2722 TREFUSIS (MISS EL.) Poems and Tales, 2 vol. *portrait,* 1808

2723 TRELAWNY (ANNE) Mary Stuart, a Tragedy from the German of Schiller, 1838—The same, *another edition, Devonport,* 1838—Lyrical Ballads, containing the Song of the Bell, &c. *ib.* 1838—Easter Offering, *Tavistock,* 1845 4 vol.

2724 TRENCH (MRS RICHARD) Campaspe, and other Poems, *Southampton,* 1815—On the Loss of an only Daughter, *ib* 1816—Sonnet on seeing Children Dance, 1817—Assize Ball, or Lucy of the Moor, *second edition, Dorchester,* 1820—Aubrey, *Southampton,* 1818 *in one vol.*

2725 TRENCH (MRS RICHARD) Campaspe, &c. *Southampton*, 1815
—Ellen, a Ballad, *Bath*, 1815—Laura's Dream, or,
The Moonlanders, 1816—Aubrey, in five cantos, *Southampton*, 1818—To Lady * * * on reading Lord ——'s
Farewell, n d—Lines on reading the 1st Canto of
Childe Harold, *ib* n. d—On the loss of Elizabeth Melesina Trench, n d—Sonnet on seeing Children Dance,
1817, and others, *with MS notes by the Authoress*
in one vol

2726 —— Laura's Dream, or, the Moonlanders, 1816—Aubrey,
Southampton, 1818—Thoughts on Education, *ib* n d—
Campaspe, &c *ib* 1815—Monody on the Death of Mr
Grattan, 1820, and others by the same *in one vol.*

2727 —— Remains, edited by her son the Dean of Westminster,
portrait 1862

2728 —— The same, second edition, *portrait* 1862

2729 TREPKA (BLANCHE SHAKESPEARE DE.) The Question, 1855—
Panthea, a Greek Tale, and other Poems, 1856 *2 vol*

2730 TREVANION (ADA) Poems 1858

2731 TREVELYAN (FRANCES A) Quarr Abbey, or, The Mistaken
Calling a Tale of the Isle of Wight, *with illustrations*
4to *Oxford*, 1862

2732 TRIMMER (MRS SARAH) Family Magazine, or Repository of
Religious Instruction and Rational Amusement, for 1788
and from Jan to June, 1789, 3 vol *plates* 1788-9

2733 —— Account of her Life and Writings, with Letters, Meditations, and Prayers, 2 vol *portrait*, 1816—Miscellaneous Pieces selected from the Family Magazine,
1818 *3 vol*

2734 TRINDER (MRS W H) Voices of Home and Nature, 1861—
The same, second edition, 1861—Trim (Alice) Wild
Flowers, *Sidmouth*, 1861—Tributary Tears to the
Memory of the Princess Charlotte, 1818—Trifle to the
Afflicted, *Bath*, 1811 *5 vol*

2735 TRIPP (MARY ANNE) Songs of La Colonna *Bristol*, 1835

2736 Triumphant Christian a Poem on the Death of Joseph
Weatherill of Southwark 1751

2737 Triumphs of Female Wit, in some Pindarick Odes, or, The
Emulation Together with an Answer to an Objector
against Female Ingenuity, and Capacity of Learning
Also, A Preface to the Masculine Sex, by a Young Lady
VERY RARE, *with autograph of Ro Mylne on the titlepage* 4to. 1683

2738 TROLLOPE (MRS F) Mother's Manual, or Illustrations of
Matrimonial Economy, 20 *plates* 1833

2739 —— The same, second edition, 20 *plates* 1833

2740 TROTTER (ELIZABETH HILL) Cindabright; or, the Fatal Flowers, a Fairy Tale, with minor Poems, *plates*, *Kensington*, 1838—TROUTBECK (ANNE) Abridged History of England, *two editions*   3 vol
2741 TRUESDELL (MRS HELEN) Poems   *Cincinnati*, 1857
2742 TUCK (ELIZABETH) Vallis Vale, and other Poems   *Frome*, 1823
2743 TUCKER (CHARLOTTE) Precepts in Practice, or Stories illustrating the Proverbs, by A L O E, *plates*, *Edinb* 1858—Glimpses of the Unseen, Poems, *ib. n d.*— White Shroud, and other Poems, *ib n d.*   3 vol
2744 TUCKEY (MARY B) Wrongs of Africa, *Glasgow*, 1838—Great Exemplar, *Dublin*, 1840—Harry and Willie, *ib.* 1844—Creation, *ib.* 1845—Old James, *n d*, &c   7 vol
2745 TUITE (LADY ELIZA DOROTHEA) *of Bath*, Poems   1796
2746 —— The same, *second edition*   1799
2747 —— Miscellaneous Poetry, *third edition*   *Bath*, 1841
2748 TUPPER (MISSES) Poems by three Sisters, dedicated to their Father, Martin F. Tupper, *frontispiece*   1866
2749 TURELL (MRS. JANE) *of Medford*, Memoirs (with Poems) collected from her own Manuscripts by Rev. E Turell   1741
2750 TURNBULL (MRS) Song of Azrael and other Poems, 1840—The King, a Drama, by Mrs Walter Turnbull, *n d*—Selections from Compositions in Miss Turnbull's Seminary, *Edinb* 1854   3 vol
2751 TURNER (ANNETTE) Children of the Mist, Conqueror, and other Poems, *frontispiece*   1827
2752 —— The same, *second edition, frontispiece*   1827
2753 TURNER (ELIZABETH) *formerly Gilding of Woolwich, Kent*, Breathings of Genius, a Collection of Poems and Essays, 1776—Sermon on her Death, with several Poems by her, 1786   2 vol
2754 TURNER (ELIZABETH) Blue Bell, or Tales and Fables, *cuts*, *Derby*, 1838—Crocus, *cuts*, 1844—Daisy, *cuts*, *n. d*—Cowslip, *cuts*, *n. d.*— Pink, with additions by Mary Howitt, *n d*—Short Poems, *cuts*, *n. d.*   1 vol.
2755 TURNER (E S and F. J) Maid of Orleans, and other Poems, translated from the German, 1842—TURNER (FRANCES) Devotional Breathings, 1852   2 vol.
2756 TURNER (MRS JOANNA) *formerly Cook of Trowbridge in Wilts*, Triumph of Faith exemplified in her Life and Experience   *Bristol*, 1787
2757 TURNER (MARGARET) the Gentle Shepherd of Allan Ramsay, in English, *scarce, portrait of Ramsay inserted*, 1790

2758 TUTHILL (MRS JACKSON VILLIERS) Songs of Past Hours, *frontispiece designed by Rev R Cobbold* 1852
2759 TUTHILL (MRS L C) Mirror of Life, *plates, Philadelphia,* 1847—Little Geography, *cuts, ib.* 1847—Nursery Book for Young Mothers, 1849   3 vol
2760 TWEDDELL (MRS) *formerly Eliza Smyth of Chorlton Hall, Manchester,* Life, *Liverpool,* 1830—TYTLER (M F) Hymns and Sketches in Verse, *cuts,* 1810   2 vol.
2761 UNIACKE (MARY) Dolls' Pic-Nic, *coloured plates,* 4to n d.
2762 United Efforts, a Collection of Poems, the Mutual Offspring of a Brother and Sister   1831
2763 Unnatural Mother (a Tragedy), written by a Young Lady   4to   1698
2764 UPTON (CATHERINE) Miscellaneous Pieces, in prose and verse   4to   1784
2765 Uptonian (The) (four numbers, published in Dec 1833, March 1834, June 1834, and June 1836) complete in one volume, VERY RARE, *with names of the Authors of most of the pieces and other additions in Manuscript*   *Upton upon Severn,* 1836
2766 VALLÍ (HENRIETTA T) Autumnal Leaves, 1834—The same, *second edition,* 1837—VARDILL (MISS) Poems and Translations, 1809—The same, *second and third editions,* 1809-16   6 vol
2767 VAN LANDEGHEM (MRS HIPPOLYTE) Exile and Home: the advantages of Social Education for the Blind   *printed for the Author,* 1865
2768 VARDILL (ANNA JANE) Pleasures of Human Life, a Poem   4to   *Edinb* 1812
2769 Varied Wreath or, Sketches in Poetry, *Southampton* n d The same *second edition, ib* 1810—Variety, a Collection of Poems, by a Lady (*of Stockton*), 1802   3 vol
2770 Variety, a Poem, inscrib'd to the God of Change to which is annex'd an Answer to an Ovid's Epistle, by Louisa   *Westminster,* 1727
2771 Various Essays, by Sylvana Sola, with Poems on Infidelity, &c   *printed for the author,* 1752
2772 Vauclusiad (The), *a Satirical Poem, with head of Laura, and a vignette of a musical Cupid at the end* PRIVATELY PRINTED   n d.
2773 VAUGHAN (MRS) Grecians, a Tragedy,   *printed for the author,* 1821
2774 VEITCH (AGNES) Songs for Children, *Edinb.* n d—The same, *illustrated edition* n d—Veleda, a Dramatic Sketch (1860) Verses Sacred and Miscellaneous, by Harriet, 1853   4 vol.

2775 Verses on the Death of H R H Princess Charlotte Augusta (including one by MARGARET HARVEY, another by SARAH JOPLIN), collected by William Garret, *only six copies printed, portrait inserted* Newcastle upon-Tyne, 1818

2776 Verses on the Present State of Ireland, by a Lady
4to 1778

2777 Village Maid, an Opera, by a Young Lady
printed for the authoress, 1792

2778 Village Rhymes, *with illustrative woodcuts*
Thames Ditton, 1831

2779 Vision (The), inscribed to Mrs Woffington, wrote by a Lady, *scarce* Dublin, 1753

2780 Voice of Faith in the Valley of Achor being a series of Letters to several friends on Religious Subjects, by Ruhamah, 2 vol. in 1
second edition, scarce Southwark, 1820

2781 Voices from the Misletoe, edited by Llodie, Birkenhead, 1847—Visit to the Castle of Truth, by a Lady, Bath, 1828—The Violet, edited by Miss Leslie, *plates*, Philadelphia, 1839 3 vol.

2782 Voltaire. La Pucelle; or, Maid of Orleans, a Poem, from the French of Voltaire, 2 vol PRIVATELY PRINTED, EXCESSIVELY RARE, *having been strictly suppressed on account of the freedom of the translation*
VERY FINE COPY ON LARGE PAPER, ON WHICH ONLY 5 COPIES WERE PRINTED, orange morocco extra, *edges gilt and gauffré* (Dublin), 1796-7

2783 Voltaire, Henriade, an Epic Poem, translated into English Rhyme (by a Lady) 4to. 1797

2784 W. (A M) Verses, with Imitations and Translations
PRIVATELY PRINTED, *morocco g e* 1812

2785 W (C J) Etchings from Nature Bath, 1853

2786 W (E H) Wailings of the Lyre Dublin 1860

2787 W (Hon Mrs) and LADY M , Entomology in Sport, and Entomology in Earnest, *coloured cuts* (1859)

2788 W (S) Seven Works of Mercy, and other Poems, edited by the Hon C L Courtenay 1858

2788*Wade (John) Women, past and present 1859

2789 WAIBLINGER (CATHERINE) Metrical Lessons and Fragments in remembrance of days that are gone, *plates*, Bedford, 1823

2790 WAKEFIELD (PRISCILLA) Variety, consisting of Anecdotes, Facts, Narratives, &c 1809—Introduction to Botany, *coloured plates*, 1818 2 vol

2791 WALKER (MISS MARION) Leaves from the Backwoods, Montreal, 1862—Walker (C E) Caswallon, a Tragedy, the Prologue *written by a Lady*, 1829—WALCOT (MARIA GRACE) Cup and the Lip, New York, 1859 3 vol.

2792 WALBEY (Mrs R. D) Thoughts in Metre, *Hertford*, 1860—WALL (Mrs Geo) *formerly Whately*, Songs of the Night, *two editions, Dublin*, 1858-61—WALES (A) Spring Buds and Autumn Leaves, 1860—Leaves blown together by Lottie (Miss C WALKER), 1865—WALKER (E A) Hymns and Thoughts, in Verse, with Introduction by Rev H Bonar, 1861   5 vol

2793 WALLACE (LADY E) Letter to a Friend, with a Poem called the Ghost of Werter   4to   1787

2794 —— The same, *another edition*, 1787—Diamond cut Diamond, 1787—The Ton, or Follies of Fashion, a Comedy, 1788—The same, *another edition, Dublin*, 1788—The Whim, *a Comedy, Margate*, 1795   2 vol

2795 Walpole (H) Catalogue of the Royal and Noble Authors of England, Scotland and Ireland, enlarged and continued by T Park, 5 vol *portraits, russia*   1806

2796 WALSH (ANNA MARIA DRUMMOND) Memorial, *with verses, &c second edition, printed for private circulation*   1856

2797 WALSH (Miss) Poems, by a Sister, *portrait of Francis Walsh inserted*   1812

2798 WALMSLEY (EMMA) Sacred Year containing Hymns and Verses for every Sunday and Holiday, *Winchester*, n d.

2799 Ward's Miscellany and Family Magazine, under the Superintendence of a Society for the advancement of Literature, Science and Religion, 2 vol   imp 8vo   1837-8

2800 WARD (CATHARINE GEORGE) Poems, *Edinb* 1805—Poems, *Coventry*, 1812—Tales of the Glen, 1813—Miscellaneous Poems, 1820—Dandy Family, *coloured illustrations*, n d   5 vol

2801 WARD (MABELLA ANN) Queen Bee or a Fete to the Blossoms, *Bath*, 1839—Kate Dashaway, an Autobiography, 1865   2 vol

2802 WARD (MARY) Original Poetry   *Bath*, 1807

2803 WARD (Miss) The Buried Bride, &c *Southampton* (1839)—WARD (Mrs) Word for Zion, *2 copies*, n d   3 vol

2804 WARD (Miss) Glimpse of Oriental Nature, Pictures with Verses by a Lady, with Preface by Rev G R Gleig, *beautifully illuminated*   oblong 4to   1866

2805 WARDLAW (LADY) *formerly Elizabeth Halket*, Hardyknute, a Scottish Fragment, *privately printed*, 1783—Another Edition, *bad copy, Glasgow*, 1745   2 vol

2806 WARDLE (CHARLOTTE) Norway, a Poem, with Translation into Norwegian by N H Jæger. half, *Christiania*, 1812

2807 —— St Alban's, or the Cursing Well, a Poem   1814

2808 WARE (KATHARINE AUGUSTA), *formerly Rhodes*, Power of the Passions and other Poems   *Pickering*, 1842

2809 WARE (MARY), *of Ware Hill, Herts*, Poems and Translations   1809

2810 WARFIELD AND LEE (Mrs) Wife of Leon, and other Poems, by two Sisters of the West *New York*, 1844

2811 WARING (ANNA LETITIA) Hymns and Meditations, 1850—The same, 2nd, 3rd, 4th, 5th, 6th, 8th and 9th Editions, 1850-63—Additional Hymns, 1858   9 vol

2812 WARING (CATHERINE M) Annuals and Perennials, or Seed-Time and Harvest, *with illustrations by T R. Macquoid* 1853

2813 WARING (S) Wild Garland, *coloured plates*, 1827—Another Edition, *cuts*, 1837—Minstrelsy of the Woods, *plates*, 1832—Meadow Queen, *plates*, 1836   4 vol

2814 WALKER (ANNA) Hymns of the Church Militant *Edinb* 1858

2815 WARREN (Miss) Asaph, or Faith's Conflict with Infidelity 1856

2816 WARREN (Mrs M) Poems, Dramatic and Miscellaneous *very scarce*   *Boston (in America)*, 1790

2817 WASHBOURN (Mrs), *of Hammersmith*, Hymns, 1822—Watts (Dr I) Miscellaneous Thoughts, *front* 1823—Divine and Moral Songs, revised and altered, n d   3 vol

2818 WASSELL (Miss M A) Rivals, or General Investigation, 1815—The same, *second edition*, 1815—The same, *fifth edition*, 1859   3 vol

2819 WATERMAN (CATHARINE H) Flora's Lexicon an Interpretation of the Language and Sentiment of Flowers, *coloured plates and woodcuts*   *Philadelphia*, 1839

2820 WATKINS (Misses), *of Stale Lane, Somersetshire*, Poems *Bath*, 1812

2821 WATKIS (FRANCES) Earl of Warwick, or Rival Roses, with other Poems   *Liverpool*, 1815

2822 WATSON (AMY ANN) Poems on Select Passages of Scripture, n d—WATSON (MARY) Poems, 1863—WATT (MRS. FRANCES) Poems, edited by J T B Landon, *Bromsgrove*, n d   3 vol.

2823 WATTS (Isaac) Horæ Lyricæ, *portrait*, 1779—Hymns and Moral Songs, revised by a Lady, *second edition*, 1787—The same, *fourth edition*, 1801   3 vol

2824 WATTS (LOUISA) Poems for Children, 1838—Other Editions, *Halifax*, 1858 and 61—Second Series, 1858—Pretty Little Hymns, n d.   5 vol

2825 WATTS (MARY), *of Yeovil*, Sculptor of Florence, and other Poems   1856

2826 WATTS (SUSANNAH) Chinese Maxims, translated from the Œconomy of Human Life into Heroic Verse, *in seven parts, front*   *Leicester*, 1784

2827 —— Poems and Translations, particularly Ambra from Lorenzo de' Medici   1802

2828 WATTS (SUSANNAH) Insects in Council, with other Poems, *Leicester*, 1828—The same, another edition, 1835—Hymns and Poems, *Leicester*, 1842   3 vol
2829 WEBB (JANE) Prose and Verse   *Birmingham*, 1824
2830 WEBSTER (ANN) Solitary Musings   1825
2831 WEBSTER (AUGUSTA) Dramatic Studies, *Camb.* 1866—The Prometheus bound of Æschylus, in English Verse, *ib* 1866   2 vol.
2832 WEBSTER (GRACE) Raymond Revilloyd, a Romance, 2 vol. in 1   1819
2833 WEBSTER (MRS M. M.) Pocahontas, a Legend, *wants a leaf of notes, Philadelphia*, 1810—WILBURN (E.) Lays for the Weary Pilgrim, *York*, 1851   2 vol
2834 WEDDERBURN (MARGARETTA) Mary Queen of Scots, an Historical Poem, with other Miscellaneous pieces, *portrait*   *Edinb* 1811
2835 WELBY (MRS.) *of Kentucky*, Poems, by Amelia, *enlarged edition, with illustrations by R. W. Weir*
     morocco, g e   *New York*, 1850
2836 —— Poems, by Amelia, tenth edition, *New York*, 1851—The same, 14th edition, *ib* 1860   2 vol.
2837 WELLS (ANNA MARIA) Poems and Juvenile Sketches
     Boston, (in America) 1830
2838 WELLS (ELIZABETH) Poems and Dialogues, 1812—Welsh Sketches, 1st and 3rd series, 1851-4   3 vol
2839 Wesley Family, Memoirs collected principally from Original Documents, by Adam Clarke, *plates*, 1823—Birds of Epworth, or Poetic Gems from the Wesley Cabinet, 1856—WESLEY (SARAH) Lines to the Memory of the First Methodist Preachers, *plate inserted*, 1828   3 vol
2840 WEST (ELIZABETH) Memoirs, or Spiritual Exercises, written by her own hand, *Edinb* 1798—Another edition, *Aberdeen*, 1836   2 vol.
2841 WEST (JANE) Miscellaneous Poetry, written at an early period of Life   4to. 1786
2842 —— Miscellaneous Poems and (Edmund Ironside) a Tragedy   *York*, 1791
2843 —— Gossip's Story, and a Legendary Tale, second edition, 2 vol   1797
2844 —— The same, fifth edition, 2 vol.   1804
2845 —— Elegy on the Death of Edmund Burke   4to 1797
2846 —— Poems and Plays, 4 vol   1799-1805
2847 —— Advantages of Education or, History of Maria Williams, second edition, 2 vol   1803
2848 —— The Mother, a Poem, 1809—Second edition, 1810
     2 vol
2849 —— Letters to a Young Lady, 3 vol   1811

2850 WEST (MRS. FREDERIC) [*Theresa C I.*] Summer Visit to Ireland in 1846, *plates and cuts* 1847
2851 —— Frescoes and Sketches from Memory 1855
2852 WEST (MRS JOHN) *formerly Harriett Atkinson*, Memoir, by John West, Rector of Chettle and Farnham, Dorset *Blandford*, 1840
2853 —— The same, second edition, 1842—WEST (MRS) Sacred Poems, 1st and 2nd editions, 1833 — Westminster Contribution, a Collection of Tales, in prose, and Scraps in verse, 1839 4 *vol.*
2854 Westmoreland and Cumberland Dialects: Dialogues, Poems, Songs and Ballads, with Glossary 1839
2855 WESTON (MARY *jun.*) *of Upton, in the County of Essex*, Account of, with Elegy on Hephzibah Knight 1799
2856 WESTWOOD (LUCY BELL) Poetical Remains, with Life by Rev J H Millard *Huntingdon*, 1850
2857 WETHERELT (MRS. DAWSON BRUCE [*C. C V. G*]) Bunyan's Pilgrim's Progress paraphrased, *portrait* *Parsonstown*, 1844
2858 —— Lays of the Troubadours 4*to* 1847
2859 WEYMOUTH (SARAH) Rural Poems, with other Fugitive Pieces *Devonport*, 1827
2860 Whalley (Thomas Sedgwick) Journals and Correspondence, 2 vol *portraits* 1863
2861 Wharton (Eliza) the Coquette, a Novel, by a Lady of Massachusetts, with preface, &c by Jane E Locke, *portrait* *Boston*, 1855
2862 WHARTON (GRACE and Philip) Queens of Society, 2 vol. *illustrations by Doyle and the Brothers Dalziel* n d.
2863 WHARTON (HON MRS.) — Idea of Christian Love, to which are added copies of verses from that excellent Poetess Mrs Wharton, &c 1688
2864 —— Temple of Death, a Poem by the Marquess of Normanby, &c with several Poems of the Honourable Madam Wharton, second edition 1695
2865 —— Whartoniana: or Miscellanies in Verse and Prose, by the Wharton Family, (including a Description of Jamaica) 2 vol. in 1, *frontispiece and portrait* *Printed in the Year* 1727
2866 —— The same [The Poetical Works of Philip, late Duke of Wharton, &c]—Another edition, 2 vol. *portrait, n d.*
2867 WHEATLEY (LOUISA) Scribblings during the Years 1841 and 1842, PRIVATELY PRINTED 1843
2868 WHEATLEY (PHILLIS) *of Boston, in New England*, Elegiac Poem, on the Death of Rev G Whitefield (appended to his Funeral Sermon, by E. Pemberton) 1771
2869 —— Poems on various Subjects, Religious and Moral, *portrait* 1773

2870 WHEATLEY (PHILLIS) Poems on Comic, Serious, and Moral Subjects, *second edition, portrait* n d.
2871 —— Poems on various Subjects, *another edition, the last leaf wanting, calf extra, by F. Bedford* Albany, 1793
2872 —— Memoir and Poems, *portrait* Boston, 1834
2873 —— The same, *second edition* ib 1835
2874 —— Memoir, by B. B. Thatcher, *portrait* ib. 1834
2875 WHELAN (MRS L MERRITT) Hours of Idleness, PRIVATELY PRINTED Lyons, 1814
2876 WHITE (CHARLOTTE) Companion for the Sick Chamber, *morocco, g e.* 1843—Hymns for the Cottage, 1817, &c.—Where is the Good Samaritan? *n. d.*—Caveat for Protestants, *Deptford*, 1826—Invalid's Hymn Book, with preface by Hugh White, *two editions.* Dublin, 1841-3 6 vol
2877 WHITE (DOROTHY) Trumpet of the Lord of Hosts, blown unto the City of London, and unto the Inhabitants thereof—Also, a Trumpet sounded out of the Holy City, proclaiming Deliverance to the Captives, &c. *in verse and prose*, 1662—Epistle of Love and of Consolation unto Israel, from the pouring forth of the Spirit and Holy Anointing of the Father, &c 1661, VERY RARE 4to in 1 vol.
2878 —— Call from God out of Egypt, by his Son Christ the Light of Life, *in verse and prose*, VERY RARE, *half morocco by W. Pratt* 4to 1662
2879 WHITE (MRS) Honoria, or The Day of All Souls, a Poem, with other Poetical Pieces 4to 1782
2880 WHITEHEAD (ANN) Piety Promoted by Faithfulness, manifested by several Testimonies concerning her, (by various Friends, Male and Female) VERY RARE 1686
2881 WHITEHEAD (EMMA) Romance of the City, or, Legends of London, 1851—Gertrude and Emmeline, and other Poems, by a Manchester Lady, 1853 — WHITEMAN (ELIZABETH HORSLEY) Sonnets and other Poems, 1865—WHITFIELD (MARY AMELIA) Accursed King, and other Poems, *Carlisle*, 1865 4 vol.
2882 WHITING (MARY) Early Piety Exemplified in her Life and Death, written by her brother, John Whiting, with two of her Epistles to Friends, second edition *very scarce* 1711
2883 WHITMAN (SARAH HELEN) Hours of Life, and other Poems *Providence*, 1853
2884 WHITNEY (ANNE) Poems, *New York*, 1859 — WHITNEY (HANNAH) Sabbaths in the Wood, 1817 2 vol.
2885 Widow of the Rock, and other Poems, by a Lady *Montreal*, 1824

2886 WIGLESWORTH (E.) Daily Life of The Christian Child, *n. d.*—Last Sleep of the Christian Child, *n. d.*—Seven Corporal Works of Mercy, *cuts*, (1860)—Seven Spiritual Works of Mercy, 1861—Child and the Angel, *Edinb. n. d.*—Child's Baptismal Name, 1862—Verses for the Christian Year, 1863   6 vol.

2887 WILBRAHAM (FRANCES M.) Perils in the Mine, a Colliery Tale, *Norwich*, (1863)—WILBY (MARIA A.) Cry from the Oppressed, and other Poems, 1838—Wilderness Records; or Memorial of H. H. of Chertsey, *Derby*, 1843—The same, second edition, 1847—Wild Flowers, *n. d.*—Wild Spring Flowers, by Alice Georgina, 1852—Wild Rosebuds, by Alice Georgina, 1853   7 vol.

2888 WILDE (LADY) Ugo Bassi, a Tale of the Italian Revolution, by Speranza, 1857—Poems by Speranza, *Dublin*, 1864   2 vol.

2889 WILKES (ANN) Poems   *Birmingham*, 1808

2890 WILKINSON (JANET W.) Sketches and Legends amid the Mountains of North Wales, *in verse* *morocco, with joints, watered silk linings, q. c.*   1840

2891 WILKINSON (SARAH) Love and Hymen, or Valentine Writer, *coloured front. n. d.*—Carvalho's Road to Hymen, or Cupid's Directory, *coloured front. n. d.*   2 vol

2892 WILKINSON (SARAH) Historical Reveries, by a Suffolk Villager, *Sudbury*, 1839—WILKINSON (REBECCA) Sermons to Children, *plates, n. d.*—WILLAN (RHODA MARIA) Flower Girl, and other Poems, 1843—Country Scenes and Subjects, *with illustrations*, 1847—WILLEMENT (EMILY ELIZABETH) Bouquet from Flora's Garden, *coloured plates, Norwich*, 1841   5 vol

2893 WILLIAMS (ANNA) Miscellanies, in prose and verse, *portrait inserted*   4to 1766

2894 WILLIAMS (CATHARINE R.) Original Poems on various Subjects, *Providence*, 1828—WILLIAMS (ANNA) Helps to Devotion, 1829—WILLIAMS (CATHARINE M.) Tales of Glendevon, *n. d.*   3 vol.

2895 WILLIAMS (HELEN MARIA) Edwin and Eltruda, a Legendary Tale (edited by And. Kippis)   4to 1782

2896 ——— Peru, a Poem   4to 1784

2897 ——— Poem on the Bill for regulating the Slave Trade, 1788—Farewell for Two Years to England, 1791—Ode on the Peace, 1783   4to. in one vol.

2898 ——— Poems, 2 vol *frontispiece designed by Miss Cosway*   1786

2899 ——— The same, *second edition*, 2 vol. *front*   1791

2900 ——— Julia, a Novel, with some Poetical Pieces, 2 vol. in 1   1790

2901 WILLIAMS (HELEN MARIA) Letters from France, with Anecdotes of the French Revolution, 4 vol. 1796
2902 —— Poems, Moral, Elegant and Pathetic, and Original Sonnets, 1803—Paul and Virginia, from the French of Saint-Pierre, *plates*, 1814—Poems on various Subjects, *portrait inserted*, 1823 3 vol
2903 WILLIAMS (JANE) Miscellaneous Poems, *scarce*
Brecknock, 1824
2904 WILLIAMS (JANE) Literary Women of England 1861
2905 WILLIAMS (M. A.) *of East Budleigh, Devon*, A Mother's Tribute, PRIVATELY PRINTED *Budleigh-Salterton*, 1858
2906 WILLIAMS (SARAH ANNE and HARRIETTE SOPHIA) First Note of the Lyre, 1815—WILLIAMS (SARAH JOHANNA) Sherwood Forest, a Poem, *Nottingham*, 1832—Williams (T.) Memoir of Queen Charlotte, *port* 1819—Hymns for the Household of Faith, edited by MRS WILLIAMSON, 1861
4 vol
2907 WILLIS (ANNA) *of Jericho L I*, Memoir by her Father, Thomas Willis *New York*, 1851
2908 WILLOUGHBY (HARRIET) History of France in Rhyme, *plates*, 1846—WILLS (RUTH) Lays of Lowly Life, *Leicester*, 1861—Second edition, *ib* 1861 3 vol
2909 WILMOPE (SARAH) Progress and Comforts of Religion, an Essay in Blank Verse
Stourport, printed for the author, 1820
2910 WILSON (ANN) Jephthah's Daughter, a Dramatic Poem
1783
2911 WILSON (ANNE) Teisa, a Descriptive Poem of the River Teese, its Towns and Antiquities
vignette on the title-page, very scarce
4to. *Newcastle-upon-Tyne*, 1778
2912 —— The same, another copy, without the vignette
4to *ib* 1778
2913 WILSON (CAROLINE) *formerly Fry*, Poetical Catechism, second, third, fourth and fifth editions, 1822-57—Serious Poetry, 1822—The same, *second, third and fourth editions*, 1823-33—Death, and other Poems, 1823—Autobiography, Letters, and Remains, *portrait*, 1850—Table of the Lord, *New York*, 1859 12 vol.
2914 WILSON (CORNWELL BARON) *formerly Harries*, Melancholy Hours: a collection of Miscellaneous Poems, 1816—Astarte, a Sicilian Tale, *second edition*, 1818—Hours at Home, 1826—Cypress Wreath, 1828—Volume of Lyrics, *plates*, 1840 5 vol
2915 —— Astarte, &c *fourth edition*, 1827—Another edition, 1840—Hours at Home, *second edition*, 1827—Petticoat Colonel, a Comic Interlude, 1831—Venus, a Vestal, *n. d.*—Maid of Switzerland, *n. d.* 7 vol.

2916 WILSON (ELIZABETH CARUS) Mother's Sermons for her Children, with Hymns and Prayers, *Kirkby Lonsdale*, 1829—Second edition, *ib.* 1839—Memoir, by W. C. Wilson, *ib.* 1842   3 vol.

2917 WILSON (FLORENCE) Boudoir Lyrics, *portrait*   1814

2918 WILSON (MRS. ROBERT) New Zealand and other Poems, 1851—Return to my Native Village, and other Poems, by a Lady [B Wilson], *Oxford*, 1853—Zadok, the Israel (by Mrs. Wilson, née Graham), *Carlisle*, 1837 —WILSON (SUSANNAH) Familiar Poems, *front.* 1811   1 vol.

2919 WINCHELSEA (ANNE COUNTESS OF) Spleen, a Pindarique Ode, together with a Prospect of Death   1709

2920 —— Miscellany Poems (and Aristomenes: or, The Royal Shepherd, a Tragedy)   1713

2921 —— Another copy, *with variation on the title-page*   1713

2922 —— Another copy, *with different title-page* *old red morocco, g e*   1714

2923 WINGROVE (ANN) Letters, Moral and Entertaining   *Bath*, 1795

2924 WINKWORTH (CATHERINE) Lyra Germanica, translated from the German, *first and second series*, 1856-8—The same, *first series, New York*, 1859   3 vol.

2925 —— The same, *illustrated edition* *morocco, antique style, g. c.*   4to. 1861

2926 —— Chorale Book for England, the tunes from the Sacred Music of the Lutheran, Latin, and other Churches, edited by W. S Bennett   4to. 1863

2927 WINKWORTH (SUSANNA) German Love, from the Papers of an Alien, translated with the sanction of the Author   1858

2928 WINTER (ANNA MARIA) Fairies and other Poems, *Dublin*, 1833—Confidant, a Poem, *ib* 1836, *presentation copy to Mrs Henry Martin from the Authoress*   2 vol.

2929 WINTER (M.) Translation of the Hermann and Dorothea of Goethe, *Dublin*, 1819 — Ice-Bound Ship, Sleeping Beauty, and other Poems, 1860   2 vol

2930 WINTER (SUSAN) *formerly Vince*, Mystic Wreath, or Evening Pastime, consisting of Poems, Charades, Anagrams, Conundrums, Rebuses, &c *with autograph letter of the authoress inserted*, 1829—Paraphrase on the Lord's Prayer, Miscellaneous Poems, in Verse, *with autograph letter inserted*, 1852   2 vol.

2931 Winter's Wreath, a collection of Original Contributions in Prose and Verse, 5 vol *plates*   *Liverpool*, 1828-32

2932 WISEMAN (MRS. JANE) Antiochus the Great, or the Fatal Relapse, a Tragedy   4to. 1702

2933 WOLFERSTAN (E. P.) Enchanted Flute, with other Poems and Fables from La Fontaine 1823
2934 —— Eugenia, a Poem 1824
2935 —— Fable of Phaeton, translated from Ovid PRIVATELY PRINTED, *with leaf of verses on reading Lady Flora Hastings' Poems* 1828
2936 —— Fairy Tales, in Verse, *Lichfield*, 1830—The same, *second edition, ib* 1833 *in one vol.*
2937 —— Golden Rules, 1811—Fairy Tales, *third edition*, 1836 *in one vol.*
2938 WOLLASTON (SUSAN) One Hundred Sonnets, translated from Petrarch, with the Original Text, Notes, and Life, *portrait*, 1841—The same, *second edition*, 1855   2 vol.
2939 WOLLEY (HANNAH) Queen-Like Closet, or Rich Cabinet, *with engraved title page, dated 1675, wanting one corner of a leaf and part of the contents*, 1669—Supplement to the Queen-Like Closet 1674   *in one vol.*
2940 —— The same, *second edition, frontispiece*, 2 vol in 1 1672-4
2941 Woman is a Riddle, a Comedy, by Christopher Bullock, 4to. 1717—The same, *third edition*, 1739—Woman's History, by Gertrude, *Glasgow*, 1848   3 vol.
2942 Woman: or Adela of England, a Poem PRIVATELY PRINTED   *Dungannon*, 1815
2943 WOOD (L.) Metrical History of England, *woodcuts*, 1857—WOOD (MARY S.) Questions for Bible Classes, *New York*, 1856   2 vol.
2944 WOOD (SUSAN) Literary Exercises, &c. *Bury St Edmund's*, 1802
2945 WOODCOCK (MRS. HENRY) of *Michelmersh, Hants*. Laura, a Tale, 1820—Peasant of Auburn, or Old Man's Tale, 1819   *in one vol.*
2946 WOODROOFFE (SARAH ANNE) of *Somerford Keynes, Wilts*. First Prayer, in Verse, 1855—WOODROFFE (SOPHIA) Lethë and other Poems, posthumously edited by G. S. Faber, 1844—Four Dramatic Poems, 1846—Sacred Lays, 1854   4 vol.
2947 WOODS (ANN) of *Normanton, and of Caythorpe, Lincolnshire*, Waking Moments   *Derby*, 1862
2948 WOODS (CECILIA FREDERICA) Spring Flowers of the Mind, *portrait*, 1848—WOODWARD (HELEN) Poetic Sketch-Book, *Bath*, 1848   2 vol
2949 WOOLVEN (MARY) of *Henfield, in Sussex*. Utterance of the Heart, Letters, Poetry, &c. *Brighton*, 1842—World (The) that God made, in easy verse, *woodcuts, Wellington, Salop*, 1821   2 vol.
2950 WORTH (MRS ANNE) Poems, Moral and Sacred with Life, *Macclesfield*, 1813—WORTH (SUSANNAH) Poems, *Plymouth*, 1851   2 vol.

2951	WORTLEY (LADY EMMELINE STUART) Poems	1833
2952	——— London at Night and other Poems	1834
2953	——— Travelling Sketches, in Rhyme	1835
2954	——— Village Churchyard and other Poems	1835
2955	——— Knight and Enchantress, with other Poems	1835
2956	——— Visionary, with other Poems	1836
2957	——— Fragments and Fancies	1837
2958	——— Impressions of Italy and other Poems	1837
2959	——— Hours at Naples and other Poems	1837
2960	——— Queen Berengaria's Courtesy and other Poems, 3 vol	1838
2961	——— Lays of Leisure Hours, 2 vol in 1	1838
2962	——— Visionary, Canto III	1839
2963	——— Sonnets written during a Tour through Holland, Germany, Italy, Turkey, and Hungary, *plate calf gilt, m e*	1839
2964	——— Eva; or, The Error, a Play	1840
2965	——— Jairah, a Dramatic Mystery, and other Poems	1840
2966	——— Alphonzo Algarves, a Drama	1841
2967	——— Angiolina del' Albano, or Truth and Treachery, a Play	1841
2968	——— The same, *proof sheets, with corrections and alterations in the autograph of the authoress*	1841
2969	——— Lillia Bianca, a Tale of Italy	1841
2970	——— Maiden of Moscow, a Poem, Cantos I-IV	1841
2971	——— The same, 21 Cantos	1842
2972	——— Adelaida or Letters, &c of Madame von Regenberg, to which are added Poems, *with corrections and alterations in the autograph of the authoress*	1843
2973	——— Moonshine, a Comedy	1843
2974	——— The same, another copy, *with corrections and alterations in the autograph of the authoress*	1843
2975	——— The same, another copy, *with corrections and alterations, and an autograph letter of the authoress inserted*	1843
2976	——— Ernest Mountjoy, a Comedietta, *with copious alterations and additions in the autograph of the authoress*	1844
2977	——— Honour to Labour, a Lay of 1851	n d
2978	——— &c [Recollections of the Mississippi, Arabesques, and Marabouts, Black Ghosts, Steam in America, Travelling, &c,], *plate*	1853
2979	——— Slave and other Poems, English and Spanish	1853
2980	——— Visit to Portugal and Madeira, *plate*	1854
2981	WRIGHT (ELIZA JANE) Navigation and other Poems, *plate* 4to	*Manchester*, 1854
2982	WRIGHT (FRANCES) Altorf, a Tragedy, *with manuscript corrections*	*Philadelphia*, 1819

2983 WRIGHT (FRANCES) Introductory Address at the opening of the Hall of Science, New York *New York*, 1829

2984 WRIGHT (MARY BESTWICK) Cypress Wreath, a Collection of Poems 1828

2985 WROATH (LADY MARY) Countesse of Montgomeries Urania, *engraved title-page* *folio.* 1621

2986 WYATT (GERTRUDE) Miscellaneous Poems 1829

2987 WYKE (ANNE) Bertha, a Tale of the Waldenses, and other Poems *Shrewsbury*, 1830

2988 WYVILL (FANNY SUSAN) Pansies, 1860—Another copy (by Fanshawe Brook on the title-page), 1860—Love and Mammon, and other Poems, 1863 3 vol

2989 YARROW (MRS.) Original Poems, including a Tribute of Justice to the Earl of Liverpool, &c. 1824

2990 YEARDLEY (MARTHA) *formerly Savory*, Inspiration, a Poetical Essay, 1805—Original Wreath of Forget-me-not, *Barnsley*, 1829—Eastern Customs, *York*, 1842—True Tales from Foreign Lands, *Scarbrough, n d*—Testimony of Devonshire House Monthly Meeting concerning M Yeardley, 1851 4 vol

2991 YEARSLEY (ANN) *a Milkwoman of Bristol*, Poems on several occasions, *portrait inserted*, 1785—Poems on various subjects, being her second work, 1787—Poem on the Inhumanity of the Slave Trade, 1788 4to in 1 vol

2992 —— Poems, *third edition* 1785

2993 —— Poems, *fourth edition, with verses in manuscript on the death of Miss Strafton* 1786

2994 —— Stanzas of Woe, addressed from the Heart on a bed of illness to Levi Eames, Mayor of Bristol, 1790—Reflections on the Death of Louis XVI. *Bristol*, 1793—Sequel to the same, *ib* 1793—Elegy on Marie Antoinette, with a Poem on the last Interview between the King of Poland and Loraski, *Hotwells n d.* 4to in 1 vol.

2995 —— Earl Goodwin, an Historical Play 4to 1791

2996 —— Royal Captives, a Fragment of Secret History, 4 vol 1795

2997 —— Rural Lyre, a Volume of Poems, *frontispiece*, 1796—Reflections on the Death of Louis XVI, *Bristol*, 1793—Elegy on Marie Antoinette, *Hotwells, n d*—Earl Goodwin, 1791 4to in 1 vol

2998 YORKE (CAROLINE JANE) Reflections for Leisure Hours on the Duties of Life &c 1845—YORKE (HARRIET) Self Exiled and other Poems, *Camb* 1850 2 vol

2999 YOUNG (ANN M) Poems, *portrait and plates* 4to *Glasgow*, 1858

3000 YOUNG (CHARLOTTE) World's Complaint and other Poems, 1817—YOUNG (MISS) The Mercy Seat upon the Ark, 1841 2 vol
3001 YOUNG (DOROTHY) Dorval or, the Test of Virtue, a Comedy from the French of Diderot, 1767—Younger Brother: or, Sham Marquis, a Comedy, 1719 2 vol
3002 YOUNG (MARY) Innocence an Allegorical Poem 4to 1790
3003 YOUNG (MARY JULIA) Adelaide and Antonine or, The Emigrants, a Tale 4to 1793
3004 —— Poems, 1798—Metrical Museum, Part 1 *plate, the work ends on page 95, with the catchword Autumn, qy if any more published, n d* 2 vol
3005 Zion's Ornaments and Offerings, with preface by W. Huntington, *scarce* 1787
3006 ZORNLIN (MISS) Vision of Isaiah concerning Jerusalem from chap. XL. to the end, in verse 1813

3007 Post Office Directory, 1863—Watkins's Directory, 1855—Memorials of King's School, Canterbury, 1865—London Diocese Book, 1866 1 vol

MANUSCRIPTS

3008 BAKER (MISS THOMASINE) Lyric for 1826, with Acrostics
3009 BARDOLPH (ROSA S.) Album, *morocco, g. e.* 4to 1860
3010 BETHAM (MATILDA) Australian Paradise Lost, and Smaller Poems, *with autograph letter of the Authoress to Mrs. Dawson Turner* 4to 1836
3011 BLESSINGTON (COUNTESS OF) Amabel and other Poetical pieces, *autograph manuscript, half morocco* 4to.
3012 BOADEN (CAROLINE) Towers of Notre Dame, a Drama translated from the French—Quite Correct, a Play 4to 2 vol
3013 BRENNAN (LOUISA) Album, *with illustrations* 4to 1844
3014 BYRNE (MRS) [Rosa Matilda] The Dream, or Living Portraits, *autograph manuscript, green morocco, portrait inserted*
3015 CAVENDISH (LADY JANE) and LADY ELIZABETH BRACKLEY, Concealed Fansyes, a Play, *copied from a MS in the Bodleian Library* folio.
3016 COLLET (JOYCE) Collections of Short Sentences out of the Holy Scriptures, *old morocco, sides richly tooled and gilt* 1635
3017 CLARK (MISS NELLY) *of Arbigland, Dumfriesshire, a correspondent of Burns,* Indian Maid, a Tale, *with various pieces by Miss Miller, also from Dumfriesshire, afterwards Mrs Colonel Jones, with note on the fly-leaf, relating to Paul Jones, the Pirate* 4to.

3018 CROMWELL (ANNA) Booke of Devotions, 1656, *modern copy* —Poems for my Children, by M A E C 1811— CROSSE (SARAH) Verses upon the Holy Women in the Old and New Testaments   4to (3)

3019 DAVIDS (MARY ANNE) *wife of Dr. Davids, of Wolverton, Bucks*, Verses   4to 1833, &c

3020 DENVIL (MRS) Ida, the Betrayed, or the Murder at the Old Smithy, a Melo-Drama   4to 1839

3021 LITTOTT (C) Hymns *half morocco*—LAZZARD (ALICE) Poems, 1855-8—LEWIN (ELIZA) Poems, 1862
    4to and 8vo (3)

3022 GOOCH (MRS) [*Elizabeth Sarah Villa Real*] Selected Poetry, 3 vol *old morocco, &c*   4to 1792-3

3023 GORE (MRS) Lords and Commons a Comedy   4to 1831

3024 —— Crazy Wedding, a Musical after-piece   *folio*

3025 GUION (MADAME) Select Spiritual Songs, translated from the French, *old morocco*   obl. 12mo

3026 GWENNAP (MRS) *wife of Rev. Joseph Gwennap of Saffron Walden*, Verses on the Death of Lewis Andrews *autograph MS*   4to 1777

3027 HAMILTON (MRS) The Lead, a Fragment *half morocco*   *folio*

3028 HAMILTON (ELIZA) Album of original compositions, 1862 —HALL (E F H) Poems— HAWKEY (CHARLOTTE) Diary in Italy, 1858   3 vol 4to and 8vo.

3029 HOLMES (ANN) Discarded Daughter, a Tragedy, and Verses by Mary More, *copied from MSS in the British Museum*   4to 2 vol

3030 HOLCROFT (FANNY) Goldsmith a Melo-Drama   4to

3031 INCHBALD (MRS) Mogul Tale, *autograph MS*   4to.

3032 —— Such Things are a Play in Five Acts *autograph MS*   4to

3033 JACKSON (RACHEL) Collection of Poetry, 1862—JEROULT (MRS) Miscellanies, 1817— JONES (ELIZA) Common Place Book, 1811   4to and 8vo 3 vol

3034 JOHNSTON (MRS) The Elopement a Comedy   4to

3035 KEE (MARIANNE) Poems, *autograph MS*   1808-13

3036 MIDDLETON (MRS) *formerly Miss Scott*, Mary the Maid of the Inn, the Lowland Romp and various other Dramatic productions by the same, by Miss Keating, &c
    a bundle

3037 MONTAGU (LADY MARY WORTLEY) Copies of Verses, Songs, Epistles, Eclogues, &c *contemporary MS half morocco*   4to.

3038 NAPLETON (MRS ELIZ) *of Pembridge, Herefordshire*, Spare Hours not Misspent, a Collection of Miscellaneous Poems   4to 1759

3039 NOEL (AMELIA) Dido Queen of Carthage, a Play   4to

3040 O'BRIEN (Mrs. MARY) Temple of Virtue, an Opera, *copied from a MS. in the British Museum*—The Patriot, a Tragedy in five Acts, 1779, *modern copy*—PETTET (LAURA) Common Place Book, 1838   3 vol.

3041 POLEWHELE (MRS.) The Frolicks, or the Lawyer Cheated, a Comedy, *dedicated to Prince Rupert, autograph MS. old morocco g. e. with autograph and book-plate of Arthur Hewes*   4to   1671

*** Mrs Margaret Hewes (or Hughes), the celebrated actress, was the mistress of Prince Rupert

3042 PORTER (ANNA MARIA) Switzerland, a Play, *autograph MS. imperfect, formerly belonged to Kean, the actor, who took a part in its performance*   4to   1819

3043 REDE (MARY LEMAN) Songs and other small Poems *green morocco, g. e.*   1820

3044 ROBINSON (MRS. MARY) Songs, &c. in the Lucky Escape, *copied from a MS in the British Museum*—Poems, by Sarah Robinson, daughter of J. J. Robinson, of Boxgrove, near Guildford, 1860   4to   2 vol.

3045 ROGERS (Charles) Common-Place Book   1719, &c.

3046 ROGERS (MARY) Ballads for the Cottager, *with pen and ink sketches*   4to

3047 ROWE (ELIZABETH) Common-Place Book. AUTOGRAPH MS. A MOST INTERESTING AND VALUABLE VOLUME *written about 1720, with a transcript of a portion of the same*   4to   2 vol.

3048 SAVAGE (L. A.) Ivy Leaves, 1862—SCOTT (M. C.) Poems —SEWARD (ALPINIA) Poems, Charades, &c. 1786-99— SHAW (MARY) Poems on Marriage, &c. 1787-8—SLINN (SARAH) Hymns and Spiritual Songs, 1779   5 vol.

3049 SMITH (JULIA) Translation of the Book of Job *autograph MS.*   4to   1803

3050 SMITH (REBECCA ELISON) The Friends, a Fable, imitated from La Fontaine, *plate*   4to   1831

3051 SNEYD (Miss) Songs and other Poems, 1790—Sonnets by ANNA SEWARD and others 1788, &c.   2 vol.

3052 Stainforth (F. J.) Manuscript Catalogue of his Library, compiled by himself, *very useful in giving the names of the authors to many anonymous publications*   4to

3053 Stainforth (F. J.) Collection of Bibliographical Notes, Biographies of Female Writers, and loose papers, a blank paper book, ruled, 4to &c.   a bundle

3054 Stanzas, Songs, Sonnets and other Poetical Compositions of Female Writers, *an interesting collection of original pieces, mounted in 3 vol. with list of contents half green morocco*   folio

3055 TABOR (MARTHA) Poems, *autograph MS.* *folio.* 1861
3056 Tale (A) of Parga, *half morocco* *folio.* 1819
3057 TAYLOR (MRS CLARA) Hymns, 1712, *modern copy half morocco*
3058 TAYLOR (JANE) Wedding among the Flowers *autograph MS* *4to*
3059 THROCKMORTON (LADY ANNE) Stanza of Lines and Verses in praise of the Bible, by Sir Arthur Throckmorton, written on the fly-leaves of the following Book, Common Prayer, *imprinted by Robert Barker,* 1611—Genealogies recorded in the Sacred Scriptures, by J. S. *n d*—The Bible, that is, the Holy Scriptures contained in the Old and New Testament (Genevan and Tomson's), *engraved title-page by Hole, R Barker,* 1611-12—Psalmes by Sternhold, Hopkins, and others, 1618

old morocco, with the name of Mary Wotton stamped on the sides *folio* *in one vol*
3060 TIGHE (MRS HENRY) Psyche, or the Legend of Love, *autograph MS portrait inserted, morocco* *4to*
3061 TREFUSIS (E) Poems, Songs, and Tales *autograph MS* *4to* *2 vol*
3062 TURNER (DOROTHY) Common-Place Book, containing entries of the Births, &c of her Children, Divine Poems, &c. 1672, *&c*
3063 VAUGHAN (ANNA MARIA) Poems, *copied from a MS in the British Museum*—VILLAIL (F R) Poems, 2 vol 1818—Poems and Letters, by Von der Heyde, 1834 *4 vol*
3064 Verses, &c including some original compositions by Lord Lyttelton, Voltaire, a page in the autograph of Horace Walpole, &c *4to*
3065 Wheeler (M A) Album of original compositions 1828-9
3066 WYKI (ANNE L B) Father and Daughter, Stanzas on Dreams, &c *half morocco* *folio* *Southampton, n d.*
3067 YOUNG (MRS H) Ida May, or Secrets of the Slave Triangle, in Two Acts, The Seamstress and Dutchess, Bertha Gray and Ben Liel, a Drama *4to* (3)

FINE ENGRAVINGS

FRAMED AND GLAZED

3068 The Silence, after Curracci, by Bartolozzi *proof before any letters, gilt frame* 1
3069 Ecce Homo, after Correggio, by Doo, *proof before letters, gilt frame* 1
3070 THE ASSUMPTION OF THE VIRGIN, after Murillo, by Lefevre, *a very choice proof on india paper before the letters, gilt frame* 1

3071 The Madonna di S. Sisto, after Raphael, proof before any letters, gilt frame — 1
3072 The Lo Spasimo, after Raphael, by Toschi, *fine proof, gilt frame* — 1
3073 Last Supper after Leonardo da Vinci, by Raphael Morghen, *fine impression, gilt frame* — 1
3074 Our Saviour's Entry into Jerusalem, and Companion, published by the Art Union, *gilt frames* — 2
3075 La Vierge au Palais Royal, after Raffaelle — 1
3076 Madonna della Seggiola, after Raffaelle, by Calamatta, *fine india proof before the letters* — 1

END OF SALE.

CPSIA information can be obtained
at www.ICGtesting.com
Printed in the USA
BVOW09s1023240817
493003BV00011B/104/P